The Reinvention of Politics

For my Mother

The Reinvention of Politics

Rethinking Modernity in the Global Social Order

ULRICH BECK

Translated by Mark Ritter

Polity Press

English translation © Polity Press 1997
First published in German as *Die Erfindung des Politischen*
© Suhrkamp Verlag 1993. Chapter 1 first published in German as
Das Zeitalter der Nebenfolgen und die
Politisierung der Industriegesellschaft
© Suhrkamp Verlag, Frankfort am Main 1996.
All rights reserved.

This translation first published in 1997 by Polity Press
in association with Blackwell Publishers Ltd.

Published with the financial support of Inter Nationes, Bonn.

2 4 6 8 10 9 7 5 3 1

Editorial office:
Polity Press
65 Bridge Street
Cambridge CB2 1UR, UK

Marketing and production:
Blackwell Publishers Ltd
108 Cowley Road
Oxford OX4 1JF, UK

Published in the USA by
Blackwell Publishers Inc.
238 Main Street
Cambridge, MA 02142, USA

ISBN 0–7456–1366–7
ISBN 0–7456–1758–1 (pbk)

A CIP catalogue record for this book is available from the British Library and the
Library of Congress.

Typeset in 10 on 12 pt Sabon
by Pure Tech India Ltd, Pondicherry India.
Printed in Great Britain by TJ Press Ltd, Padstow, Cornwall

This book is printed on acid-free paper.

Contents

Introduction

There is an essay by Wassily Kandinsky (1982) with the peculiar title 'And'. In it, Kandinsky inquires as to the word that characterizes the twentieth century in contrast to the nineteenth century. His surprising answer is that, while the nineteenth century was dominated by Either–or, the twentieth was to be devoted to work on And. Formerly: separation, specialization, efforts at clarity and the calculability of the world; now: simultaneity, multiplicity, uncertainty, the issue of connections, cohesion, experiments with exchange, the excluded middle, synthesis, ambivalence.

The vagueness of And is the theme of the latter world, which is ours. Its farewell to order, its overflowing chaos, its extravagant hope for unity, its helplessness in the face of merely additive growth, its limits and limitlessness, the increasingly illusive borders and the anxiety that they arouse – all that lures and thrills in And. The Either–or does not really terminate in the inconclusiveness, one could even say the undifferentiated mercifulness, of And. If so, then only imperfectly, vaguely and dangerously. Certainly, the irredeemable globality of the world speaks in favour of And. The And even worms its way through the armed borders, but this only makes the dangers general and indefensible.

Every new era of political existence has its key experience. The monarch's 'divinity under law', his divine right, ended with the storming of the Bastille in 1789, and democracy, 'the rule of the people' within the boundaries of the nation state, began its increasingly questionable triumphal march. Two hundred years later, the breakthrough of And is characteristically announced by two experiences: the reactor disaster in Chernobyl and the collapse of the Berlin Wall. In the first, the Either–or institutions of industrial society and their claims to exercise control and provide security are being refuted by the global risk society. In the second, the Either–or categories of East–West and left–right have collapsed as well.

Precisely because the second fundamental experience of And, in Kandinsky's sense, flew by so quickly, it is important to preserve it in memory. Communism was not swept from the world-historical stage by brutal force, nor with bound hands in front of a firing squad, nor in some blood-soaked big bang. It disappeared like a nightmare upon waking, like a fairy tale in reality.

'The year 1989 was just coming to an end,' writes Peter Handke,

> a year in which, from day to day and from country to country, so many things seemed to be changing, and with such miraculous ease, that he imagined that someone who had gone for a while without hearing the news, voluntarily shut up in a research station or having spent months in a coma after an accident, would, upon reading his first newspaper, think it was a special joke edition pretending that the wish dreams of the subjugated and separated peoples of the continent had overnight become reality. This year, even for him, who had a background devoid of history, and a childhood and youth scarcely enlivened, at most hindered, by historic events (and their neck-craning celebrations), was the year of history: suddenly it seemed as if history, in addition to all its other forms, could be a self-narrating fairy tale, the most real and realistic, the most heavenly and earthly of fairy tales . . . now that history was apparently moving along, day after day, in the guise of the great fairy tale of the world, of humanity, weaving its magic (or was it merely a variant on the old ghost story?). (Handke 1994: 57f)

Nineteen eighty-nine was the year of And. The dancing at the Berlin Wall symbolizes the peaceful revolution of And, starting from nowhere and unexplained, unexplainable, to this day. If the borders in Europe that had fallen away are now being reconstructed, invoked and re-flagged, this still remains a reaction – a reaction to the sheer intolerability of And.

The global, diffuse and formless character of And is upsetting to many people. The dis-alienation of the alien and the concomitant dis-possession of that which is one's own, both involuntarily produced by the age of And, are experienced as a threat. Without Either–or, they say, they cannot live and, they add, cannot even conceive of the And. So And is by no means the beginning of paradise on earth. Circumstances of a completely new type are probably beginning here. The world of Either–or in which we think, act and live is becoming false. In one way or another, this is the beginning of conflicts and experiments *beyond Either–or*, or, in the terms of this book, the *reinvention of politics*.

A book that has as many versions and facets as this has flown under a number of flags in its journey. It set off as *Beyond Left and Right*, and that is how it was announced. Now it has the proud and controversial title *The Reinvention of Politics*, to which should be added 'after the end of the East–West conflict order'. The title could also have been short and simple: *And*. If I lacked the courage to do this, then it was because the book is even less able to meet this expectation.

The book circles around the difference between two epochs of modernity – simple or industrial versus reflexive modernity, which is now coming into view and calling for the reinvention of politics. If one wanted to simplify and condense to the greatest possible degree the assessment which is tied up with this, one could use the words of Kandinsky: the 'age of *and*' is destroying and replacing the 'age of *either–or*'. But as has been said, that would be too ambitious, perhaps too hopeful, even clairvoyant, exceeding even the powers of a frivolous sociologist. Yet it remains true; this tiny little word 'And' with its modesty bordering on invisibility contains keys to new modernities.

Kandinsky published his essay in 1927 (see Kandinsky, 1982: 706). It is depressing how little has been contributed since then to the discovery and clarification of the riddles hidden in the three letters '*And*'. And yet it is a reassuring insight that all the insanity of this century has emphasized the urgency of the task of coaxing the secrets out of this conjunction. What Kandinsky foresaw for the twentieth century will thus perhaps be passed on to the next: the question of *And*.

It does not seem exaggerated to say that sociology, as well, will have to be reinvented after the end of the Cold War. Of course, a conceptual renaissance of sociology presumes sociological and social controversy over the guiding theoretical and political ideas. A contribution to this is to be presented here. The concept of 'reflexive modernization' is at the centre. This does indeed connect up with the traditions of self-reflection and self-criticism in modernity, but implies something more and different, namely, as is to be shown, the momentous and unreflected basic state of affairs that industrial modernization in the highly developed countries is changing the overall conditions and foundations for industrial modernization. Modernization – no longer conceived of only in instrumentally rational and linear terms, but as refracted, as the rule of side-effects – is becoming the motor of social history.

Industrial modernity is disintegrating, but something else is coming into existence. Both are possible, necessary perspectives and questions that are opened up by the theory of reflexive modernization. This must be elaborated, therefore, in two quite different ways of seeing, studying and arguing: the disembedding question and the re-embedding question. Both are to be treated here, as far as possible, and even more space will be devoted to the issue of what happens if, in Max Weber's terms, the 'guiding value ideas' of industrial modernity dwindle and fade.

When does modernity start and when does it end? How is modernity to be understood as 'simple' or 'reflexive'? Are there multiple modernities? An indissoluble ambiguity clings to questions of this type. Not just because the concept of modernity is so pale and so broad, so apparently strict and yet so vague that there is room in it for everything from minor repairs all the way down to a complete renovation of the very foundations of Enlightenment. It depends on the dividing lines, which the surveyors who lay out cultural periods tend to place quite differently. There is an attempt in chapters 1 and 2 at least to begin answering these questions.

In order to be assessable, comprehensible and judgeable at all, the catchword 'reflexive modernization' must be elaborated in several dimensions. These cannot be pressed between the covers of a book. They even point to different genres of literature. As a theory-forming idea, 'reflexive modernization' must get into the ring with other contenders, that is, it must take on the modernization theories of Weber, Simmel, Durkheim, Marx, Parsons, Foucault, Habermas and Luhmann, all the way to Giddens, Bauman, and many others, by being sharpened, contoured and relativized; in short it must prove itself.

A second way of illustrating the specific features of this theoretical view is oriented more according to socio-structural descriptions and can be developed as a phenomenological diagnosis of our times. Here one can deal with love, individualization, social inequality, the proliferation of science, ecology, law, economics, and so forth, in order to demonstrate in all these fields that which falls under the general category of 'reflexive modernization'. Of course this concept no more has one single unambiguous empirical correlative than does the concept of 'fruit', and since the empirical description must be presented differently and to different audiences than the theoretical structure and comparison, it is advisable to separate these two levels, if not absolutely, then at least relatively to one another. This book is concerned *not* with the general and comparative theory of reflexive modernization,[1] but instead with its consequences for political action, indeed for the concept of the political in general.

This is precisely where the essential difference lies with respect to my books *Risk Society* (1992) and *Ecological Politics in an Age of Risk* (1994).[2] Whereas the new globality of hazards is illuminated in the latter, here 'reflexive modernization' is being both generalized and analysed with regard to changes in the concept, site and subject of *politics*. The conjecture is that the second modernity into which we slid some time ago is a *political* modernity, a modernity, that is, which stimulates the *reinvention of politics*.

An additional difficulty of comprehension that is inherent in the concept of 'reflexive modernization' is that theoretical/empirical and normative/moral statements appear to be surreptitiously connected and fused together here. This concept can be used like a magician's top hat, out of which one can pull, at one time, diagnoses, and, at another time, suggestions and formulas. The diagnosis states that industrial modernization is undermining industrial modernization; ethics, on the other hand, argues that industrial modernization is becoming a problem for itself, perhaps making much more possible: more knowledge, more reflection, more criticism, more publicity, more alternatives, the way into a better modernity of self-limitation, of And.

The two must be kept strictly separated: there is no automatic transition from the discomfiting of classical industrial society to reflection on this self-abolition and self-modification. Whether the disembedding and re-embedding of the structures in industrial society will lead to a public and scientific policy-forging self-reflection of this epochal change, whether this will seize hold of and occupy the mass media, the mass parties and organized agents, whether it will become the object of broad controversies, conflicts, political elections and reforms, all this depends on many conditions and initiatives which cannot be theoretically decided and pronounced in advance. Quite to the contrary, self-abolition and self-modification in industrial modernity can equally well turn into and end up as types of *counter*-modernization.

The analytical core of this theory states, quite amorally and free of any hope, that reflexive modernization generates fundamental upheavals which either can provide grist for the mills of neo-nationalism and neo-fascism as counter-modernity (if the majority appeals for and grasps at new–old rigidities) or can be used in the opposite extreme for the reformulation of the goals and foundations of Western industrial societies.

Between the two extremes lie, at least in potential, the 'ambivalences of modernity' (Zygmunt Bauman). As will be shown in detail in chapter 2, 'The Construction of the Other Side of Modernity: Counter-modernization', these provide new developmental opportunities for 'counter-modernity', understood as 'constructed certitude'. In this view, nationalism, ethnocentrism, xenophobia and violence are not the expression or eruption of suppressed atavism continuing to be a potent force behind the façades of civilization. They are instead responses to the fundamental experience of And, the product of a never-finished dialectic of modernization and counter-modernization.

This can be reconstructed retrospectively for the eighteenth and nineteenth centuries (for instance, in the 'naturalization of femininity' by the rising natural and human sciences and the concomitant restriction of women to the role of mother and housewife), but applies just as well to the present and future. The modernization of barbarism is not all that improbable as a variant for the future which is being enabled by reflexive modernization. Or in Kandinsky's simple terms, the onset of And can lead to a renaissance of Either–or in various forms of counter-modernity, from esoteric beliefs or new spiritual movements and religions to violence and nationalism all the way to the revival of old hatreds and wars.

Just how much disintegration can a person stand? The fact that reflexive modernization makes chaos even more chaotic, therefore leading to intolerable conditions, forces the question: what type of counter-modernity, what rigidities might be or become acceptable, and based on what criteria? This issue is discussed at the conclusion of chapter 2 on the example of the environmental crisis and the opportunities it presents for a remoralization of all fields of social action ('Ecological ligatures').

The conflict between counter-modernization, on one side, and renewal and radicalization of modernity, on the other, is by no means purely theoretical; it will determine the coming years and decades, and this book takes a position in it. My position is based on a view that informs the entire book and struggles to find full expression in it: after the Cold War, the West has slid into a victory crisis and the goals of social development must be spelled out all over again.[3] What modernity is, can be or wants to be is becoming palpably unclear and indeterminate. An entire political and social lexicon has become obsolete in one stroke, and must now be rewritten. That is precisely what the *reinvention of politics* means.

The model of Western modernity, that occidental mixture of capitalism, democracy, a government of laws, and so forth, is antiquated and must be renegotiated and redesigned. That is the core of the much-discussed crisis of Western party-political democracy. Radicalization

and reform are now possible against the background of our streng-
thened self-confidence following the end of the East–West conflict.
The achievements of European modernity – parliamentary democracy,
a government of laws, human rights, individual freedom – are not at
stake, but how they are cast into the moulding forms of industrial
society certainly is. Much is needed, particularly a type of active
thinking that will open our eyes to fundamental alternatives.

What, then, does the reinvention of politics mean? Not just rule-
enforcing but rule-altering politics, not just politics for politicians, but
politics for society, not just power politics, but political design, the art
of politics. It can be shown on all levels and with all topics: there is no
longer any security system in Europe, because the contractual parties
that made the agreements no longer exist, nor do the political terri-
tories to which they referred, nor the interests they were supposed to
bring to agreement. In that sense the drama in the former Yugoslavia
cannot be isolated. Military conflicts are a threat everywhere, even
between nuclear-armed neighbours, such as Russia and the Ukraine.
Only the invention of a new European security system (at a European
congress to be convened for that purpose) could lead out of this
dangerous imbalance. That is nowhere in sight, and this is only one
example: such things that do not exist but need to be created have been
an essential source of the general malaise in Europe for some time.

Reinvention of politics thus does not mean a universalization of state
and welfare state politics; not every action is political in the old sense
of that term. Nor does this mean the 'long march through the institutions' envisioned by the student rebels of the seventies. What is meant
is that more and more often we find ourselves in situations which the
prevailing institutions and concepts of politics can neither grasp nor
adequately respond to. This is of course nothing terribly new.

Politics and political institutions were never copied down or over-
heard somewhere, never derived from immutable natural laws; rather,
they were always invented. Politics and art, and technology as well,
bear this seal of self-creation. In this sense, the history of politics is the
history of the invention of politics – from Greek democracy, through
Machiavelli's theories of power, Hobbes' or Max Weber's theories of
the state, all the way to the provocative assertion in the women's
movement that 'the personal is the political' and the instructive though
empty slogan of an 'ecological restructuring of industrial society'. The
principles of democracy, proclaimed today like the Ten Command-
ments, had to be invented against the resistance – and the empirical
data! – of undemocratic systems. Their intellectual leaders were thus
unable even to glean a hint of the speed of the changes and the

globality of the situations and hazards that would be set in motion with the triumph of the democratic industrial system.

In short, just as it was necessary in Greek antiquity to invent the forms of local democracy, and to invent those of national democracy in the eighteenth and nineteenth centuries, so it is necessary today to invent the forms of global democracy. Of course, no book and no author in his right mind can set himself such objectives. This is a bit more realistic: to argue a way free for this objective and make it a part of broad public awareness, that is, to open up the concept of politics in this special sense to the challenges of global industrial civilization at the turn of the twenty-first century. This would – perhaps – be a response to the challenge of 1989, the year of And.

In a small article with the suddenly pertinent title 'The German as Symptom', Robert Musil writes: 'The current condition of the European mind is in my view not a disintegration, but an uncompleted transition, not overripeness but underripeness.' And somewhat later one reads:

> A sea of complaints have been poured out over our lack of a soul, our mechanization, calculability, and lack of religion, and the achievements of both science and art are regarded as excesses of these conditions. People need only check and, so it is said, see that even humanity's allegedly greatest scientific achievements are nothing but excesses of this calculation drive . . .

'The old ties – faith, pre-scientific ways, simplicity, humanity, altruism, national solidarity and civil subordination, the sacrifice of capitalistic individualism and its way of thinking – are recommended to the rootless people,' Musil continues. His passing remark 'socialism is full of this as well – people believe they must cure a decay' can be ignored, since that belief system has itself decayed and is probably facing a long period of treatment. Then comes this assessment: 'It is very seldom recognized that these phenomena represent a new problem which has no solution as yet; I am scarcely aware of a presentation which would even recognize this contemporary problem as a problem, albeit a new one, and not as an incorrect solution' (Musil 1967: 15)

Not decay, not a wrong solution, not overripeness, but underripeness and a transition; everywhere the non-solutions of yesterday are struggling with those of the day before yesterday to master a future which is bursting all its boundaries. Breaking up these false alternatives with (an at least conceivable) *radicalization of modernity* is the concern of the *reinvention of politics*.

– There is a significant difference between the original German edition and this English translation: chapters 2 and 3 of *Die Erfindung des Politischen* have been replaced by a new chapter 'The Age of Side Effects', which is the English translation of my revised chapter for the German translation (published by Suhrkamp Verlag, 1996) of Beck, Giddens and Lash: *Reflexive Modernization* (Polity Press, 1994). The distinction between first (simple) and second (reflexive) modernity will be elaborated and applied (chapter 1, 'The Age of Side-effects: On the Politicization of Modernity').
– Then in chapter 2, 'The Construction of the Other Side of Modernity: Counter-modernization', this will be confronted with the theory of counter-modernization.
– Following that, the concept of politics will be supplemented and expanded with the concept of subpolitics in reflexive modernity (chapter 3, 'Subpolitics – The Individual Returns to Society').
– Two chapters follow, 'Ways to Alternative Modernities' (chapter 4) and
– 'The Reinvention of Politics' (chapter 5), both of which explore the thought experiment of a self-application of modernity, in order to open up fundamental alternatives.
– The book ends with an essay on 'The Art of Doubt', which sketches out and attempts to illustrate essential guideposts and highlights of reflexive modernity in the theory of science and philosophical ethics.

This structure of the book can also be understood from the attempt to elaborate the coordinates of politics in reflexive modernity, however tentatively. In chapter 1, the contrast *safe–unsafe* is developed. Chapter 2 revolves around the dichotomy *inside–outside*, in a specific way; the constructions of 'counter-modernity' are conceived as conditions of this delimitation. In this way advance clarification of the issue of strangers in global risk society is undertaken. The following chapters 'Subpolitics', 'Ways to Alternative Modernities', 'The Reinvention of Politics', vary the main contrast of this book: *political–unpolitical*.

One result of the analysis can be anticipated at this point: none of the dichotomies permits *a clear social opposition and group formation*. A constant feature of the conflict axes in reflexive modernity is rather that they tend to diffuse in one way or another. Relating this to chapter 2, even the 'stranger' is being detraditionalized in global risk society; the boundaries between intrinsic and extrinsic are becoming indistinct. This does not nullify the conflicts; rather, it intensifies them and makes them more erratic. In a word, the conflicts of And come into being.

No one writes a book alone. I must admit that without the calm – and uproar – of the *Wissenschaftskolleg* [Institute for Advanced Studies] in Berlin, the reader would have been spared this. Everyone can draw his or her own conclusions. In any case, I found the stay there extraordinarily enjoyable. This is the happy example of a cosmopolitan German institute that produces ideas which produce more ideas. The book was also written, rewritten and rewritten once again in sight of and under the protection of Lake Starnberg. It was discussed, commented on, encouraged and fought over in conversations with many people who have accompanied me in my work over the years. My mode of production, which forms the ideas while they are being produced, and the accompanying flood of manuscripts may have robbed many of both nerves and time. I beg pardon from and at the same time warmly thank: Wolfgang Bonss and Christoph Lau, who opened up their treasure chest of ideas for me; this book owes much more to them than can be documented here and in the notes. Ronald Hitzler spurred on many assessments and arguments with his lively encouragement and contradiction. Elmar Koenen often asked me questions to the point of speechlessness and stimulated a reform of the whole thing. Michaela Pfadenhauer has a way of wrinkling her brow and the ability to throw in a word of praise in just the right way to make me change or correct the direction of arguments. Martin Mulsow kept me informed on the crudest philosophical errors of my text. Angela Behring read closely and drew my attention to irritating omissions.

How can I thank the one whose company is present everywhere – in life as in the book – Elisabeth Beck-Gernsheim? Quite simply, I think, by just writing one book fewer in the future.

Anyone who draws the conclusion from all of this that the author is the writer and compiler of suggestions given him by others is not too far wrong.

Ulrich Beck

1

The Age of Side-effects: On the Politicization of Modernity

What does 'reflexive modernization' mean?

We hear talk of the end everywhere – the end of the nation state, modernity, democracy, nature, the individual. It is time to inquire into the beginning which is hidden in every end. The perspective of reflexive modernization connects both inquiries; the question of what is breaking up is confronted by the question of what is coming into being, the question of the contours, principles and prospects of a second, non-linear, global modernity in a 'cosmopolitan intention' (Kant). Posing this question, of course, by no means implies being able to answer it.

For practically all fields of social activity, a gradual or eruptive collapse of previously applicable basic certainties is being asserted. The striking point is the ambivalence. What seems like decay and crisis to one person is a departure for new shores to the others. This is clearest in foreign policy where the 'eternal truths' of the East–West conflict reigned until 1989, but also in domestic policy, as well as in the left–right schematism of the political parties. NATO, the Bundeswehr, the European Union, the CSCE, first world and third world – everywhere empty linguistic formulas, broken coordinate systems and gutted institutions.[1]

Yet the erosion of industrial modernity, as it developed since the nineteenth century in Europe and later radiated or was proselytized across the world, is not a consequence of 1989. In the beginning was the environmental issue. It called into question basic premises of European thought and activity – the notion of limitless growth, the certainty of progress or the contrasting of nature and society.[2] The questioning of industrial modernity has for some time no longer been limited to the alarms from the environmental crisis; it is beginning to gnaw at almost all ordering models of society. In industry and industrial sociology, people are beginning to speak of the end of Fordist mass production and Taylorist hierarchies in the division of labour, even of the end of plants ('system rationalization' Bechtle and Lutz 1989; Beckenbach and van Treeck 1994; Lash and Urry 1994). There is turbulence in business, management and trade unions (Alfred Herrhausen Gesellschaft für Internationalen Dialog 1994). Nuclear family models and the analogous role formulas have lost their grip in view of the very commonplace confusion of marital or non-marital cohabitation and separation in one or several households, the possibilities of formal or informal divorce, on the one hand, and of post-marital parenthood, on the other (Lüscher, Schultheis and Weberspann 1988; Beck-Gernsheim 1994.

New insecurities are infiltrating the secure milieu of the welfare state and erupting there. These may involve the loss of formerly secure benefits, threats to health or life itself from toxins, criminality and violence, or the loss of such certainties as the faith in progress, science and experts. The consequence is a new fragility of social positions and biographies – even behind the façade of established prosperity. How it should be understood, withstood and investigated no one really knows.

This is all the more true as social identities that developed along with industrial society – status-based class cultures or the separation between a man's world of careers and a woman's world of the family – are rapidly being disembedded (Beck 1992: part II). Thus the irritations of post-feminism are becoming the new trump card in the battle of the sexes (for instance, cf. Haraway 1993). Of course, such processes of individualization (Beck and Beck-Gernsheim 1993a, 1994)[3] go hand in hand with processes of globalization (Wallerstein 1986; Giddens 1990; Robertson 1992; Lash and Urry 1994: part 4). 'We are the first generation that is living in a post-traditional order of cosmopolitan dimensions,' writes Anthony Giddens (1990). That also means that the old boundaries between public and private no longer shield us. New global communication networks and monopolies are coming into existence. Neighbourhood is becoming place-independent and global social movements are becoming a possibility. All this adds up to a fully mature 'victory crisis' of the political institutions and legitimations of the West after the end of the Cold War. The European project of democratically enlightened industrialism is disintegrating and losing its foundations.

Anyone who takes a look at the shifts and erosion in the basic structure of European modernity must ask the question of how and where new structures, coordinate systems and orientations will come into being. If the issue of disembedding dominated the stability context of the seventies and eighties, the issue of restructuring is becoming central in the milieu of insecurity after the Cold War. And this is of course a central problem: if people look for new structure formations at all, they tend to do so in the old categories.

People count on the pathos of the nation to undo and unseat individualized society. Marriage, parenthood, love, living together and maintaining a household drift apart; the result of this is none the less squeezed into the comforting little word 'family' with all the unabashed ease provided by blindness to history. Economic growth is glorified without simultaneously seeing and recording the growth of hazards connected to it. We mourn the growing unemployment in and despite an economic recovery, but do not dare to ask how a society based on work that is running out of work must change its self-concept, how social identities and security are possible beyond work or can become so. That means that all the changes must start in thinking, with work on concepts. This is the reason why it is necessary to distinguish systematically between a *first* (simple) and a *second* (reflexive) modernity.

'Reflexive modernization' is initially a keyword in group formation, comparable to such keywords as 'Dadaism' or 'Expressionism' in art, a concept which does not pin much down but does indicate a tendency and permit distinctions. This community of opposition is seen first in the pronounced aversion to all varieties of an automatic, action-free and thus ultimately unpolitical 'modernization as usual' in society and sociology. These conceptions of simple modernization may feud with one another (as functionalism and Marxism did for a long time). They are accused and convicted of intellectual slovenliness. A modernization that makes an exception for itself, that does not subject its own premises and social forms to the law of disembedding and re-embedding of modernization, is no modernization at all. These *linear* modernization theories, positing themselves as absolutes and refusing to apply and relativize themselves to themselves, are struck by the fate that modernity keeps in store for everything it encounters and overruns: they become antiquated and ossified, the ideological relic of their own pretensions.

A second delimitation and restriction concerns the cognitive rituals of *post*modernity.[4] Many of its theorists and theories are certainly exciting, even productively stimulating for a theory of modernized modernity, because they (often involuntarily) conceive of it or anticipate it. Most, however, peter out on the sand of arbitrariness on which they consider modern industrial democracy to be founded. There is one contrast, however, which always defines their perspective. Postmodernism renounces what the theory of reflexive modernization recalls: the demand of the Enlightenment, especially when it is turned on itself.

The third delimitation is perhaps clearest in the case of the antimoderns, now raising their voices provocatively everywhere. Theories of reflexive modernization develop a critique of industrial modernity which definitely gets down to the fundamentals; more precisely, they follow the self-criticism which is self-created and publicized in the conflict between functional subrationalities, or, most clearly, in the scientifically illuminated ecological crisis in society. In that sense their criticism is aimed at further development, not refusal, of modernity, at opening it to the challenges of a world of 'global homogeneity',[5] which has lost the security of its foundations and oppositions. Theories of reflexive modernization try to capture the new savagery of reality with a conceptualization and theory formation that have learned from the idea of the radicalization of modernity. In that sense there is little in common with types of counter-modernization that ·attempt to turn back the wheel of modernity in theory and politics, no matter what the political camp to which they may belong. Theories of reflexive modernization are not nostalgic. They are permeated with the knowledge that the future cannot be understood and withstood in the conceptual framework of the past.

The competition among theories of reflexive modernization is thus the expression of an avant-garde demand. The institutionalized boredom of the ingrained routines in both science and politics is to be broken open and broken through, in the self-confrontation of modernity as stagnated in the model of nation state, capitalist and democratic industrial society with its own origins, claims and self-generated challenges. This is also an incitement to a struggle against prejudices in people's heads. Sociology should never be innocuous – particularly not when it calls its own foundations into question along with the foundations of modern society.

'Inside the West,' writes Gottfried Benn in his famous Berlin letter of 1948,

the same group of intellectuals has been discussing the same group of
problems with the same group of arguments relying on the same
group of causal and conditional clauses and has been reaching the
same group of results, which they call syntheses, or of non-results, which
they call crises – the whole thing seems a bit tired, like a popular libretto.
It seems rigid and scholastic, it seems like a genre play relying on painted
backdrops and papier-maché. (Benn 1986: 45)

Theories of reflexive modernization attempt to break out of these
intellectual backdrops and arouse awareness of the excluded middle.
This is tantamount to a reversal of the Feuerbach–Marx controversy:
thinking must be changed so that the world of modernity can be
renewed with its own origins and demands. The space for political
reforms, even a reform of the Western, only apparently eternal symbiosis of capitalism and democracy, must first be earned and opened
up by the power of the concept. We must learn to *see* that the fatalisms
that dominate our thinking are antiquated, that they cannot stand up
to the test of a decisive self-confrontation of modernity.

The discontent of Western culture with the consequences of its own
dynamism is old, and at the latest in the seventies it took on a new
drama, even a dominance, due to public awareness of the globality of
the challenges. The theory of reflexive modernization takes this consciousness of self-endangerment seriously. Indeed it is the decisive
attempt to make this challenge itself the compass and the historical
validity criterion of social theory and research. Reflexive modernization is the attempt to regain a voice and thus the ability to act, the
attempt to regain reality in view of developments that are the consequences of the successes of modernization. These developments call the
concepts and formulas of classical industrial society fundamentally
into question from the inside, not from crisis, disintegration, revolution or conspiracy, but from the repercussions of very ordinary
'progress' on its own foundations. To many, Western modernity appears unreformable. Is this not a confusion of thought with action?
Does unreformability not point to limits and orientations of thought
that can and must be broken up?

'Reflexive modernization' is supposed to mean self-transformation
of industrial society (which is not identical to the self-reflection of this
self-transformation), the disembedding and re-embedding of its dichotomies, basic certainties, indeed its anthropologies; that is, the changing of the social foundations of industrial society modernization by
industrial society modernization.

The phrase 'self-transformation of industrial society' throws characteristic light on the global situation. The overwhelming majority of

countries are now running more or less hopelessly after the goals of simple industrial modernity, at the same time as those goals are becoming dubious in the centres of developed modernity and entering into political flux as they become the objects of decision-making (Menzel 1994; Senghaas 1994; Zürn 1994). To many societies the institutions of the first modernity appear as enticing as they are unattainable. They have neither a guaranteed control of the military and police nor a government of laws, and thus not the combination of those two items, a constitutional state. Moreover, they do not have a functioning economy. Large parts of their population can neither read nor write and thus live below subsistence level. At the same time (the contradiction of different epochs existing side by side) the foundations and objectives of industrial modernity are becoming dubious even in the centres of the modern world. On the one hand, this exponentially raises the uncertainties and intensifies the dependencies. On the other, the West's monopoly on rationality and development is also collapsing and the cultures of the world are now able for the first time to open themselves to the global dialogue. A global exchange is necessary on what 'development' can and should mean for the future – not just in the so-called 'underdeveloped' but in the 'highly developed' countries as well (Menzel 1994).

At the turn of the third millennium, civilization finds itself in a chaotic simultaneity of the non-synchronous: the transition into simple modernity now shaking the post-communist world and the countries of the South has its foundations and goals snatched away by self-transformations of industrial society.

> The actual core of the development dilemma lies in the non-synchronism of the modernization processes from one country to another, the out-of-phase development of competence and power in individual countries and the resulting pressure on less successful societies.... The established world of the old West thus faces pressure from a variety of problems.... Competition to survive and migration are ... only two sides of the same coin, extremes in the effects of the non-synchronism of successful, failed and so far unsuccessful modernization processes, as sketched out above. (Menzel 1994: 92)

To this we must add: 'and of reflexive modernization processes calling themselves into question'.

Reflexive modernization therefore means a change in the foundations of industrial modernity which occurs in the wake of *normal*, autonomized modernization, *un*planned and gradually, and, with an unchanged, possibly intact political and economic order, aims at three things: a *radicalization* of modernity which *breaks up* the premises and contours of industrial society and opens paths to new modernities or counter-modernities.

Reflexive modernization therefore asserts exactly what is considered out of the question in unanimous antagonism by the two main authorities of simple modernization, Marxists and functionalists, namely that there will be *no* revolution but there will be a *new* society. The taboo that we are breaking in this way is the tacit equation of latency and immanence in social change. The idea that the transition from one social epoch to another could take place unintended and unpolitically, bypassing all the forums for political decisions, the lines of conflict and the partisan controversies, contradicts the democratic self-understanding of this society just as much as it does the fundamental convictions of its sociology.

In plainer terms, reflexive modernization means a *heightened* modernization of *society-changing* scope. In the conventional view, it is, above all, collapses and bitter experiences which signal social upheavals. That need not be the case, however. The new society is not always born in pain. Not just growing poverty, but growing wealth as well, and the loss of an Eastern rival, produce a fundamental change in the types of problems, the scope of relevance and the quality of politics.

More participation by women in work outside the home, for instance, is welcomed and encouraged by all political parties, at least on the level of lip service, but it also leads to an upheaval at a snail's pace in the conventional occupational, political and private order of things. Temporal and contractual flexibilization of wage labour is striven for and advanced broadly in view of horrendous unemployment figures, but in sum it breaks up the industrial boundary lines drawn between work and non-work. After the security of the welfare state, we now appear to be threatened by the insecurity of widespread underemployment; poverty and the hazards of early capitalism in new forms are being 'modernized' under the catchword of 'flexibility'. Precisely *because* such small measures with large cumulative effects do not arrive with fanfares, controversial votes in parliament, programmatic political antagonisms or under the flag of revolutionary change, that is, because they do not make use of 'illegitimate' or spectacular means, the reflexive modernization of industrial society occurs on cats' paws, as it were, unnoticed, even by sociologists, who unquestioningly continue gathering data in the old categories. The insignificance, familiarity, and often the desirability of the changes conceals their society-changing scope. More of the same, so people believe, cannot produce anything qualitatively new. *The desired + the familiar = new modernity*. This formula sounds and seems paradoxical and suspicious.

The talk of reflexive modernization refers to changes of social and sociological foundations, the foundations of institutional action or of sociological thought and research. The two levels cannot be imaged in one another or derived from one another. In terms of an example, the ecological reform of society need not lead to or be matched by any ecological reform of the sociological conceptualization and theories of industrial society. Sociology can become an antiquary's shop specializing in industrial society, in other words. Conversely, however, a reflexive modernization of the premises of sociology must proceed reconstructively, that is, it must indicate the way to a transformation of the fundamentals in the institutions.

What is at stake everywhere in the phase of reflexive modernization is the continued existence of premises – conventional ways of life, work, production, organization, and hence of specialized fields in sociology (see above). Normatively and in actuality, scientifically and politically, the issue is whether and how basic self-evident certainties can erode or continue to apply, how they can be renewed and protected against questioning and questioners. At least part of the reason why highly specialized and routine-prone social research tends to report stability and constancy must be that it is neither prepared nor equipped for this mammoth question of the transformation of categories and premises. How can I dismantle the ship of sociology on the high seas and refit it for the new challenges? Thus even the inquiry into the possibility of a reform of the fundamental concepts in sociology is ostracized as a completely erroneous (not an overdue) provocation.

Highly specialized empirical social research presumes a constancy of categories and hence a high and actually rather rare social stability. How a historical society that is transforming itself categorically can be observed by social science remains an unanswered question. Western sociology presumes not only stable clientele relationships, but also a non-revolutionary social order constructed upon long-range – more precisely, industrial – certainties and antagonisms, which are 'calculable' in the truest sense of the word and change according to probabilities. Collapses, the division of countries, the blurring of coordinates and the disappearance of entire groups of countries and military structures are not foreseen. Even the unification of the two German states is, strictly speaking, a sociological non-event, at least for a sociology so specialized in the status quo that it becomes the status quo itself. As a corrective measure, it is necessary to 'invent' and standardize methodologically a regulated opposition of social theory, social empiricism and social experience that will permit even external, extreme and explosive things to be incorporated within the horizon of that which is sociologically conceivable, observable and explicable. Otherwise, the horizon of sociology will actually shrink down to the mathematically expanded horizon of the nouveau-riche middle-class imagination, which excludes everything that transcends or threatens it: eruption, erosion, transformation, reformation. As long as such a methodology is lacking,[6] hypotheses must be gathered and put together into empirically substantive theories.

Politically as well, reflexive modernization, as a broad-scale, loose-knit and structure-changing modernization, is a major phenomenon which requires the greatest attentiveness. For one thing, it implies difficult-to-delimit deep insecurities of an entire society, with factional struggles on all levels that are equally difficult to delimit. At the same time, reflexive modernization encompasses only *one* developmental dynamism, which by itself can have precisely the *opposite* consequences, although against a different background. In various cultural groups and areas this is joined by nationalism, mass poverty, religious fundamentalism of various factions and faiths, economic crises, environmental crises, possibly wars and revolutions, not to forget the states of emergency produced by great catastrophic accidents, that is, the conflict dynamism of risk society in the narrower sense.

From the multitude of problems and issues touched on above, two are to be illuminated and discussed in greater detail below. In a first line of argumentation there is an attempt to define and formulate the theory of reflexive modernization more exactly in a *comparison of sociological modernization theories*. The assessment is that the various schools of sociology, including their antagonisms, are still largely circumscribed by the experience and problems of simple, industrial modernity. In contrast to that, a typology of modern societies is to be developed here that will permit us to learn and teach how to distinguish between primary and secondary modernity.

In a second stage of the argumentation, there will be an attempt to illustrate the categories and principles obtained in selected fields of special sociological research. It will be asked in conclusion to what extent the distinctions to be presented between simple and reflexive modernization can also be considered and interpreted as lines of a future conflict. Are we on the eve of a new Reformation?

The sociology of simple and reflexive modernization – a comparison

The grand consensus on modernization

Sociology came into being in Europe in the context of the 'social question', the 'class issue', and reconstructed it theoretically and politically in a debate with Karl Marx with reference to the distinction between labour and capital. The confusion of social and sociological issues reaches the point 'that frequently "socialism–sociology–social issues" were equated in society, just as sometimes occurs with "feminism–women's studies–women's issues" ' (Müller 1994: 121). Two things are noteworthy in this respect, however.

First, the relationship between labour and capital remains the central axis of sociological argumentation in one form or another, despite all the criticism (Luhmann 1986). This theme has not really been superseded, nullified or overcome to this very day. Other figures of argumentation have been added and have fundamentally changed the relative significance of the political–economic approach into one view (or one system) among others. That approach remains central, however, with a significance that can be reactivated at any time. Many consider political economy to be sociology's ace in the hole, which can always be counted on for a trump in the future. Thus, after the collapse of the communist sphere of power, it ought not to be very long before relatively clever theoreticians of late capitalism begin breathing new life into theories of economic crisis, considering the lack of any competition between communism and capitalism, the growing mass unemployment, the dismantling or reconfiguring of the welfare state and the general erosion of social structures and institutions.

Second, this confirms that the social sciences have generally tended to underestimate the level of abstraction of political and economic theories in their reception of them. This is a sufficiently general theoretical model that will remain interpretable for historically quite different, indeed even opposing, contexts.[7]

That Max Weber and all who followed in his footsteps have outdone the abstractness of the political and economic starting point is no contradiction to this. Characteristically, Weber does not reach out for a systematic critique of the economic foundation of social theory, its foundation in economic criticism, but criticizes it instead only as an objective constriction, and replaces the notion of a capitalistic *accumulation process* with the more abstract and open notion of a *rationalization process* on the social scale. In parallel, the 'labour force' is replaced as a socio-economic category by the more general concept of '(social) action' (Weber 1968, 1978). No one can deny that these fundamental elements of a theory of modernity in industrial society have remained very effective to this day. The characteristic thing here is that Max Weber assumes a *linear* increase of bureaucratization and rationalization, which accordingly tend increasingly to take on the character of compulsions to 'social action'. In this linear model of modernity, the escape from the 'shell of servitude' is relegated to the field of fearing and hoping. According to Max Weber, it is only possible by means of the charisma of a figure of historic significance – a leading idea, the resemblance of which to the ideological motif of a leader (*Führer*) is not entirely coincidental. After all, this motif had considerable credibility among national-liberal intellectuals in Kaiser Wilhelm II's Germany long before its fascist premiere. This tension between subjectively intended meaning and the graduated, supra-subjective objective constraints of prevailing rationalities has been retained in the social sciences to this day. Social scientific functional-ism and the products of its decomposition continue to gnaw on this 'conceptual bone' and are nourished reasonably well on the scraps.

Now that even the industrial demand for rationality and control-lability has been theoretically and morally worn down (by the environ-mental crisis, for instance), the question must be raised of whether similar, differently directed steps of abstraction are not needed and possible today. In fact two principles, *globalization* and *individualiza-tion*, offer themselves for this purpose. The former breaks the horizon of the nation state and its ideology theoretically and politically, and the latter has the same effect on sociology's virtual fixation on the priority of groups and collectives. (This cannot be pursued here for now.) Since the 1960s, horizons of questions and problems that have so far gained little influence on the core of sociological argumentation have opened up in political and scientific debates; these include the ecological issue (environmental and anti-nuclear movements), the women's issue (feminist movements) and the democratic issue (col-lapse of the Eastern Bloc). Viewed in this way, it is obvious that, overcoming all theoretical antagonisms, a largely unbroken *grand Ma(r)x-Weber consensus on modernization* still generally prevails in sociology.

Sociology seems to be a controversial science. Expressed in positive terms, it has a wealth of different theoretical languages and basic theories (known as 'paradigms' in the specialist jargon, borrowing from Thomas Kuhn) and these are often very difficult to relate to one another.[8] This theoretical pluralism can easily deceive us, however, into thinking that in the eye of the hurricane there is the calm of a basic consensus: across all the differences in wording, modernization is conceived of in a structurally very analogous manner; it is thought out and researched with very related questions (cf. Berger 1988).

This persistent Ma(r)x-Weber consensus on modernization is called into question by the theory of reflexive modernization. That means this theory must contend against two competing tendencies and sharpen its contours and assert its assumptions in the dispute.

On one side there are the dominant theories of *simple*, classical, industrial-society modernization. For all their variety and internal antagonisms, these theories share the characteristic equation of modernization with industrial-society modernization. Within the simple modernization camp, however, there are two intensely feuding schools – the *functionalists*[9] and the *Marxists*,[10] which in turn have developed the variants of *post-industrialism* (Fourastié 1954; Bell 1973; Touraine 1974) and *late capitalism* (Offe 1972; Habermas 1987), respectively. In theories of post-industrialism, for instance, the horizon of possible futures is narrowed down to a shift in the centre of gravity from the industrial to the service sector. This and only this is explored theoretically, thought through and researched. But in the process, the equation of modernity with industrial-society modernity remains unquestioned.[11]

On the other side, the theories of *postmodernity* have taken up their positions.[12] Not only do these theories chronically deny the environmental issue, they actually boast of having dismissed the principles of modernity in one way or another. This too is based on a confusion of modernity with industrial-society modernity, only this time with negative conclusions. Because modernity and industrial-society modernity are considered indissoluble, people jump straight from capitalist democratic industrial modernity into postmodernity, not a new modernity, when the historical falsity of the earlier model begins to dawn on them. Thus, at the first signs of a structural transformation, people desert the battle, and the principles of modernity as well as the diagnosis of a radicalized modern society are cast aside like rifles in the proverbial retreat.[13]

Both of the competing positions thus rule out the subject of the present discussion, that is, the multiple modernities arriving in the wake of inherently dynamic modernization-as-usual, through the back door of side-effects (more precisely, slipping in behind the side-effects under the cover of ahistorical general ideas).

If simple modernization means the disembedding of traditional social forms and then the re-embedding of industrial ones, reflexive modernization means the disembedding of industrial social forms and then the re-embedding of other modernities. The difference between the two phases of modern society is therefore that, in the first case, pre-industrial traditions and, in the second, the 'traditions' and sources of security of industrial society itself become the object of disembedding and re-embedding processes. This is precisely what self-application means: in the wake of autonomized modernization, industrial society is overrun, even 'abolished', just as industrial-society modernization disembedded status-based and feudal society and re-embedded itself.

The motor of social transformation is no longer considered to be instrumental rationality, but rather the side-effect: risks, dangers, individualization, globalization. A series of things that go unreflected add up to the structural rupture that separates industrial modernity from the second modernity. This is precisely where questions arise which will now be taken up. In the age of instrumental rationality, how is it possible to conceive of 'reflexive' modernization as unreflected, automatic, reflex-like modernization which is still a part of social history? In alternative terms, how can a typology of different modern societies be based on the category of side-effect?

Fundamental assumptions of the sociology of simple modernization

With the triumph of industrial, that is, simple, modernity – so the broad sociological consensus goes – certain everyday ways of life and systemic organization principles become dominant. These can be grouped into three assumptions of simple modernization theories.

1 Life situations and life courses are socially organized and representable in *classes*. These absorb status-based antagonisms and cultures, but have their foundation in the position of a person in the industrial production process, in the antagonism of labour and capital. Endless debates proliferate around this point, regarding the number, boundaries, behavioural relevance and ideologies of 'classes' and later, less pointedly, 'strata'. Characteristic of these political conflicts and scientific controversies, however, is this: the occupational position in the production process radiates outward or, more precisely, determines how and where someone lives, what kind of consumption and recreation habits he or she has, what kinds of political views and commitments are to be expected, and so on. The dynamics of social inequality are interpreted in unambiguous, delimited and politically contrary or contradictory *large-group* categories. Multiple and passionate controversies may break out inside these historical 'a priori forms of intuition', not about *whether*, but only about *how* large

groups are to be conceived, defined empirically and politically and interpreted (socialistic or capitalistic models of society, for instance).[14]

2 The disembedding of the traditional order – this is a point on which the classics also agree, for all the disparity in their diagnoses – takes place as a revolutionary process, either openly and explosively (like the French Revolution) or permanently and eruptively (like the Industrial Revolution). The situation of the new order that replaces the 'divinely willed' feudal and status order is correspondingly precarious. Modern society, as Hans Freyer puts it, 'is negative, critical and revolutionary for all the great systems of sociology. It has neither a meaning nor a foothold within itself, but always pushes beyond itself. It has lost order and not yet found the new order' (Freyer 1930: 165, quoted in Berger 1988: 226).

From Spencer through Parsons and Luhmann, order in industrial society has been conceived in sociology as *functional differentiation of subsystems*. Accordingly, modern (that is, industrial) societies obtain and develop their special abilities of adaptation and achievement from an 'art of separation' (Michael Walzer). In the wake of profound shocks, the political sphere splits off from the economic one, the scientific sphere from the political one, and so on. All these differentiated subsystems develop and elaborate their own 'laws' or 'binary code' (Luhmann).

Quoting a suppressed author, who continues to exert an effect precisely because he has been suppressed, 'Let us assume that in the moral field the ultimate distinctions are good and evil; in the economic field, beneficial and harmful or profitable and unprofitable. . . . The specific political distinction to which political actions and motives can be traced back is the distinction between friend and enemy' (Schmitt 1963: 26). This ultimate decisive point on which Carl Schmitt based his theory of politics has been widely, in fact, almost universally, condemned (at least in theoretical terms). And yet it is striking how extensively the formulations coincide, even down to the microcosms of Luhmannesque conceptualization, in the fundamental notion of 'autonomous binary-coded subsystems'.

3 These 'subsystems' are dominated by their own *sovereignty*. That is to say, the law of motion of modernity is a rationalization process in the sense of instrumental rationality, which may take many shapes, but is still conceived as linear and one-dimensional. This implies more and different, 'intelligent', 'ecological' technologies and mega-technical systems, new markets, experts and patents. For instance, the reaction to environmental dangers is the invention and production of patentable microbes to eat up the industrial toxins. This transformation by

a linear increase of rationalization can and must be conceived and advanced on all levels and by all the means of society, by new organizations, new careers, new specialities, new fields of law, new consulting initiatives and the like, but with the same old rationality, the same presumptions of control and security in enhanced and refined form.

'Rationalization' here also means (technified) *reflection*. The subject and type of reflection may change (experts, public sphere or individuals). The assumption remains, however, that

> with its split from tradition, modern society is forced to ground itself exclusively within itself. A type of society arises that builds on its own foundations. This state of affairs is expressed in the growing flood of reflection concepts with which people attempt to understand the basic structure of modernity: self-utilization (Marx), self-production (Touraine), self-reference (Luhmann), growth of self-regulatory capacity (Zapf). (Berger 1988: 226)

Characteristics of simple and reflexive modernization theory

Second or reflexive modernity – in the non-normative, empirical and theoretical sense – must be clearly distinguished from these reflection concepts native to sociology. *Reflexivity* of modernity and modernization need by no means automatically imply reflection on modernity or on self-abolition of industrial modernity. The change of principles and the accompanying uncertainties may also, for instance, give impetus to various types of counter-modernity. Even the talk of 'self-reference' and 'self-referentiality' drives the logic of Either–or to an extreme and misunderstands the ambivalences which irrupt along with reflexive modernity, understood non-normatively. This is precisely where those assertions become questionable. This 'self' (the contour) of industrial modernity gets lost in the modernization process, which shifts its own foundations and coordinates; it is replaced by another self which must be reconstructed, theoretically and politically (Beck 1992: 91ff; Berger and Hradil 1990; Beck and Allmendinger 1993; Berger 1993).

That the dynamics of industrial society undercut its own foundations recalls the message of Karl Marx that capitalism is its own gravedigger, but means something else. It is not the crises, but rather the triumphs (let us say) of capitalism that produce the new social form. At the same time, this implies that normal, continued modernization, not class struggle, breaks up the contours of classical industrial society. Nor does the constellation which that produces have anything in common with the now discredited utopias of a socialistic society. The assertion is instead that high-powered industrial dynamism is skidding into a new society without the big bang of a revolution, bypassing political debates and decisions in parliaments and governments.

The conceptual model for this is the environmental issue. As is known, this issue is in fact created by abstraction from itself, by untrammelled economic growth. Aiming exclusively at growth and screening out the environmental consequences only exacerbates the environmental crisis (not necessarily in the consciousness of people or in the public sphere).

Another distinction immediately sticks out here. In contrast to the environmentalism debate, reflexive modernization aims not at self-destruction, but at self-modification of the foundations of industrial modernization. Whether the world perishes is not only a completely open question, but, more than anything else, it is completely uninteresting to sociology. Only the threatening doom is the topic (though certainly the great and so far unexplored topic) of a sociology beyond the faith in industrial progress.

Thus the sociology of reflexive modernization is not a crisis or class theory, but instead a theory of the unintended disembedding and re-embedding of industrial-society modernity by something which seems to be taken for granted – 'normal' inherently dynamic modernization. Applied to methodology, to the techniques and experiments of thought, this means self-application of modernization to industrial-society modernization. The characteristics of simple and reflexive modernization (theory) can be contrasted as follows (with some schematic simplification).

1 Reflexive modernization disembeds and re-embeds the cultural prerequisites of social classes with forms of the *individualization* of social inequality. That means, on the one hand, that the disappearance of social classes and the abolition of social inequality no longer coincide. Instead, the blurring of social classes (in perception) runs in tandem with an exacerbation of social inequality, which now does not follow large identifiable groups in the lifeworld, but is instead fragmented across (life) phases, space and time (Hradil 1987; Lau 1991; Kreckel 1992: 107–211).

On the other hand, it is no longer possible to extrapolate the ways of life, life situations and lifestyles of people from their (vocational) position in the process of labour and production. The assertion of reflexive modernization thus comes down to the assertion of the *diminishing covariation* of economically determined milieu differentiation and subjective interests and situational definitions. The consequence of this is, in turn, that theories of large-group society are increasingly less able to describe current developments. At the same time, social institutions – family and social law, but trade unions and political parties as well – find themselves deprived of the socio-structural order on which they build. 'The classical conflict pattern of modernity, the conflict between more or less stable interest groups, gives way to a theme-centred *vagrant hostility* oriented according to mass-media publicity' (Lau 1991: 374).

2 The questions of functional differentiation are replaced by the questions of *functional coordination*, cross-linking, harmonization, synthesis, and so on. Once again, this undermines the Either–or, even in the realm of systems theory. Differentiation itself is becoming a social problem.[15] The way systems of activity are delineated becomes problematic because of the consequences it produces. Why does one delimit science from economics, economics from politics or politics from science in this way, and why can they not be intermeshed and 'sectioned' any other way in regard to tasks and responsibilities? How can subsystems be conceived of and organized as both functionally autonomous and coordinated? How are 'systemic harmonizations' that allow both autonomy and coordination possible (Willke 1992: 292ff)? Empirically considered, does modernity actually roll along in the form of further and further differentiations? Or can one not observe the exact opposite in the field of science and technology development, where the boundary between basic research and technology development is just now being abolished (Krohn and Weyer 1989; Halfmann 1990; Lau 1991)? Are there not concrete And experiments underway everywhere, in which the 'binary codes', thought to be strictly separated in simple modernization theory, are being applied to one another, combined and fused?

Just why must the binary codes of the respective subsystems be based exclusively on these fundamental differences as conceived by system theorists? Even the comparison hints at arbitrariness and decisionism. Carl Schmitt distinguishes *friend and enemy* and Luhmann *elected and non-elected* for politics and the political system. Do these represent differences of temperament or differences in political and theoretical ideology? Why one, why the other, and on what basis is that measured and decided? Is the difference between utility and non-utility still of any utility or not? Can the coding 'beautiful–ugly' be identified as beautiful or ugly? Or is the *type* of binary coding immune to the distinction with which it operates? But what does it then rely on? An idea? The *Zeitgeist*? The self-understanding of the elites in the respective institutions? On fundamental experiences which the theorist shares – with whom? Or on what else?[16]

3 The concept of linearly increasing rationality has the double significance of a *descriptive* and a *normative* model. This normative part of classical modernization theory can be demonstrated with Talcott Parsons and his theory of 'evolutionary universals', but also, in a more political and pragmatic sense, in the work of Wolfgang Zapf (for example, 1992). The assertion is that modern societies have developed certain inventions which make them more adaptable and hence better suited to survive in complex environments. Among these 'basic institutions' Zapf includes competitive democracy, the market economy and the affluent society with mass consumption and a social safety net. Zapf also sees challenges impending for modern societies. For him it is inconceivable, however, that the latter cannot be mastered with the institutions just mentioned.

'In a perspective in which modernization is viewed as an evolutionary process of failing and successful reforms and innovations,' Zapf writes,

> even such basic institutions as competitive democracy, the market economy and the affluent society are not guaranteed eternal existence. At present, however, I do not see any more capable alternatives to these institutions. The size of problems such as the environmental crisis is not in itself an argument for a transformation of the system. Even large problems can be transformed by spatial, temporal, objective and social division into problems that can be mastered with reforms and innovations. . . . In this sense I speak of advancing modernization as transformation in detail with general constancy of direction in the foreseeable future. (Zapf 1992: 207)

Thus modernization is equated in the theory of simple modernization to linear rationalization. In political terms this implies that, ultimately, there is *no alternative to the basic institutions*. The answer given here to the question 'how will you deal with the challenges?' is: with the known and familiar repertoire, that is, more technology, more markets, and so on.

What are self-abolition and self-endangerment?

This is just what the theory of reflexive modernization disputes, empirically and normatively. It breaks empirically and theoretically with the assumption of linearity. That is replaced by the 'self-endangerment argument' that further modernization abolishes the foundations of industrial-society modernization. This thought is neither as original nor as unambiguous as it seems. It is already present in classical sociology.

First, the thesis of the *loss of community* has been asserted and embellished (often with a nostalgic and culturally pessimistic attitude) by Tönnies, for instance, but up to the present day by Jürgen Habermas, Daniel Bell and, with renewed vehemence, by the 'communitarians'.

Second, there has been early and extensive exposition of the view that the division of labour creates integration but also may generate disintegration in certain forms that became dominant with industrialism, resulting in apathy, violence and suicide (the early insights of Durkheim serve as guides here).[17]

Characteristically, both self-endangerment arguments are presented in classical sociology with restrictions of a certain type. The resultant problems, so goes the assumption, do not ricochet back at the institutions, organizations or subsystems; they do not threaten their claims to monitor and control society, nor do they threaten the self-referentiality and autonomy of the subsystems.

This is based in part on the dualist theory of individual and system, organization and private lifeworld, which are conceived of as being largely autonomous with respect to one another. Additionally, the diagnosis of loss of community and disintegration in classical sociology is justified 'ecologically', as it were. The starting point is the assumption that modern societies do indeed use up 'resources', nature and culture, on which they depend, without being able to see to their preservation and renewal. Yet these self-endangerments – and this is where the optimistic faith in progress lies concealed – can be shifted off onto the environment. 'Optimization in one sphere of action triggers difficult-to-control consequent problems in other spheres of action' (Berger 1988: 37), but not in the system itself.

An argumentation figure of self-dissolution, scarcely noticed today, was presented by the elder Joseph Schumpeter in his classic work *Capitalism, Socialism and Democracy*. For him the foundations of capitalistic management are eroded by the very same dynamics which set and keep capitalism in motion. The interesting point is that Schumpeter reaches Marx's conclusion, but by taking Max Weber's path. It is not the class struggle which causes capitalism to ossify and die off on its own accord, in this view, but rather rationalization, bureaucratization and delegitimation.

> If capitalist evolution – 'progress' – either ceases or becomes completely automatic, the economic basis of the industrial bourgeoisie will be reduced eventually to wages such as are paid for current administrative work excepting remnants of quasi-rents and monopoloid gains that may

be expected to linger on for some time. Since the capitalist enterprise, by its very achievements, tends to automatize progress, we conclude that it tends to make itself superfluous – to break to pieces under the pressure of its own success. The perfectly bureaucratized giant industrial unit not only ousts the small or middle-sized firm and 'expropriates' its owners, but in the end it also ousts the entrepreneur and expropriates the bourgeoisie as a class which in the process stands to lose not only its income, but also what is infinitely more important, its function. (Schumpeter 1950: 134)

Independently of how one assesses this argument, it is by structure a classical self-dissolution argument in the sense of reflexive modernization. The bourgeoisie undermines its crucial position not by crises, but by the victories of quite ordinary modernization (the development of organized employee structures, for instance); it forfeits the support of the intellectuals and thereby loses its legitimacy as an agent of social innovation. This argument is not exhausted or decided empirically either, considering the environmental issue, on the one hand, and the challenges of an industrial society without industrial labour, on the other.

In a common variant of this argument, self-endangerment is replaced by self-modification. This heralds not doom, but rather a change of scene, or, more precisely, a double theatre. Two plays are performed at the same time, disrupting one another on the same stages: the familiar and the new distributional struggle for 'goods' and 'bads'. The former involves desired goods, the wealth produced by instrumental rationality in all the forms in which it could be desired (capital, jobs, opportunities for consumption, and so on), and the latter, usually concealed in it, but gradually pushing more and more into the foreground, concerns the denial, disposal of and redefinition of risks and dangers.[18]

In the daily alternation between news of toxic crises and stories about unemployment, it is possible to study how these two scenarios supplement and undermine one another and what kind of contradictions and curiosities erupt in the process. The roles described and decorated, so it would seem, only for the old struggles for position can be and must be 'played' and fleshed out. It is as if one were performing a mixture of Marx and *Macbeth*, or the collective bargaining negotiations for civil servants juxtaposed with Goethe's *Sorcerer's Apprentice*.

A second variation of the same thing can be observed and displayed in the erosion of male and female roles. At first sight, the argument sounds familiar enough: equality, the catching up of women on the labour market and in careers is negating the familial foundations of industrial society. This only means that the basis of the division of labour, its self-evidence, is dribbling away. With that, the 'classical' roles of men and women are mixed and broken down, and in an explicitly reflexive way as well. This should be equated neither to destruction (as in the environmental crisis), nor to the transposed double scenario (as in the overlapping of economic and risk conflicts). Instead, and more modestly, it means the loss of self-evidence and security, the need to make decisions and negotiate, and so on, but conversely as well: the repercussions on intra-organizational activities.

Then the hard core of the reflexivity argument begins. This theory contradicts the built-in naiveté of simple modernization, its practical optimism of a predestined, one could almost say divinely willed, controllability of the uncontrollable. A whole series of arguments can be forged from this.

First, and somewhat broadly, this concerns the *globalization of 'side-effects'* in the nuclear state and in the creeping ecological disasters (the ozone hole, climatic changes, and so on). As Günther Anders, Hans Jonas, Karl Jaspers, Hannah Arendt and many others have impressively shown, the possibility of deliberate or inadvertent collective suicide is in fact a historical innovation, one which bursts apart all moral, political and social concepts, even that of 'side-effect'. This entire constructed mirage of man-made risk makes the talk of 'externalizability' a joke, a symptom of the prevailing 'blindness to the apocalypse' (Anders 1980).

Second, the assumption of externalizability in classical sociology is called into question in multiple ways by *circular, cumulative and boomerang effects*. Side-effects devalue capital, destroy trust, make markets collapse, confuse agendas, and split apart staff, management, trade unions, parties, vocational groups and families. This applies even to costs in the narrower sense in view of insurance constraints and legal reforms that redistribute burdens of proof. The issue of *how* externalization collapses can certainly remain open initially (cf. Hildebrandt et al. 1994).

Third, individuals bring the resultant problems back into plants and organizations in their consciousness, in their basic orientations and in the conflicts that ensue. To the extent that the environmental issue has penetrated and percolated through a society, even the inner circles and cores of the modernization agents in business, politics and science can no longer shield themselves against it. If one assumes that 'organizations' are in essence interpretation efforts, the products of interpretation by individuals in social contexts, then it becomes clear that only a metaphysics of the system can protect the differentiated subsystems from the repercussions of the self-endangerment they provoke. Externalizability is thus a belief, perhaps *the* belief of simple modernization theory, which shatters and becomes absurd as the side-effects grow.[19]

Fourth, this argument broadens. It applies as well in the case of the equation of modernization to scientization. Simple modernization sociology combines two optimisms: the linear perspective on scientization with the faith in the rapidly progressing controllability of the side-effects, whether the latter are 'externalized' or can be processed by 'more intelligent' surges of rationalization of the second type and transformed into new economic recoveries. Precisely this doubled optimism of control is contradicted by historical experience and, with it, the theory of reflexive modernization.

On the one hand, so this contrary argument runs, scientization undermines itself. Both insecurity and compulsions to justify grow. One conditions the other. The inherent pluralization of risks also calls the rationality of risk calculations into question. On the other hand, society is changed not only by that which is seen and desired but also by that which is *not* seen and *not* desired. The *side-effect*, not instrumental rationality (as in the theory of simple modernization), becomes the motor of social history. (That this side-effect must be seen, understood and broken up as a side-effect in order for the thesis to be meaningfully formulated and substantiated in the first place will only be noted here and left for subsequent clarification.)[20]

Industrial society as semi-modern society

One objection to the classical sociology and politics of industrial-society modernization has been that under the flag of a non-partisan universalism they practise Americanization, Europeanization or Westernization, in short, imperialism. This objection brings to a point a contradiction that is difficult to formulate and invalidate within the sociology of simple modernity. In one way or another, this always makes an absolute of a historical status quo, a certain model. That even modern societies can be modernized, that is, revolutionized, is ruled out here just as much as is the question of which aims (other than the nameless aim of further and further modernization) modern societies can and should pursue.

By contrast, the theory of reflexive modernization asserts that no such thing as a 'modern' society exists anywhere. What a modern society 'is', what it would look like, whether it would be liveable or unliveable, these are things no one knows because the type of a society more modern or more radically modern than industrial society has not even been conceived or anticipated. In so-called 'modern', that is, industrial, societies, we are always dealing with *'semi-*modern' or partially modern societies, in the architecture and structure of which modern 'components' are combined and fused together with elements of a *counter- modernity.*[21] The universalism of human and civil rights is granted or denied according to national criteria; the market economy is based on families, a model of 'selfless love' that runs directly contrary to the exchange laws of the market. As a thought experiment, one need only think through to completion the equality of men and women in professions and the family, now so casually spoken of, in order to see that even the complete implementation of fundamental principles of modernity is tantamount to the abolition of the industrial mixed model of modernity and counter-modernity.

The talk of 'modernization' in semi-modern society thus becomes ambiguous. It can be conceived and pursued either within the ways and categories of industrial society, or as the assertion of modernity against industrial divisions and limitations, as a disembedding of industrial society by radicalizing modernity. The possibility exists here, of course, that the former type of modernization is desired and the latter is produced. Precisely this ambiguity marks the difference and antagonism between the sociology and theory of simple and reflexive modernization.

Diagnostically, the equation of industrial and modern society signifies a collective self-deception and an exclusive focus on oneself. It closes its eyes to the fact that in the societies we inhabit in developed Western countries, modern elements are limited, permeated and fused with elements of a counter-modernity. For Claus Offe,

> This raises the question of whether the talk of 'modern' society is not more likely an unjustified euphemism and whether we ought instead to speak more precisely of a society which has indeed gone through varied processes of increasing the options in sectors, and consequently has at its disposal a really modern administration and art, modern industries and communications links, a modern military and educational system, but as a society, it does *not* have options as to how one could control the ensemble of partial modernities and their connections. Rather, it appears that society's deficit of modernity becomes that much greater the more modern the subsystems become; on this macro-level the helpless experiencing of blind fatalities becomes the rule to the extent that the rational increase in capacity of the subsystems progresses. The modernization of the parts, so it would appear, is to the detriment of the modernity of the whole. Precisely because of the subsystems' openness to the future and of their innovation-accelerating sectoral rationalities, society itself appears

to have become incapable of conceiving of its own future as a project or even of regulating it to basic standards. Thus the other side of modernity is a thoroughly paradoxical fixation on the status quo and an immobility of society which have nothing to do with the fundamental motive of modernity, the increase in the ability to command and select things. (Offe 1986: 105)

Now one could object that the distinction between modernity and counter-modernity is not much more than a terminological nicety. Not at all! This involves revealing, understanding and concentrating attention on a repressed side of so-called 'modern' society and its origin and future as well. The terminological muddling through, the linguistic self-perfection of semi-modern society, if you will, covers up the glaring problem that the revolt leading to modernity always takes place in cages, exclusively for certain groups and according to a clear plan of inside and outside. The bourgeoisie said 'humanity' but meant – at best – 'nation'. Democracy has always come into being only as a national democracy, not just limited but domesticated by the opposing forces, armed to the teeth militarily and protecting itself against its collective enemies. Its universalist pretension was never politically un-national, never formulated and intended to be directly universalist. If the universal was ever thought or considered beyond national considerations, then typically as a connection or alliance of republics (as in Kant), an international of national democracies, but not as a democracy of humanity. This would only redeem politically that which is generally floating in the air and the minds of people.

Modernity, the explosion of claims to generality and universality, has always been practised under restrictions from the opposing tendencies. In other words, modernization, the triumph of the principles of modernity (democracy, paid labour, decision-making and the requirement to justify actions) and counter-modernization, the exclusion and absorption of the principles of modernity, are, first of all, equally original. It is therefore necessary to contrast the history of successes and crises in modernization with a history of counter-modernization's successes and failures. To this end, it is necessary to trace, clarify and illuminate the concepts, theories, instruments, strategies, institutions and figurations of counter-modernity and counter-modernization.

Second, this dialectic of modernization and counter-modernization is not just a question of the past, of sociological historiography, but an issue in the present and future. Phases of modernization are and will continue to be followed by phases of counter-modernization. It is not certain and never has been that a certain level of modernity is irreversible (contrary to the arguments or more accurately, hopes of the sociology of simple modernization). This is the bitter and bloody teaching of the twentieth century. Modernization and the modernization of barbarism are not mutually exclusive; instead they supplement and perhaps even interpenetrate one another under certain conditions. This is the native language of more than just fascism and communism. The potential of mega-technical world reform (genetic engineering, genetic medicine, and so on) forces us into this pessimistic realism. The future of counter-modernity is also the theme of a sociology that has been rudely awakened from the really rather nice fairy tale of further and further modernization.

To oversimplify, the premise of irreversibility in the sociology of simple modernization contrasts with the reversibility premises of reflexive modernization theory. Modernization is viewed not just as a multi-level process with contrary tendencies and structures, but, more sharply, as an unfinished and unfinishable dialectic of modernization and counter-modernization. This is a dialectic, of course, which plays itself out in objective form behind the backs of individuals, but is by nature also fought out and elaborated in action, thought and conflict, in short, in politics.

A test case for this theory of counter-modernization is the eighteenth and nineteenth centuries, the implementation phase of industrial society in the centre of Europe. The model of techno-economic innovation was implemented, made permanent and autonomous in an eruptive or revolutionary manner in this period. The ideas of political and cultural modernity were disseminated and given material form in the corresponding institutions – the installation of parliamentary democracy, universal suffrage, a government of laws and the universalist principles of human rights as set down in the American Bill of Rights. However, the 'dark side' was also designed, produced and implemented against opposition – the oppression of women, their cementing into the role of housewife and mother, the nationalism and racism of the nineteenth century, the industrialization of war-making, the general mobilization including universal conscription, the militarization of all of social life and its explosions in the form of world wars, concentration camps, re-education camps, and so on. All of this was created with and programmed into the structural image of modern society that claims the monopoly right to modernity.

This simultaneity and opposition of modernity and counter-modernity is not a coincidence or an accident – we must open our eyes to that and keep them open – but is instead caused by the system and systemically linked to it. In this dialectic of modernity (dubiousness) and counter-modernity (certitude) I am drawing on the reflections

regarding the boundaries and turning points of reflexive modernization which were so emphatically laid down and defended by Scott
Lash (1993) in the context of the communitarianism debate.

Counter-modernity is not at all a shadow of modernity; it is a
project, a deed and an institution just as authentic as industrial modernity itself. It is intended and produced, with all the means and
resources of modernity itself: science and research, technology and
technology development, education, organization, mass media, politics, and so on.

This can be illustrated today, for example, with the social and political significance of genetics and the public debate on it. 'The genes are at
fault' is the motto of this wave of scientific counter-modernization.

> In America it is once again permitted to say it out loud: blacks are less
> intelligent. By birth. Richard Herrnstein, the recently deceased Harvard
> psychologist, and Charles Murray, a political scientist, . . . have written a
> book on a topic that is moving America, namely intelligence. In their
> 845-page tome with the lovely title *The Bell Curve* they demonstrate that
> intelligence is mainly a matter of genes. In short, society is divided for the
> authors into a group of gifted haves (generally of northern European or
> Asiatic descent), whose children become more and more gifted, and a
> group of less gifted have-nots, whose future is as dark as their skin colour.
> The same applies to their offspring.
>
> The two authors are not isolated in their opinion. The educational
> scientist Seymour Itzkoff considers it to be demonstrated that the less
> intelligent part of the American populace has already triumphed, because
> it is reproducing more rapidly. In his polemic entitled *The Decline of
> Intelligence in America* he demands a type of national emergency pro-
> gramme: an end to liberalism, cuts in social programmes, more rigorous
> selection in universities and stricter immigration regulations for 'geneti-
> cally weaker races' and peoples.
>
> Such tones are nothing new. Years ago already, Daniel E. Koshland,
> editor of the respected American scientific journal *Science*, announced
> that mass social phenomena such as homelessness, poverty, criminality or
> drug dependence were the product of improperly programmed genes.
> And in his own publication he made no secret of his conviction that these
> phenomena could be eliminated by improvements in the genetic
> substance of the affected parties. The new aspect in the debate is
> that these shrill voices are finding an ear in broad groups of American
> society.
>
> Biologism is in vogue in the media. Dorothy Nelkin, sociologist at New
> York University, has investigated the fervour with which they plunge into
> the realm of genetics. The gist of her findings is that 'The threatening
> decline of the gene pool, the heritability of character and behavior,
> dominate American newspapers and television programs'. Particularly in
> women's magazines such as *Glamour*, *Mademoiselle* or *McCalls*, Nelkin
> finds a profoundly fatalistic attitude to life. From wearing showy buckles

or drinking cold coffee to church attendance and eating disorders – everything is genetically conditioned. The *Boston Globe* proclaims that geneticists now have the last word in matters of child-raising; the *Philadelphia Inquirer* runs the title 'Personality Above All a Matter of Genes'; in a report in the *New York Times* on a fourteen-year-old murderer, the question emerges of whether such behaviour cannot 'be explained from bad stock', and a woman who suffers from a genetically caused disability is confronted with questions as to whether her parents shouldn't have considered abortion.

Are these precursors of a new world in which people are divided up into biological castes? What are the consequences for education when limits are already laid out for children in pre-school? What are the consequences for jurisprudence if a murderer no longer is granted any time for remorse and resocialization – once a criminal, always a criminal? Or for the labour market, if a genetic fingerprint replaces a personal resumé? Or for the insurance industry, if the monthly premium of a citizen depends on the number of mutated genes he has? And what are the consequences for politics, science and business, if there is no longer any culpability, just regrettable deficient natures? (Albrecht and Rückert 1995: 39f)

First and second modernity: contrasting features

François Lyotard, the French theorist of postmodernism, begins an essay with the statement that all attempts to delimit modernity and postmodernity off against one another and assign them to certain periods of history must fail. In his view, even the programme of a temporal succession, an ordered sequence, is pointless.[22] The problem is solved for him by his giving that which is known here as 'reflexive modernity' a certain non-periodic meaning. This is expressed even in the German title of his essay, 'Revising modernity'. In French and English, his presentation bears the titles 'Reécrire la modernité' and 'Rewriting modernity'. This approaches rewriting or reinventing modernity. Lyotard casts the programme of reflection and reform he envisions in concepts borrowed from psychoanalytical practice: 'remembering', 'repeating', 'working through'. Reflexive modernization means here that the modernity of our societies must again be inquired into, determined, fought for and obtained by interpreting and reinterpreting past, present and future.

It is not evident, however, why this critical, even self-critical recollection of modernity, its dark sides and hopes, its victories and defeats, cannot be tied to a contrast of first and second modernity as is attempted in the present work. One can even go a step further; only the (ideal-typical) distinction between different, and differently modern, societies allows the 'revision' of modernity that Lyotard invokes. Then how are the periods and theories of simple and reflexive modernization distinguished? Six contrasts demarcate the horizon.

First, linear models (and atavistic control fantasies) in optimistic modernization are replaced by varied and multi-layered figures of argument that involve self-modification, self-endangerment and self-dissolution of foundations and forms of rationality in the power centres of industrial modernization. This occurs as an uncontrollable (side)-effect of the triumphs of autonomous modernization. Uncertainty returns.

Second, while simple modernization ultimately situates the motor of social change in categories of instrumental rationality (reflection), 'reflexive' modernization conceptualizes the motive power of social change in categories of the side-effect (reflexivity). Things at first unseen and unreflected, but externalized, add up to the structural rupture that separates industrial from 'new' modernities in the present and the future. 'Reflexive' thus also implies reflex-like and simultaneously historic modernization (which, of course, as the present enterprise evidences, can be conceptualized, that is, reflected).[23]

Third, the sociology of simple modernization elevates industrial society to modern society per se. The sociology of reflexive modernization discovers industrial society as a contradictory historical symbiosis between modernity, pre-modernity and counter-modernity, a semi-modern society that is being disembedded because of continued modernization and radicalization of modernity and re-embedded as different types of 'modern' or 'counter-modern' societal forms. That is, the issue of counter-modernity is now becoming central. At the turn of the twenty-first century, modernization is being analysed in a simultaneous opposition of reflexive modernization, which deepens and broadens insecurities, and counter-modernization, which inscribes, promises and elaborates new and old rigidities and limits.

Fourth, in regard to life situation, life conduct and social structure, there is a conflict of large-group categories and theories versus theories of individualization (and intensifying) social inequality.

Fifth, the problems of the functional differentiation of 'autonomized' spheres of action are replaced by the problems of functional coordination, cross-linking and fusion of differentiated subsystems (as well as of their 'communicative' codes) (cf. Münch 1991).

Sixth, beyond distinctions of left and right – the spatial metaphors for ordering politics that established themselves along with the industrial epoch – political, ideological and theoretical conflicts are beginning that can be outlined with axes and dichotomies such as safe–unsafe, inside–outside, political–apolitical.[24]

This distinction of a first, simple, industrial modernity from a second, reflexive, global modernity is not just burdened with all the tentativeness of a hypothetical draft. Above all, this is the sketch of a theory for which the empirical, historical and methodological elaboration and testing remains to be done, aside from a few aspects and studies. That is true of possible confirmations, but equally well of possible refutations. Studies with this focus are easily caught in the circle of intending to prove (clarify or refute) these theses of new realities within the horizon of old categories. The mere inquiry into the conditions and opportunities for a change of the foundations in society and sociology raises methodological problems that have scarcely been discussed so far, let alone clarified.

As long as these unclear areas remain, we shall have to take recourse to the following criterion. It was the theorist and historian of science Imre Lakatos (1970) who suggested the criterion of *positive* (or *negative*) *problem shift* for assessing complex research programmes (including the implicit and explicit theories contained in them). This means in essence that what matters for assessing theories is not only the individual corroborative or contradictory facts contained in them. As the history of science teaches us, those facts always exist. What should be decisive is rather to what extent new theoretical arguments dethrone old positions and make new experiences and research projects possible. Productive movement must be introduced into the landscape of research. Crucial in this view is the extent to which facts, problems, falsifications and developmental perspectives that had previously been in the shadow of dominant theories and controversies can be uncovered and made the object of interesting research and public debates.

I would like to appeal to this criterion of a 'positive problem shift' and not just because the self-discrediting of industrial modernity and the further development of its foundations are made into empirically investigable research problems by the perspective of reflexive modernization. This mode of thought has yet to prove its productivity in specific topic fields – politics, the family, social classes, economics, labour, publicity and mass media, the nation, the (welfare) state, religion, science, and so on. In plain language, it is necessary to specify the theory of reflexive modernization in medium-scope analyses and to elaborate it and spell it out in related research and controversies. In the present context, this can and will be indicated and illustrated in only three steps by way of example:

1 the issue of reflexive democracy;
2 the issue of the politicization of corporate rationality;
3 the issue of the new fragility of social life in a second global modernity.

Reflexive democracy

Reflexively modern societies, to wrap up the previous argumentation, are characterized in that they largely produce of their own accord the problems and challenges which confront them. Conversely this means that the foundations of modernization in industrial society are called into question by that very modernization. The issue below is what this means for the ground rules of democracy.

The foundations of democracy belong to the protected realm of secular religion. Calling them into question is tantamount to violating a taboo. Yet the opposite is true: self-confident doubt is the original expression of scepticism in a civil citizenry. The self-renewal of democracy, its continued development beyond internal and external boundaries (the general conditions of the nation state, for instance) need not fear doubt; indeed it needs doubt to prepare the way. The secular miracle of a new beginning, which constitutes the mystery of really secularized politics for Hannah Arendt, is made possible only by doubt in the limitations and narrow-mindedness of democracy under the conditions of industrial society.

As preconditions of democratic processes, the foundations of democracy are (largely) removed from change within such processes. They are treated as if they were eternal. Their historical character is recalled, at best, in the foundation myth of a 'bourgeois revolution', but is not held open to revision and reformation in the sense of a future that can be shaped.[25] There is good reason for this. The parliamentary rule system is the answer to all the transitoriness that modernity brings into the world. Where all the security of traditions, values and scientific truth is dissolved and replaced by procedures, methods and modes of voting, it seems that an abyss is opening up when these modes in turn become transitory and malleable. Or at least this is true so long as it remains unclear which rules will replace or supplement the democratic rules of the game and which rules in turn govern the transformation of the rules (given all the questions this stirs up as to what, how and who). Still, it must be stated that this is exactly what is happening all around us in anticipation of the unsolved and unspoken problems in the air. The examples are legend; they need only be recalled by a few key words.

The distinction between public and private spheres is part of the protected basic stock of modern democracies. This distinction is precisely what is put at stake by the success of the women's movement, because the same problems (not limited to women) remain invisible and insoluble behind the walls of both the private and the public spheres. In the old pattern of thought, the politicization of the private sphere is considered a horrific idea. Against the background of premises considered immovable, it must be conceived of as politicization by the state or by parties, that is, from the top down and from outside. The special quality of self-politicization of a private sphere that is losing the security of its industrial-society social forms (class cultures, internalized complementary roles for men and women or parents and children) can then only be conceived of negatively and pessimistically, as loss and breakdown, not as a beginning and a departure to a new chapter of modernity.

Democracy in industrial society rests on the fiction that technological decisions of industry cannot nullify and modify the foundations of social coexistence and cooperation. Consequently, they do not require special public articulation and consent and are instead implemented in accelerated fashion by a business sector and politics attuned only to unrestricted growth. At the same time, the political justification of technocracy (like all democratic politics) is tied to the revisability of decision-making. As interpreted by political science, the change of governments is the central operational criterion which gives an essential indication of a society's democratic quality. Over the past two decades, social movements (anti-nuclear, environmental, criticism of genetic and human engineering) have persistently criticized generations of permanent technological change for which revisability, a 'change of governments', is either ruled out, or is tied to almost insuperable difficulties, as in the case of nuclear energy and weapons technologies. In fact, blinded to the consequences by the central ideology of economic growth, and with the blessings of a policy that invokes safety and order, predictably unpredictable side-effects are continuously unleashed that are irreversibly binding on future generations, which are excluded from the decision-making process and for which no one can be held liable.

Whereas these so-called new social movements aim at an expansion, that is, ultimately a democratization of democracy, the demand for changing the foundations does not remain limited to this political spectrum; instead, it is placed on the agenda by the opponents of those movements and implemented in the sense of a de-democratization of democracy. Even here, the general rule becomes clear that reflexive modernization is not a political one-way street. What is beginning to move here can be used and mobilized by all political tendencies for all

possible purposes. This historical form of the self-questioning of democratic rules of the game is no more an extreme function for liberation
than it automatically favours the construction of imperial democratic
forms of a strong state. At any rate, when one considers the power of
a 'new policy of the strong state' (Heribert Prantl), it becomes obvious
that not just social movements outside the political institutions, but
also social counter-movements inside the political system know how to
use the spaces of reflexive democracy.

> Not a day passed in 1994 without a call for new laws. Not a day without
> complaints about laws that are too soft. Those in charge of judicial and
> home affairs in the two major German parties acted as if the state were a
> weakling. They gave the impression that the main characteristic of a free
> government under law is cowardice in the face of the criminal enemy.
> The words 'organized crime' are used like a skeleton key to open every-
> thing – every taboo and every constitutional right. The judicial system
> built up over the last 45 years is being softened up. 'Extrajudicial discre-
> tion' is being called for not just in criminal law, but even in administrative
> law. (Prantl 1994: 8)

Prantl mentions 'enhanced telephone surveillance', intended to allow
the police to tap and monitor telephone lines without judicial per-
mission in suspicious cases, as well as the Crime Fighting Act. It
abolishes the strict separation between police and secret service which
has so far always been the foundation of democracy in the Federal
Republic of Germany. Criminal law, police law and the law of the secret
services, regulated quite differently until now and for very good reason,
are beginning to dissolve into a uniform law of internal security.
    That implies that the backdrops of perception and action in risk
society are transferred to the 'risks of civilization in the liberal
state' (Hitzler 1996). A generalized suspicion of apathy takes the place
of technical or ecological dangers. This is how the foundations of liberal
democracy in a government of laws are put at stake and renegotiated.

> Politics is in the process of developing a new state. In the security state of
> the year 2000, the point will no longer be to prosecute crimes and prevent
> concrete dangers, but instead to avoid even conceivable risks. In this
> state, therefore, every individual citizen will be viewed and treated as a
> risk factor. Such a state, which conceives of itself as a risk-avoidance
> organization, will permit fewer and fewer freedoms to the people. Their
> fear of crime, just like their fear of refugees, is a governmental measure,
> which finds general approval so long as it promises more security. The
> people in such a state will at first believe they are in a well-patrolled
> holiday resort, and will not notice until it is too late that this is a posh
> prison. The type of 'public spirit' demanded by conservative policy of late

fits in here. It implies the renunciation of individuality and the rights of
individuals. (Prantl 1994: 12)

This deliberate and reflexive questioning of fundamental principles
of democracy is not confined to social movements inside and outside
the institutions; it also occurs as a result of automatized modernization
processes. This is the case, for instance, where it dawns on people that
the production of social consensus depends on traditional forms of
solidarity – social and moral milieus, status and class cultures, familial
forms, regional, national and ethnic traditions, as well as the power of
religious traditions – all of which are being diluted and consumed in
the wake of continuing modernization. They are being replaced by the
tribulations of finding (or inventing) commonality and communal
spirit in the variety and contradictions between situations and topics of
fluctuating individual (self-)interpretations.

If one conceives of these forms of direct and indirect self-questioning
as phenomena of reflexive modernization, then one can say in regard
to the institutions and procedures of political decision-making in the
narrow sense that *democracy is becoming reflexive*, and not as some
desktop thought experiment, but as a concrete experiment in almost all
fields of social action.

This has so far only been presented schematically, but it can easily be
generalized. The issue may be the reduction, the revision, the basis or
the ideology of the welfare state, or it may be the extent to which
national sovereignty has already become an illusion, in view of global
economic and security interdependence, so that the arenas for making
democratic decisions and the genuine dependencies appear to be almost
impossible to join back together. In all such questions, which will
embellish and adorn ceremonial debates on the occasion of the turn of
the millennium, the horizon of reflexive democracy is at stake. Quite
independently of whether we like it and approve of it, regardless of
whether it is considered progressive or catastrophic, the Western world
has glided into a phase of reflexivity, in which the foundations of
democracy are analysed, questioned and set into motion one way or
another. A series of questions that have sped far past any possible
answers have been unleashed and now require a change from simple
and linear to reflexive democracy theories and models in the observer
perspective of the social and political sciences.

Without being able to plumb, much less illuminate, these areas
(abysses?) of self-questioning of democracy in this study, we can
distinguish two directions in which it can be done. These are, on the
one hand, vertically (or intensively) and, on the other, horizontally (or

extensively). In the vertical dimension, the point is to focus not on individual democratic political institutions (parties, parliament, government, the relationship of law and politics, that is, the jurisdiction of the Constitutional Appeals Court, and so forth), but on the principles of democracy itself. These latter are either confronted with the challenges of reflexive modern societies, against which they must prove themselves (examples might be issues of the destruction of nature, international interdependency, global impoverishment, safety in the atomic age, and so on), or are measured against their own principles and demands.

Modern democracy relies on the axiom of the self-control of individuals: each person is master of himself and of no one else. This principle was postulated and analysed in the political theory and philosophy of the Enlightenment, but at the same time the principal problem that results from it, the fundamental dilemma of all theories of democracy, was stated with enviable clarity. How can the principle of self-determination of individuals be formulated and how can masses of individual self-determinations be bound together such that the result is a community, a common will, and how, in turn, can the state, with all its institutions, agencies and authority, be based on this?

At least two common answers can be recognized as insufficient. On the one hand there are all the purely negative models of a democracy restricting the arbitrariness of the state and the governing group, protecting the citizens from excesses, but ultimately only an enlightened authoritarian democracy at best. After all, this view presumes that which is to be legitimated and substantiated, from the bottom up: the state with all its authority, power and force.

A second variant, the seemingly so obvious *majority principle*, was already criticized and rejected by Immanuel Kant. This view holds that the individual must bow to the quantitative superiority of the multitude. Kant considers the domination of the individual by the majority 'despotic', for the quite understandable reason that it rules out the individual self-determination demanded by democracy; indeed, it stands that principle on its head. Dictatorship from below, the dictatorship of the majority, is a real possibility and it uses democratic methods. Democracy and totalitarianism are not mutually exclusive; they can complement and ratify one another. 'Among the three forms of government, *democracy*, in the proper sense of the term, is necessarily a *despotism*', Kant writes, because it establishes an executive power in which 'all citizens make decisions about and, if need be, against one (who therefore does not agree); consequently, all, who indeed are not all, decide, so that the general will contradicts both itself and freedom' (Kant 1983: 114).

If one asks us Germans for our ticket to the age of democracy, we do not have a French, an American or even a British revolution to show, but we do have Immanuel Kant. Our revolution answers to the name of Enlightenment (which as *Aufklärung* sounds much better to us than 'enlightenment' in English, with its connotation of excessive rationalization), carries the noble title of *Critique of Pure Reason* (an early classic of 'rational correctness') and can be printed, read, given as a gift or eaten and reduced to dust by bookworms. Now we have to note with a certain displeasure that our official philosophical revolutionary, our enlightener Kant, was quite obviously not in conformity with our Federal Republic constitution. For him, democracy of the majority is despotic, as stated, for two reasons.

First, the general will, which Rousseau praised so highly, is necessarily a 'common will', because it cancels the autonomy of the individual. Second, 'everyone' is not in any event involved in or intended to be involved in the decision-making process. It is always a matter of *representation* of one type or another. If a general power of attorney or blank cheque of consent is issued in the process, an equally unlimited shock from a politics elevated above consent cannot be far behind. This, in turn, contradicts the freedom and self-determination of the individual which is proclaimed by democracy.

The *republican* form of state, which Kant contrasts to the democratic–despotic one, presumes not a unity created, for instance, on the rule of the majority, but rather an indissoluble diversity. Dissent, not consensus, is the norm here, the consensus, as it were, on which political decisions must be constructed and made binding. Freedom is measured on the freedom not just to express a dissenting view, but to assert it; thought out to its logical end (although Kant does not go this far), freedom is the fundamental right to civil disobedience (Arendt 1989: 119–60).

However one evaluates these arguments, even they show how much the foundations of democracy, measured against its most essential demands, are floating in the air. In all the central stages of mediation – in the transition from individual autonomy to the general will (popular sovereignty), from there to the decision-making rule (the majority principle), from there to a functional constitution which sets down and legitimates the order and power distribution of the state-principled objections can be raised. These are not brought in from the outside, but in fact they turn the fundamental principle of democracy against its own institutional arrangements.

'There is no form of human coexistence, no institution, no constitution that one could not cause to fail with the postulate of individual self-determination,' writes Count Peter Kielmansegg.

> Democratic constitutions thus appeal to norms that can always also be turned against them. Democracies, to formulate the same issue somewhat differently, always face the danger of being overtaxed by their own normative premises. They cannot escape this dilemma.
>   It might appear at first sight as if this were more a problem of theory than of practice. In fact, people are often not aware of the peculiar weakness of the foundation of democratic constitutions. A constitutional consensus, the shared readiness to accept a certain constitutional order as 'democracy', can and often does conceal the impossibility of rigorous, unambiguous derivations of the constitution from its own premises. There is no guarantee of the durability of such a consensus, so that the foundational dilemma can turn from a theoretical into a practical problem at any moment. (Kielmansegg 1977: 121)

This is exactly what happens in reflexive modernization, in this case when democracy becomes reflexive. If referred back to Immanuel Kant, Kielmansegg's point, with its undertone of a fading of democracy, can aim at the further development of democratic into a republican modernity with a cosmopolitan intention.

Alongside the vertical dimension, the question of reflexive democracy, as distinguished above, can also be elaborated in the *horizontal* dimension. The sovereignty of individuals established by democracy is connected to the sovereignty and the boundaries of the nation state, and, within the latter, restricted to that which is political in the narrower sense. Democracy has hitherto been conceived of as horizontally bounded. Seen in that way, it seems to many not only incomprehensible, but reprehensible and dangerous to speak in some sense of 'democratizing' the family, business or industrial labour (not to mention science). One aspect of this horizontal reflexivity of democracy will be taken up and elaborated below, namely the impossibility of limiting the basic rights of the citizen to a single field (that of the state and politics, for instance). Instead, the perspective that will be sketched out is this: to the extent that workers, women, children, Christians, soldiers, and so on, become citizens, this will radiate out into all areas and fields of action with the consequence that society will be transformed.

Reflexive democracy, understood horizontally, thus means that collisions and syntheses of logics specific to particular fields with the principle of democracy are inevitable, observable and reconstructible. This will be traced in the example of the business operation.

The politics of rationalization

As many of his followers do to this day, Marx criticized civil rights as 'empty' since they exempt the capitalistic labour contract. In that way they buttress the power of the bourgeoisie, integrate the workers into a system hostile to them and block the socialist revolution. Today, in the nineties, after the collapse of the communist state system, we must set this view, which had been stood on its head, back on its feet. (Only now can we begin an unbiased reading, appreciation and criticism of Marx, now that the dogmatism of a military–ideological confrontation has ended.) With only a degree of exaggeration, one can say that a good bit of actual socialism has been implemented along with civil rights within capitalism (which was changed categorically by this process). Meanwhile, the socialist revolution led straight to the (anti-socialist) patronization of citizens because of the rights withheld from them, and this is not the least important reason for that revolution's failure.

The decisive objection to this view remains the existence of the capitalistic labour contract. This is viewed by many as the key continuing element of capitalistic class relationships (Bravermann 1974, for instance; cf. Giddens 1983 as well). It may be true, so the argument goes, that people's consciousness and way of life are drifting ever further away from class thinking and action, but as long as the core structure of domination, the capitalistic labour contract, remains *the* basis of economic action, society will continue to bear the 'capitalistic' seal. This view relies on two intermeshed postulates: first the separation of politics and economy and, second, the renunciation of control of one's own labour power to its purchaser, the entrepreneur or manager. Both aspects are sanctioned by the capitalistic labour contract, it is argued, with the consequence that civil rights must be left at the door to the workplace, and remain 'empty' in that sense.

These principles are characteristically justified not by the legal form of the labour contract, but rather by the concrete power relationships between those who control the means of production and those who can only sell or rent out their own skins, their abilities and knowledge, that is, their labour power. This argument can be turned the other way around, however. To the extent that the legal equality of the labour contract is filled out with elements of shared and self-control over the expenditure of one's own labour power, or, putting it another way, to the extent that civil rights achieve validity in the economic sphere as well, this last pillar of the antagonism between labour and capital will collapse.

In fact, it can be shown that the continuing wave of rationalization in all fields of the economy cannot be interpreted as an extension of linear rationalization or automation in the sense of Taylorism and Fordism (for instance, Bechtle and Lutz 1989; Ortmann 1994). It must instead be interpreted as a rule-altering rationalization, a rationalization of rationalization, in which the power and rule systems of operational action themselves come up for decision-making and must be renegotiated and established. This implies an immanent (sub)politicization of the forms of industrial labour and of the relations of production. That is to say, politics (understood in a certain sense outside of party politics) is entering the sphere of business.

At the same time, open conflicts arise over the integration of civil rights into the labour roles and the power relations in companies. This conflict can be observed in the (self-)control of the procedures, content, results and modes of labour.

The results of this struggle over the abolition of 'divided democracy' in industrial labour, the establishment of civil rights within the sphere of labour and business, are certainly open, and are ambivalent in any case. The opportunity, however, that has opened up in plants (or what is left of them) can no longer be understood on the model of a linear rationalization as conceived by a post-Tayloristic Taylorism. Instead, it involves at the very least *also* a fusion of democratic reforms and capitalistic rationalization which is altering the foundations of business action. This is a (re)form of labour which is organized and designed along the lines of civil rights and is, in that sense, post-capitalistic. Ultimately, the abolition of residual capitalism inside residual capitalism is at issue here.

The consequences would be drastic. To the extent that the legal equality of the labour contract could be socially *honoured*, by placing buyers and sellers of occupational skills *materially* on the same level, by allowing control over expenditure of labour power to be exercised by the workers, the antagonism between labour and capital would really be shunted onto the side-track of history. On the one hand, this would redeem the old ideology of the capitalist mode of production, in which the owners of the means of production and the owners of ability and knowledge are all pulling their oars in the same boat, for instance by uniting to defend against ecologically oriented critics and the resultant threats to markets and products.

On the other hand, fewer and fewer citizens have the opportunity to enjoy this 'liberated' work enhanced by civil rights. This implies in turn that a new and deep gulf is emerging between the owners of the means of production and jobs, on the one hand, and the growing army of those not (gainfully) employed and also no longer exploited, on the other. Not least important, the subject of this democratized labour would no longer be a proletarian. He or she would be a proudly professional citizen, whose self-confidence feeds on two sources: professional ability and attained freedom and civil rights.

Talk of 'the end of the division of labour' (Kern and Schuhmann 1985), of the 'end of mass production' or of 'system rationalization' (Altmann et al. 1986) would thus be replaced by issues of a *theory of the rationalization of operational rationalization*. This is distinguished from the conceptions above in a number of respects.

Re-rationalization is understood to be a form of *politics*. This opposes, first, those conceptions that insinuate in one way or another that *objective logics*, whether of technology or of the economy, are played out in the rationalization process more or less without any space for discretion. Second, it sets itself off against the view that the outcomes and results of these arrangements are predetermined, or that they can even be defined and calculated. That is, the contingency of politics is emphasized against the predictability of rationalization.

This political interpretation is expressed particularly in the fact that the boundaries between the political and the economic spheres become porous in two senses. For one thing, the processes and results of the rationalization of rationalization can no longer be understood purely inside business, capital or a concern. What is also, and centrally, at stake here is the assertion of political civil rights within the world of work, a synthesis of democracy and economics yet to be invented. Action within the operation becomes dependent on publicity, legitimation and also on consent.

Furthermore, the foundations and rule systems of operational rationalization themselves become the object of conflicts, decisions and, hence, rationalization. This is not an extension and application of known principles of operational rationalization, but rather their self-modification. What is at stake, in other words, is a rule-modifying, not a rule-applying, rationalization policy. Creating and maintaining awareness of this rationalization of rationalization as a space for opportunity, interests, conflict, decisions and publicity remains to be done. This is equally true in the sense of the necessity for an ecological re-rationalization.

To exclude any misunderstanding, the politicization of rationalization does not contain any automatic mechanism leading to a democratization of wage labour, which would then probably no longer be 'industrial labour'. It is a journey without any evolutionary insurance policy. Even the installation of new types of monitoring or an intelligent version of Taylorism are certainly possible, indeed even probable, but they too would be the result of a give-and-take, a politicization of rationalization in the aforesaid multiple sense. Whoever conceals these opportunities for arranging society, these contingently political horizons in the core fields of the old industrial society where the objective constraints are forged, is attesting to the reality of the prevailing illusion of 'capitalist determination'.

Rule-altering politics cannot only establish constitutional rights. It can also abolish or undermine them, for instance those which Marshall calls 'economic civil rights', the right to form trade unions, conduct collective bargaining and strike. To put it quite clearly, the politicization of rationalization means that fundamental norms of human coexistence – in this case, industrial labour and production – become subject to decision-making. That *could* affirm Foucault and, in a successive and subversive demolition of basic rights, lead to an installation of the 'electronic collar' (Gilles Deleuze) inside and outside of work (Hitzler and Koenen 1994).

The chances of this happening are perhaps not even all that bad. They result from the fact that the arguments of self-abolition, self-modification and self-dissolution almost all concern only *one* side of the conflict of labour and capital, namely labour, while the 'capital side' at first seems unaffected. In terms of the sociology of domination, this does not come down to a capitalism without classes, but rather a capitalism without a *working* class, while 'capital' (whatever that might mean) can celebrate victory by default. What could emerge would be a classless capitalism of capital, an 'intelligent', socially irresponsible capitalism across the board, a militant neo-laissez-faire movement, which pursues the demolition of the civil rights won by the labour movement and the early bourgeois revolution, perhaps even with the (extorted) consent of the vitiated labour parties.

Calls for solidarity and the corresponding restoration of the old organizational forms (trade unions, labour parties, and the like) are of no help against this. What could help is the theoretical and political treatment of the question: how can the evolved demands for a life of one's own, for cooperatively and self-determined labour and collaboration, be reattuned to the foundations of the social order? How can citizens be tied together, seized and engaged beyond labour and capital? Citizens' movements, organizations and parties inside and outside the world of work which defend fundamental freedoms and push forward a democratization of divided democracy could offer one future perspective of the political organization of individualized society.

On the fragility of social life

Along with the ecological crisis, the knowledge has spread that the institutions of modernity in industrial society, particularly technology and industry, cannot control many of the effects they unleash. This thought is more barbed than it might seem at first. Everyone is reminded of the figure of the sorcerer's apprentice. But this misses the point in a double sense. First, these are effects that are systematically blocked out and therefore grow exponentially; second, the lack of controllability is measured by the failure of the achieved and available control instruments. For instance, a cleverly devised system of acceptable level provisions has been set up. On closer analysis, it turns out that this does not solve the problem because, to cite one example, only a limited number among the multitude of new substances are subject to these regulations, so that the whole system of acceptable levels resembles a Swiss cheese in which, as we all know, the holes are an essential part. Moreover, that attempt at a solution surreptitiously turns into a significant cause of problems. Substances that have been legalized by not being regulated are free to poison the air, water, ground and foodstuffs, with the consequence that following the rules, not exceeding them, is what poisons the 'environment'.

The striking aspect of this and numerous other examples is the noteworthy transformation of institutions for *overcoming* problems into institutions for *causing* problems. Putting it in other terms, second-order problems are the problem for industrial modernity. Whereas first-order problems refer to a pre-modern world – nature, tradition, unbroken constraints of transcendentally based systems of domination – against which the pretensions to problem-solving and progress in early modernity can develop their pathos and power of conviction, second-order problems stem from the institutional system of industrial modernity itself. The consequence is that anyone who calls on the recipes established in these institutions against the second-order problems is not only not contributing anything to solving them, he is indeed creating and intensifying them. Elaborate arrangements are needed to keep this from becoming apparent. Second-order problems must be denied or downplayed; the mere recognition of them should be hampered or prevented.

In dealing with uncertainty and unforeseen effects (designed to be so by a certain organizational pattern) the distinction between *risks* and *dangers* has become established for this contrast between problematic situations of first and second order (Beck 1994; Bonss 1995; Lau 1996). Risks are effects of industrial production and technical systems that are still 'controllable' by the established institutions (according to certain, socially negotiated rules); that is no longer the case for dangers. A very rough distinction is provided by the principle of private insurability. Wherever insurance companies step out of the picture or refuse to enter in the first place, based on their internal standards of economic rationality, the alarm systems for uncontrollable effects light up, even if engineers and managers assure the harmlessness of their ventures.

Whatever this may be like in detail, the issue of interest here is the fundamental fact of second-order problem situations. The arrangements that were created and implemented to overcome issues and situations change camps in the further modernization of modernity and metamorphose from sources of problem solutions into causes of problems, while their principles and practices remain constant. The maddening part is that they are simultaneously source and cause, and this blocks both the recognition and the overcoming of this reversal of functions, this functional defection. The mere example of the environmental crisis and the dangerous consequences of technological mass-produced change (as in genetic engineering and human genetics) shows that this is far from being understood (Beck 1992, 1994, 1996a; Luhmann 1991 deals with this only peripherally). The dimensions of the effects still are reflected and operate there in a dimension of speechlessness that is difficult to perceive socially. Yet, as we are now coming to realize, this defection from the side of problem solutions to the side of problem causes reaches well beyond the group of institutions that have been spotlighted by an alarmed public in the environmental crisis (the chemical industry, certain professions, technical advisory and standardization committees, environmental administrations, and so on). Analogous problems can be demonstrated in schools, the Employment Office, labour law and in the services of the welfare state. Their achievements appear to be tied to side-effects that have so far been insufficiently appreciated, and they frequently impede the solution. Thus they create and intensify the problematic situations to which they are supposed to respond, to a degree that mocks all reason and especially the institutions' claim to provide solutions. The extent of this discrepancy may correspond to that of the ecological self-endangerment, but there is a crucial difference: in this case the effects have eyes, hands and weapons.

The most striking examples are the ghettos of the excluded, the lumpenproletariat of civilized society, not just in India, South America and Africa, but in all the metropolises of the world (cf. Peterson 1991; Wilson 1991; Wolch 1991; Lash and Urry 1994). Twenty per cent of the population in the United States lives below the poverty line and the number of new illiterates is incalculable. Children must pass through

metal detectors to enter school buildings to prevent them from stab-
bing or shooting one another or their teachers. These are only a few
rough indicators that such effects are also not 'environmental effects'
that can be externalized; they remain present in and act upon the
centre of society. The concept of 'environmental destruction' corresponds to that of 'ghettos of poverty'. Both give the illusion of what is
becoming impossible: the exclusion or eradication of the 'side-effects'
in the centres of modern society.

The first step towards revealing this is to destroy the fictions of simple
industrial-society modernity, according to which these are first-order
problems. That would imply that more schools, more welfare, more
social work, more economic growth, more jobs or more police and
more prisons, in general, more government, would solve the problem of
the excluded, or at least push it down below the level of public scrutiny.
This misunderstanding is based on the confusion of first and second
modernity. It represses what must be recognized: that schools, welfare
institutions, law and order policies, and so on, extend problems and
produce new ones rather than solving them, and why this is so.

We cannot answer these questions at this point, but we can at least
address them. We are being reduced to naked survival interests, to
violence arising from no purpose other than a personal thrill and
criminality that has become so normal because the idea of legitimate
legality seems to belong on a different planet, so that the meaning of
violating the law can only be enforced from the outside. This may be
bringing about new tribal rituals, loyalty and forms of rule, but they
have nothing to do with primeval, pre-civilized savagery. This is a new
form of *constructed barbarism*, that is, these are second-order problems. This barbarism is the paradoxical and scarcely understood sum
of all attempts to prevent, found and construct a humane society. The
expression 'barbarism' is apt in the sense that it designates the opposite
of civilization and re-emerges at the culmination of civilization.

The decisive point can be located in the reflected image of individualization. All types of life conduct in modern society are highly
societalized. This means that, even if the image of individual autonomy
flutters around in people's minds, such ways of living can be practised
only by participating in and being dependent upon a variety of institutions (Beck and Beck-Gernsheim 1996). This is based in essence on
the fact that all opportunities and prerequisites for self-sufficiency are
cut off in the approach to modernity. Farmers are the exception that
proves the rule, since even they obtain a good (or bad) part of the food
they need from the supermarket. Everyone is therefore working for
something with which he cannot personally do anything in the sense of

assuring his own subsistence. Thus work for others becomes the key to living in modernity, along with everything this presupposes: not just training, but also available jobs; not just a certain subjective ability, but demonstrable licensed competence; and not just that but also readiness and ability, as well as a diurnal, annual and life rhythm appropriate for learning and working.

Individualism (as understood here) is precisely the process in which individuals (more or less) succeed in this. Individualization can thus be decoded as a positive circle in the interplay between the acquisition of prerequisites, the opportunities they open up, and the maximization and utilization of such opportunities. In this case, someone manages to get access to higher education, hence to a career, hence to an attractive residence, all of this of course against the backdrop of stable citizenship and guaranteed rights to political freedom. In sum, this easily leads to a melancholy affluence with no real prospects besides a comfortable life.

Alongside a number of intermediate and transitional forms, the logical opposite and shadow of the above, there is also the negative circle. It is the summation and exponentiation of 'exclusions' (Niklas Luhmann) which demonstrate and denounce the civilized origin and constructed nature of barbarism. People caught in these circles of exclusion not only have no opportunities, they in fact collide with a bureaucratic wall of futility. The crucial thing is that this wall is just the other side of the highly cultivated entry prerequisites and their interdependencies, which the individual has difficulty seeing through and certainly cannot control.

It begins with the shifting prerequisites for a job, which represents the key to survival. Suddenly the labour market has a new lock, so to speak, so that the old keys – for instance, a secondary modern or special school certificate – no longer open anything. Thus education, or, better, the gradation of school types, changes from a stairway upwards into an escalator downwards, which one must run up in order to reach any promising floor. If an occupationally qualified educational certificate is missing, then the only remaining position in life is a life on the dole. Still, there are cases where even a school certificate lies out of reach atop a Mount Everest of bureaucracy. Families who live on the street (in India, but in Brazil and the United States as well) cannot provide a legal residence, which makes it impossible for their children to attend school. Those without proper identification will be sent to jail if suspicion arises, cannot vote, marry (legally), and so on.

The modern biography with its inherent dependency on institutions has been compared to a marionette dangling from the strings of bureaucratic rules. It is now becoming clear that the contrary existence of cut strings can force people into an uncivilized or anti-civilized life within civilization. The situation of the excluded is the obverse of the elevated demands of institutions which, at least to a large extent, were invented precisely in order to prevent such collective collapses. The excluded are not excluded at all in another sense; indeed, they are omnipresent. The scandal of their exclusion reflects back into the centre of modernity in industrial society and not just in the form of violence and loss of civility. It is reflected equally in the disruption or even destruction of the pretensions and foundations of institutions that live on the fiction of overcoming the problem of such 'enclosed outsiders'.

It goes without saying that functional differentiation cannot give order to its exclusion range, although because of its universal social self-concept it also extends there; that is, it does not distinguish money according to the hand which spends or receives it. It makes laws apply to everyone, and does not deny anyone the right to marry and start a family (or make that right dependent on official approval). This logic of functional differentiation comes into conflict with the facts of the exclusion. The improbability and artificiality of that logic become visible. Its codes apply and do not apply in the same society. If things become difficult and can no longer be marginalized, one can draw the conclusion that society is 'supercoded' by the distinction between inclusion (with loose integration) and exclusion (with solid integration) and that one must first orient oneself according to this difference, if one wishes to find one's way.

This certainly reacts back onto the functional system itself, which can no longer meet its own demands and begin to adapt to that fact. What does it mean for an educational system that the illiteracy rate does not decline, but increases for reasons that cannot be controlled in schools? What does it mean for the political system if in more and more areas peace (= freedom from violence) can no longer be assured? What does it mean for the legal system if the exclusion range and then the police as a communication organization between inclusion and exclusion and finally politics as well are no longer bound by a government of laws, but can act just as well and just as successfully as legally? What does it mean for the economic system if large parts of the population are excluded from the marketplace, but cannot support themselves in the manner of a subsistence economy either, so that it becomes obvious that the economy is not capable of delivering sufficient food wherever it is needed? So far we have no justification for the assumption that these conditions could lead to a global collapse of the functional systems. Autopoiesis in those systems is too robust for that. If one pays attention to structural developments inside these systems, one will no longer be able to ignore the effects of an increasing harshness and of the predominance of the difference of inclusion and exclusion. Vis-à-vis the ecological problem considered dominant today, a trend may be beginning here that deserves at least equal attention and generates at least as much perplexity. (Luhmann 1994: 88–91)

The constructed fate of exclusion results from the connection of absoluteness to helplessness, with which the exclusion is generated as a 'side-effect', on the one hand, and accepted as a type of 'natural fate', on the other. This naturalization and fatalization of hopelessness has absolutely nothing to do with nature. Everything which constitutes this different nature of those ejected by civilization is highly modern. This includes the dependence on access to institutions in order to be able to make a living and build up a life history and outlook, the interdependence of the exclusions of which the hopelessness is made, even the disintegration of the subsidiary circles of security – marriage, family, parenthood, a functioning neighbourhood. Characteristically, only the churches appear to be spared, at least in part, from this failure. All of this is modern in origin and much is even reflexively modern. An additional factor is the institutions' blind spot in perceiving problems. If people even find it difficult to view themselves as the cause of problems, which therefore cannot be solved among other people, then this type of self-referentiality appears virtually out of the question among social institutions. The old Chinese proverb 'Whoever would change the world must first look around his own house' is in crass contradiction to the prevailing institutional egoism.

It will be necessary to distinguish different fundamental forms of biography in modernity: risk biography, danger biography and the catastrophic existences and situations of constructed barbarism. The term 'biography' would be a euphemism for the latter, since it presumes elements of modern individualism. These downsides of the hierarchies of institutional access do not add up to class situations, however, because the latter presume that which has been cut off here: (dis)integration through gainful (un)employment. Luhmann attempted to show that this 'exclusion range', in contrast to functionally differentiated society, is 'highly integrated': 'highly integrated because the exclusion from one functional system almost automatically leads to the exclusion from another one' (Luhmann 1994: 41).

This impression is deceptive, in my view, or applies only in a very limited, functionalist sense. When viewed for themselves, rather than in the uniformity of institutional exclusion, no situations which are somehow integrated are originating here; instead these are tentative forms of forced self-organization, resembling the Hobbesian state of nature in late modernity. Here it is necessary to steal or snatch together opportunity to survive from the instrumental exploitation of the unseen and rejected – gaps in the law, refuse, and so on.

The modes of surviving on the dark side of modernity are certainly not easily accessible or comprehensible to the possibilities of institutionalized social science. But this fundamental feature of being cut off from precisely those institutional strings on which making a living hangs in modernity differentiates them from risk and danger biographies.

These latter two modes of living have in common the fact that there is something afoot in them. Both are possible fragmentary biographies, now a bit more, then a bit less. That is to say, no matter what the appearance of wealth and security, these are biographies in which skidding off or falling are always tangibly present. This reflects the enormous exertion which the success of a do-it-yourself biography implies for those who must continually create and hold together with threads from their hands and minds the patchwork magic carpets they appear to be riding.

In the case of risk biographies, the available resources (of whatever type) still appear to correspond to the demand for (and feeling of) control, while danger biographies have passed beyond this threshold of perceived controllability. Here the individuals find themselves in situations of tension, in which with their possibilities of control they run hopelessly behind the out-of-control problems. In contrast to the institutional meltdown of exclusion situations, these danger biographies still presume the desire and compulsion to lead a life of one's own. Only on this horizon does the feeling of uncontrollability, the feeling of being overtaxed and overrun come out, as is mentioned in so many social science interviews.

A new Reformation?

An answer, albeit grossly oversimplified, to the question of what reflexive modernization means, namely a change in the foundations of modernity, was played through in this chapter. Yet this answer retrospectively raises a number of new questions.

Which foundations change and for whom? By what means? Do they change conceptually? In action? Who sees the 'unseen' side-effects and keeps records of them? How can it be decided in a methodologically understandable manner whether certain foundations of certain institutions remain the same or change?

That the foundations of the modes of living and working changed in the transition from nomadic existence to settled society was only discovered *post hoc* and has now been widely accepted. How the Renaissance differs from the Middle Ages and the modern era remains controversial. Sociology, of course (with the cultural theory of Mary

Douglas forming one of the few exceptions) has largely agreed that a systemic breach exists between traditional, status-based, agrarian, feudal societies, on the one hand, and modern, industrial, capitalist, democratic societies, on the other. This is the topic of both the classics of sociology and modernization sociology since the forties, which began characteristically as the sociology of development and developing countries. The theory of reflexive modernization, on the other hand, must struggle against three types of difficulties. First, it does not place the period boundary between modernity and non-modernity (in the sense of tradition or postmodernity) but asserts instead a typology of different and diverse 'modern' societies. It thus assumes a continuity of 'modernity' (in the sense of a development of certain basic ideas and principles in intellectual history, on the one hand, and their political implementation and generalization in the model of classical industrial modernity, on the other) and asserts a change of foundations within unchanging structures (parliamentary democracy or the private market economy, for instance). This is therefore a theory of the inherent transformation of foundations.

A second difficulty is tied to that. Not only must a concrete distinction be made between that which remains the same and the premises, categories and foundations that change. It is probable that many basic assumptions in the minds of many people, on paper, in law, in routines and in the strategic action of organizational elites, will remain completely unbroken, perhaps even be deliberately defended, initially against attacks 'from outside', from the public, the parties, the social movements, and so on.

That already addresses the third difficulty. Insofar as reflexive modernization is not conceived on the plan of unseen side-effects, it marks a social conflict that unfolds in the conflicts among agents in plants, publics, social movements, as well as in political and scientific elites, and it will probably intensify in the future. Viewed in that way, the theory of reflexive modernization refers to an ongoing process, the outcome of which cannot be anticipated by anyone today.

If one recalls these three basic difficulties – immanence, simultaneity of continuity and rupture, and fundamental openness and unpredictability – of contentious, reflexive modernization processes and one looks around for historical comparison, one encounters the *Reformation*. As early as 1974, the political scientist Robert Nisbet speaks in this sense of the possibility of a 'new Reformation':

> My reference . . . to the possibility of a new Reformation taking place or beginning to take place in our age was not entirely casual. There are

junctures in history when some dominant institution reveals incapacity to sustain any longer the loyalties of populations living within its authority. There came a time, as we know, when the Christian church, which had penetrated almost every corner and crevice of Western life, had become, as a rising number of gifted minds thought, top heavy from absorption of functions, responsibilities, powers and privileges. However we choose to describe the events of the sixteenth century, under whatever larger rubric we place them, there is abundant evidence that among intellectuals and laymen there came a time when the church, in its visible institutional form, had ceased to be able to maintain order, supply consensus or reach out for the allegiance of human beings to the degree that it formerly had.

Has the national state reached this position in our time? No one can be certain, of course. . . . Possibly we are at the beginning of a Reformation, this time with the state rather than the church at its centre; possibly we are going through one of the many small and transitory evolutions that history records, with damage, yes, but not lasting alteration of landscape. We shall see, no doubt, in due time. (Nisbet 1974: 631)

In fact, instructive parallels do exist between the 'religious conflicts' of Protestants and Catholics, on the one hand, and reflexive modernizers on the other. Both sides refer in each case to the same foundations – in the former case, the Christian religion (Bible), in the latter, the claim to modernity, rationality and enlightenment. Simple modernization no longer expresses itself, of course, in a theological orthodoxy, but rather in a business, economic, political and social science 'orthodoxy', which also has a way of selling indulgences: the absolution from ecological sins (by the granting of seals of ecological approval for products). The conflicts no longer take place in the context of the Christian church, but rather in the scientific, economic and political institutions and the theories that sustain them. What is publicly demanded and debated is in fact equivalent to a reformation of industrial dogmatism.

It is possible to speak of a 'reformation' of industrial modernity if, first, influential intellectuals, but members of the political and economic elites as well, crossing all party loyalties, publicly withdraw their consent to certain central articles of faith in industrial modernity.[26] Of course, the combination of capitalism, democracy and nation state that developed in the form of 'occidental rationality' (Max Weber) has never had to complain of a lack of fundamental criticism.

Second, it is therefore essential that the criticism relate to a new quality of challenges, which engage public debate in such key words as 'global issues', 'human issues', the global economic society, global security, ecological devastation, migration movements, the disintegration of political loyalties, and so forth. The characteristic feature is that the challenges are interpreted as consequences of the successes (or failures) of social modernization processes. Only in that way can they count as an expression of reflexive modernization.

This discontent with modernity can of course provide grist for very different, even antagonistic, political mills. Third, therefore, it only makes sense to speak of a 'reformation' if it is associated with a call not for a 'strong state', but rather for global economic, ecological and other reforms, for the corresponding rethinking and new ways of acting on both small and large scales. Criticism is necessary but not sufficient. The existing institutions (including personal behaviour patterns in the private sphere) must be surrounded and besieged by fundamental alternatives. What is at stake are attempts at revitalizing the Enlightenment against its seeming demise in the institutional structure of modernity as embodied in democratic market economies. Reformation thus means the radicalization of modernity against its limitations and division in industrial society. This presumes social inventions and the collective courage to engage in political experiments, that is to say, inclinations and qualities that are not exactly frequently encountered, perhaps no longer even capable of garnering a majority. And yet, many signs indicate that in the confusion of the future, the struggle over a reformation of industrial orthodoxy will play a significant role.

2

The Construction of the Other Side of Modernity: Counter-modernization

Reflexive modernization does not necessarily lead, as was emphasized, to a reflection on modernization and its consequences, but may well give rise to forms of counter-modernization.

To use Kandinsky's differentiation, the And is permeating the Either–or. But it does not really nullify it thereby. On the contrary, the ambivalences of the And favour a renaissance of the Either–or.

Many components are present in this. First, the And can tolerate the Either–or only so long as the Either–or does not abolish and deny the And. But the Either–or is erasing the And. When all is said and done, the Either–or, not the And, prevails among the two. (At which point the And crosses over somewhat to the Either–or under force of necessity.) Second, the And becomes concrete and to just that extent intolerable in the world of shortages and dangers. So that, third and in conclusion, the significance of the Either–or grows once again in people's consciousness and behaviour.

'The supreme difficulty of our generation', according to an article from London's *Economist* from 1930 cited by the historian Paul Kennedy,

> is that our achievements on the economic plane of life have outstripped our progress on the political plane to such an extent that our politics and our economics are continually falling out of gear with one another. On the economic plane, the world has been organized into a single

all-embracing unit of activity. On the political plane, it has not only remained partitioned into sixty or seventy sovereign national States, but the national units have been growing smaller and more numerous and the national consciousnesses more acute. The tension between these two antithetical tendencies has been producing a series of jolts and jars and smashes in the social life of humanity. (*Economist*, 11 October 1930: 652; cited in Kennedy 1993: 329)

Reflexive modernization abolishes boundaries – of classes, business sectors, nations, continents, families, gender roles and so on. Counter-modernization asserts, draws, creates and solidifies all boundaries over again. We have long been living under a 'domestic policy of global dimensions' (Carl Friedrich von Weizsäcker) and that is why the fences are being renovated and new flags are raised and why the barriers in thought and action take on such a seductive glow for many people. This coexistence and opposition between reflexive modernization and counter-modernization will now be investigated.

Counter-modernity means constructed certitude

The concept of 'counter-modernity', as the very name suggests, is conceived of as an antithesis to modernity. There would be nothing very surprising in this negation if this contradiction/connection were not conceived within modernity as an integral design principle of modernity itself. If modernity means questions, decisions and calculability, then counter-modernity means indubitability, indecision, incalculability and the attempt to force this indecision, contrary to all modernity, into a decision in modernity. Here too the And shows up again; indecision and decision, modernity and counter-modernity. This occurs precisely as a reaction to the questioning of modernity, with this very limitation of modernity in modern society (despite all its inherent and yet characteristic contradictions) giving contours and a framework to industrial modernity and strengthening them.

In the term 'counter-modernity' the word 'modernity' thus also has an adjectival sense: modern counter-modernity. That is, contrary to the substance of key counter-modern concepts such as nation, people, nature, woman or man, this does *not* involve something ancient, beyond time, anthropological or transcendental (or whatever one wishes to call these status words of inexorability). It involves something that came into being relatively late, namely with modernity and against it. Being invented belongs to the concept of counter-modernity just as much as green to grass. People say 'nature' but intend and are engaged in 'naturalization'. More precisely, this is renaturalization, because the naturalization is a reaction to questioning. That is what counter-modernization intends and does.

Counter-modernity must, first, be constructed or chosen, so that it is a project and a product of modernity (requiring substantiation and so on). Second, it contradicts modernity; third, it limits it in a way that creates a structure; fourth, it is not endangered in its open contradiction of modernity by continuing modernization; instead, fifth, it obtains its structure-forming stability only through special (counter-modern) modes of legitimation. In this sense, Max Weber's typology of legitimate rule would need to be supplemented by counter-modern forms of legitimation, the other side of modernity, so to speak.

In this sense I define 'counter-modernity' as *constructed and constructible certitude (hergestellte FraglosigKeit)*, more precisely liquidation, disposal of the question into which modernity has disintegrated. Counter-modernity absorbs, demonizes and dismisses the questions raised and repeated by modernity. (Instead of 'constructed certitude' the definition could have also read 'constructed indecision', 'constructed ascription', and so on, all of which would change only the indicator of the definition.)

In this not just active, but also conscious certitude lies the basis of a puzzle of counter-modernity. It connects that which appears to be ruled out – consciousness, awareness and its abolition or disappearance in certitude. This is also the basis for the central difference between the concept of institutionalization and the concept of counter-modernity. Both intend and aim at autonomization or, adopting the formulation used here, constructed certitude. Institutionalization means, however, a temporary, not a lasting certitude. By contrast, by its very concept, counter-modernity quite consciously absorbs questions.

To cite an example: pointing to women's ability to give birth is not a surreptitious or tacit, but an explicit attempt to construct in a single stroke the certitude of their subordinate position in 'modern' society. This makes three things evident: First, the modernity of counter-modernity is justified. Second, these justifications with which counter-modernity transforms doubt into certitude are often supplied by the sciences. In the example of women, this is well documented for medicine, biology, law and philosophy. The high-priests of simple modernity are thus revealed as the agents of counter-modernity. They supply at least, in advance or retrospectively, the cognitive instruments that enable and protect the restriction and division of modernity in the 'structure' of industrial society and its future mutations. Third, because it is explicit and required to substantiate itself, counter-modernization can also be 'desubstantiated' in the wake of continuing modernization and scientific critique. The above is an example of this; because of the historical and systematic work in women's studies, the attempt to base the old order of the sexes in the bedroom, the kitchen, professions and politics on the transhistorical ability of women to bear children, even in modernity, must be considered a failure in empirical-analytical terms.

Counter-modernity is thus not just constructed and modern in that sense. It permits, protects and produces certitude within the horizon of awareness. Thus it is active and conscious.

Even counter-modernity can of course be institutionalized, that is, it can become a matter of taken-for-granted routine. In that sense both modernity and counter-modernity can be institutionalized. Each can be made to appear 'self evident'. But counter-modernity achieves something which seems absurd and unthinkable when considered from the concept of modernity, that is, it abolishes, transforms and limits the infinity of questioning down to certitude, deliberately, or at least consciously.

Just this characteristic, this riddle, justifies the attraction and the irresistibility of counter-modernity in the living conditions of modernity. Exactly for this reason, counter-modernity becomes so promising for modernity, tormented by doubts and uncertainties in thought and action. Not some brutal destroyer of questions, but rather the conscious allowing of questioning to disappear in constructed, sometimes even scientifically fortified certitude makes the anti-civilizing impulse the possible victor over the self-restraint of civilization.

The characteristic of the *construction* of certitude is internally ambivalent; it remains open who does the construction, as well as how and against whom it occurs. One can highlight two types of understanding. One means construction in the sense of the negation of old, natural and anthropological; this emphasizes the historical character of counter-modernity, more precisely its origin together with industrial modernity in the eighteenth and nineteenth centuries. In the other view, constructed certitude can also arise from action, as can be shown in the example of violence.

On the small scale (ambushes) as well as on the large scale (wars), the threat to life forces the greatest possible simplification, as shown most insistently and apologetically by Carl Schmitt. This radicalization of the Either–or selects the questions and doubts of the And as its first victims.

In ordinary violence and retaliatory violence on the street, young people are therefore trying out a question trap which they know how to manipulate. This yields another essential feature of counter-modernity, namely praxis, that is, not just standardization, values, knowledge and awareness, but action. The counter-modernity of violence absorbs questions with action. It is internalized and rehearsed in action. It floats on action, washing away the questions in the stream of action.

This priority of the reality-creating force and power of action characterizes the superiority of counter-modernity, but also its inferiority. After all, acting always means the end of discussions, questions and ambiguities. Thinking refreshes itself in the Either–or of action and in the power of creating this Either–or against all the ambiguities of the And. Counter-modernity therefore rules by the 'language' of deeds, which undermines the eternal back-and-forth of doubt, puts an end to it and is therefore rewarded with the fruits, the simple brutalities and the brutal simplicities of reality.

Furthermore, if modernity appeals and fights with understanding, *ratio*, doubt, basis and cause, counter-modernity plays on the keyboard of the orphaned and dried-up emotions: hate, love, fear, mistrust, intoxication, sex and instinct. Belonging is practised and exercised emotionally, lived in and lived out. Certitude arises from and with the prevalence of a 'magic of feelings' (to use a modern term), an emotional praxis that sweeps away the trembling and hesitation of questioning and doubting with the instinctive and reflex-like security of becoming effective and making things effective in action. This is not, of course, intended to say that all feelings or appeals to emotion are by nature counter-modern (no more so than is all action). But counter-modern constructions are founded in emotions (compulsions to act or, more exactly, defend oneself). This is the source of their (convincing) force and power. Emotion and active assertion are their two main ingredients.

So it is not just active, constructible certitude, but the accomplishment of it, the success with it in the broad daylight of consciousness which characterizes counter-modernity. This quality of being able to douse the fires of questioning is acquired by counter-modernity while disappearing into the unambiguous milieu of action, which is superior to reality, as well as in an emotionalization with a distinctly intellectual note, the deepening, coloration, binding and stratification of this action. Here orders that are simply *established* emotionally, not substantiated, with clear profiles of intrinsic and extrinsic (that is, friend/enemy stereotypes) are acted out and made routine underneath the continuing doubtfulness of modern life.

Let us clarify and illustrate this concept of counter-modernity with a subject that avoids the negative aftertaste and values: love, sexuality, the option to love out one's urges. All the characteristics of counter-modernity are gathered here. Seemingly an ancient subject, it has achieved its everyday dramatic power only relatively late in history with romanticization, moral breakdown and individualization. This is reflected not only in advertising and the mass media, but also in the turbulences of 'serial polygamy', of which the high divorce rate gives only a superficial indication.

Private life both opens up and closes. That is, the priests retreat from the bedrooms where they used to be present by virtue of the confessional. Law does the same. This is how *the* opposition to calculating modernity – love, with all the heavens and hells of its promises and disasters – develops. 'The idea of civilized war, well-behaved killing and bomb-dropping', writes Katharina Tutschky, 'is as absurd as the idea of a sexual relationship conducted by the book' (*Süddeutsche Zeitung-Magazin* 10, 12 March 1993: 16).

People know about asking questions and are therefore able to dispose of accustomed, enlightened sexuality by questioning. This is how they manage to submerge themselves in a voluntary unquestioned following of their urges, even in hostility to questioning. Robert Musil speaks of how people turn into 'raving fools' in the intoxication of love. (One really ought to add: 'want to turn into'.) There is scarcely a more apt image. Something similar applies to violence and war, the other related stages of counter-modernity.

All the concepts that modernity dismantles, unmasks and delegitimates are sacred to counter-modernity; of course this includes 'tradition' and the 'cultivation', that is, invention of it, but also nature, religion, the nation, the distinction between ourselves and 'strangers', we–they identities and hence their extreme intensification, friend–enemy relationships. Violence is the magic wand of resimplification, whether in the governmental form of the military (police), in international wars, in civil wars between various subgroups or, finally, in street violence, all of which penetrate into the now porous state monopoly on force and live from its decay and loss of legitimacy. All of this implies, however, that the concentration on the concept of tradition narrows one's perspective and horizon. It underestimates the variety available, one could say, the functional equivalence of counter-modern elements and institutions, which arise and come to prominence in the industrial era. It therefore also misses their differences and antagonisms in pattern and mode of functioning, as well as, let us not forget, their attractiveness in modern or, more exactly, hypermodern circumstances.

By contrast, the dialectics of modernity and counter-modernity will be placed in the centre here. For good reasons, Max Weber analysed modernity as a process of disenchantment. Simultaneously, however, a process of sanctification, naturalization and tabooization is taking place. The deconstruction of traditions can be contrasted to processes of reconstruction. Unmasking and remasking go hand in hand. Indeed, the latter processes seem, paradoxically, to support and enable the former. In short, a more complex view is necessary, one that discovers the simultaneity of contradictions and dependencies of reflexively modern and counter-modern elements and structures in the image of 'modern' society.

The proponents of counter-modernity are compelled, as Helmut Dubiel writes, 'to work on the ground of modernity' (Dubiel 1992: 753). Yodelling and high-tech, hatred of foreigners and superindustrialization are presented and represented as mutually enabling contradictions.

Counter-modernity and its theoreticians live under a contradiction. They can never honour what they propose. By their recourse to the costumes of the past they limit (if successful) the autonomous course of modernity. The masquerade of the past is performed on the stages of modernity as a real-life drama by contemporary people with modern means (including the generation of reality and efficacy by the mass media).

> The hybrid European – all in all, a tolerably ugly plebeian – simply needs a costume: he requires history as a storage room for costumes. To be sure, he soon notices that none fits him very well; so he keeps changing. Let anyone look at the nineteenth century with an eye for these quick preferences and changes of the style masquerade; also for the moments of despair over the fact that 'nothing is becoming'. It is of no use to parade as romantic or classical, Christian or Florentine, baroque or 'national', *in moribus et artibus*. But the 'spirit', especially the 'historical spirit', finds its advantage even in this despair: again and again, a new piece of prehistory or a foreign country is tried on, put on, taken off, packed away, and above all *studied*: we are the first age that has truly studied 'costumes' – I mean those of moralities, articles of faith, tastes in the arts and religions – prepared like no previous age for a carnival in the grand style, for the laughter and high spirits of the most spiritual revelry, for the transcendental heights of the highest nonsense and Aristophanean derision of the world. Perhaps this is where we shall discover the realm of our *invention*, that realm in which we, too, can still be original, say, as parodists of world history and God's buffoons – perhaps, even if nothing else today has any future, our *laughter* may yet have a future. (Nietzsche 1966: 340)

Here the most effective masks are those at which no one can laugh. In Europe, and, in particular, in Germany, one is allowed to do almost anything after the end of the East–West conflict, from sitting naked in the subway to plastering one's hair into spikes and painting them garish colours. But when someone shouts 'Heil Hitler!' and scrawls 'Juden raus!' on walls, this hits a sensitive nerve of our century and provokes shock waves that are felt around the world.

Counter-modernity is modern and therefore in need of substantiation. As Martin Riesebrodt (1993) shows in a comparative study of American Protestants early in this century and Iranian Shiites since the sixties, these fundamentalist tendencies need to defend not just their beliefs and readings of the holy scriptures, but their way of life as well, against effective competing interpretations and demands. In the dawning experience of relativity in modernity, faith becomes a matter of decision and reasons, but this is certainly not a matter of visions of celestial justice. Rather, in view of the alternatives that are impinging – from women working outside the home, to the diminishing ability of parents to reach their children, all the way to the frequency of divorce and 'permissive' sexuality – the core of traditional ways of life is being put at stake. In this sense Riesebrodt sees a 'patriarchal protest movement in a great variety of forms' being articulated and forming into ranks in modern fundamentalism.

All of this results in a fundamental problem: how is it possible to institutionalize certitude and push through counter-modernity with the means of modernity? How can constructed certitude be legitimized with the means of modernity? To explore this, four exemplary questions will be dealt with below. First, how are modernity and counter-modernity intermeshed and fused together in the model of the *democratic nation state*? Second, how are the *contradictions of democratization and militarization* neutralized in the model of the nation state and when and how do they erupt? Third, how can *naturalization* be interpreted as constructed certitude? What is its characteristic and how can it be illustrated by the example of the naturalization of women? Fourth, and in conclusion, the dilemmas that result for a construction of the stranger in the global risk society will at least be indicated.

The invention of the nation: national democracy as restricted modernity

How do nations come into being? What was the origin of the model behind ordering the world according to the Either–or nation states?

> Two passengers in a railway compartment. We know nothing about
> them, their origin or their destination. They have made themselves at
> home and have commandeered the little tables, coat-hooks and baggage-
> racks. Newspapers, coats and bags lie around on the empty seats. The
> door opens and two new travellers enter. Their arrival is not welcomed.
> A distinct reluctance to move up, to clear the free seats and let the
> newcomers share them is evident. The original passengers, even if they do
> not know one another, behave with a remarkable degree of solidarity.
> They display a united front against the new arrivals. The compartment
> has become their territory, and they regard each new arrival as an
> intruder. Their consciousness is that of natives claiming the whole space
> for themselves. This view cannot be rationally justified. It appears all the
> more deeply rooted. (Enzensberger 1994)

'Nevertheless, matters rarely get to the point of open conflict', Hans
Magnus Enzensberger continues this scene, because the 'territorial
instinct' of central European passengers in a train compartment is well
trained and civilized. 'The railway compartment is . . . a location
which serves only to change locations. . . . The passenger is the negation of the sedentary person. He has traded a real territory for a virtual
one. Despite this, he defends his transient abode with sullen resent-
ment.'

It is strange and noteworthy that this 'territorial instinct' shows its
universal reflex-like absurdity precisely at this transitory place of
coming and going, comprehensible to everyone, because everyone has
'driven away intruders' from empty seats with (more or less civil)
territorial behaviour.

> Two new passengers open the compartment door. From this instant, the
> status of those who entered earlier changes. Only a moment ago, they
> were intruders; now, all at once, they are natives. They now belong to the
> sedentary clan of compartment-occupants and claim all the privileges the
> latter believe are due to them. The defence of an 'ancestral' territory that
> was only recently occupied appears paradoxical. The occupants do not
> empathize with the newcomers, who have to struggle against the same
> opposition . . . (Enzensberger 1994: 105f)

And so it continues. The associations and conclusions arise almost
automatically. Is it not often 'foreigners', Greek workers in Germany,
perhaps, who express distaste for others 'of their kind', such as Turks
who live and work in Germany? Are 'Germans' themselves not an odd
mixture, a condensate of various nomads stuck in one place who now,
bound together by their 'territorial instinct', quite similarly to those
travellers in the speeding train, are directing their national territorial-
ism against newly arriving 'foreigners'? Is the aggressiveness that has

built up and is now beginning to express itself not just a natural hiccup, a 'violent burp' that comes from the national 'gastric fluids' and thus can scarcely be suppressed? Do not all attempts to suppress this archetypal mistrust end up in the undesired promotion of the undesirable – violence against foreigners?

The moral of Enzensberger's clever railway parable is that 'Sectional self-interest and xenophobia are anthropological constants which pre-date every rationalization. Their universal distribution suggests that they are older than all known societies' (Enzensberger 1994: 106). That is meant to promote calmness, which is so quickly lost in post-(yet never completely post-)Nazi Germany. And yet the question really is precisely this: is the 'territorial reflex' that is dressed up anthro-pologically here with infectious clarity not itself the product of a consciously or unconsciously concealed Eurocentrism? As an ana-chronistic thought experiment, imagine a primitive group in a German train and one of their own walks through the sliding door. What rejoicing! The proverbial Indian dances would upset all the German train schedules, perhaps even the train itself. But if an 'outsider', for them, that is, were to enter, he would (letting all our prejudices run wild for a moment) either be adored as a deity or eaten after being roasted on the seat frame.

The conclusion of the thought experiment: does the way a person sitting in the express train drives away an outsider not presume the express train, that is, the mobile world? To put the question another way, does this 'border-drawing instinct' not arise only at the end of a long European evolution with the goal of the full differentiation of individuals? Is the defensive reflex of everyone against everyone else, as depicted so forcefully by Enzensberger, not an almost exemplary outcome of late individualization? Is that not why it appears so 'natu-ral' and hence so completely self-evident to us moderns and hypermod-erns? Is this just an expression of our modern 'anthropology', elevated to such generality, yet ultimately amounting to individualized es-trangement from all others? Is this then a perfect example of con-structed certitude?[1]

The initial insight into 'counter-modernity' can be illustrated using, and simultaneously questioning, the evidence of the Enzensberger example. Let it be granted that there is such a thing as a 'border-draw-ing reflex'. It may be that people who grow into a certain family acquire an archetypal trust in one another, coloured by language and history, something for which German has only concepts that have been abused. It may be that it relaxes and strengthens democracy to admit this.

Yet it is also possible that an anthropologizing view would also fall prey to the very same *naturalization* with which counter-modernity ornaments and disguises itself to strengthen itself. One thing is clear, however; it is *never* possible to found the state and society model of nationalism and the nation state with this 'primeval ethnic need', much less the eruptions of violence and xenophobia in Europe embroiled in a hot war now that the Cold War is over.

The national is certainly not a subterranean circulation system of history that was forgotten and repressed and (for that reason, among others) is now once again erupting and bleeding. This naturalizing view is initially not moral at all, but historical, and thoroughly false in that respect (as Enzensberger also sees and says quite clearly[2]). 'Nationalism is not the awakening of nations to self-consciousness,' writes the historian Ernst Gellner. Instead, the advocates of the 'national heritage' attempt to generate and strengthen a legend by all means available: family trees, genetic and racial theories. Gellner continues, 'it invents nations where they do not exist' (Gellner 1964: 169; quoted according to Anderson 1983: 15; cf. Gellner 1983 as well). This 'invention of the nation' (Benedict Anderson) is an exemplary process; in fact it is the founding act of both modern and counter-modern industrial society. As has been well researched by historians, the contradictions of modernity and counter-modernity – democracy and people – are welded together here almost seamlessly in the model of 'national democracy' or 'popular rule'. This work of art, this masterpiece of divided modernity, is now breaking up with the advent of globalization. This is to be examined.

A 'nation', as defined by Anderson,

> is an imagined political community – and imagined as both limited and sovereign. It is *imagined* because the members of even the smallest nation will never know most of their fellow-members, meet them or even hear of them, yet in the minds of each lives the image of their communion. . . . The nation is imagined as *limited*, because even the largest of them, encompassing perhaps a billion human beings, has finite, if elastic, boundaries, beyond which lie other nations. (Anderson 1983: 15f)

The appeal to the national is therefore, to use a phrase of Robert Musil, 'of virtually ironic irrationality' (Musil 1967: 15). Not even the most glowing nationalist would dream of a state comprising all of humanity, as Christians quite certainly once dreamed of a 'wholly Christian planet' (Anderson 1983: 16).

This concept is counter-modern, not primeval, for at least two reasons. First, this image of an anonymous yet sovereign community of the 'people' turns on its head the social model that prevailed for centuries, dynasties that denied any legitimation to the people and derived their rights and dominion from God with the support of the church and its priesthood and the believed religion of their subjects. The idea of the people as sovereign or the sovereign meant more than blasphemy, it could mean one's head. It was necessary, therefore, to cut the tie that bound the earthly to the heavenly realms. In that sense, the linguistic forms and formulas – popular sovereignty, fatherland, mother tongue, and so on – that are minted and put into circulation here are coinages of a secularized religion.

The idea of the unity of the 'folk community' hardly sounds any less bizarre. It was necessary here to do violence to the original diversity that prevailed everywhere. This could be successful only to the extent that a written language was invented, and that word is really appropriate here. This could no longer be the Christian, dynastic language of dominion and administration. Instead it had to be 'cast' from a language unifying the numerous spoken dialects, one for which two things are characteristic. First, opening up linguistic space and making it generally present and available. That is, it was necessary to create what was later known as a 'mother tongue'. Second, this space also had to be filled in a quite ordinary way, one that could be lived and experienced on the pattern of the 'anonymous community' of the nation. The symbol for this, as Anderson shows, is the daily reading of newspapers.

Newspapers are the literary equivalent of mayflies, and reading them is a kind of mass ceremony that is performed in nomadic isolation and at the same time standardized in form. Hegel made the remark that the newspaper was modern man's excuse for morning prayers (quoted in Anderson 1983: 39).

Not until the invention and mass consumption of the newspaper was the linguistic space filled out (or cluttered up, one might almost say today), the space that keeps that anonymous national community up to date with 'news' changing daily and even hourly, and in that way creates the community. Nations are therefore nations of people influenced by the same newspapers. This presumes an infinite number of things: the invention of printing, the invention of written languages, the displacement of Latin, the liberation of speech and books, even the invention of the capitalistic market for speech and books, of rapid and mass consumption, of current events and their decay time, to demonstrate only this line of the constructibility of a public understanding itself to be 'communal' and 'national' in reading and in the knowledge of reading. Language must be crowned by *national* poets, it needs *national* heroes, from the Olympics to the cemetery.

Only with the aid of the newspaper market can the necessary uniformity of the national, the 'mother tongue', be directed inward and established. The nation and the national language usually deny and violently suppress the diversity of ethnic groups. Only in that way can it be set off from the outside, acquire uniformity and contrast and stabilize itself. Mediation is aspired to by minority rights, which, however, are always granted only with great restrictions, as history shows. Among other things, capitalism and its motive forces are the prerequisite to make the idea of that nation as a bounded, anonymous community of newspaper readers who stick their noses into the same puffed up matters every day capable of becoming reality at all.

These only apparently clear, but certainly not old language barriers, which made the national and national consciousness possible in the first place, therefore literally had to be *created*. Only when it was capable of being reproduced by printing did the national become possible! That only prepared the space, however. It was then filled with a collection of more or less curious ideas and plans to make those ideas a reality. That is the origin of that 'nation state cocktail' mixed from *ethos* and *demos* which was later made absolute. There was particular success in the British colonies of North America in mixing basic rights, a constitution, popular sovereignty, citizenship, republican institutions, capitalism, faith in technology, religiosity, the national flag and the national anthem, the musical paternoster of the nation, spiced with a general mood of revolution and rebellion, so much so that all of America, and one is by now inclined to say the rest of the world as well, is still on the trek into the Wild West.

This nation state intellectual and political formula radiated or threatened, depending on the side from which one viewed it. It was a great provocation to the dynastic model that ruled the world: monarchist institutions, absolutism, willing subservience, inherited nobility, serfdom, and so on. One thing that makes one somewhat sceptical, of course, is how unquestioningly slavery was integrated into the origins of American democracy. Thoreau, that arch-American who dreamed the American dream so infectiously and rebelliously that movements of civil disobedience all over the world draw sustenance from it even today, died with the firm belief that his struggle against slavery had been in vain.

This is how in the early nineteenth century the model of the nation state crystallized out, a model whose seductiveness for political elites of whatever colour lies in the fact that it confers the old idea of divine right, at least for a while and externally. After all, sovereignty implies superiority to all other institutions, restrained only by its own weakness or the military force of other states. Accordingly, as Anderson (1983) writes, this model was open to intellectual theft.

There have been attempts from above to *naturalize* the areas of dominion, which are quite mobile after all, in order to strip them of their historicity and dubitability and to eternalize them with the aura of the 'natural', but it is interesting that they have all failed. One can say they had to and still have to fail. For neither is the ethnic group an original category nor do the nation state boundaries coincide with those of the dynasties, nor is the nation state itself an ethnically uniform structure. Appeals to self-determination therefore always remain threatening. Every ethnic group that has any respect for itself and its elites can insist on its independence with the aid of the nation state model and can separate from the state group, with force if need be, in the name of self-determination.[3]

There are many examples for this failure of 'official nationalisms' (Seton-Watson), of which the Russian empire, including the decay of the Soviet Union, is only the most grandiose. This always involves the fruitless attempt 'at stretching the short, tight skin of the nation over the gigantic body of the empire', as Anderson puts it (Anderson 1983: 82). The image drawn by Enzensberger is more likely to be correct in this regard: nations are transit stations for people who try to prevent others from entering with the aid of their shared reading of newspapers. Of course the simile of the railway carriage is slightly incorrect, in a characteristic way, because all sorts of newspapers are read in that mobile site in the train.[4]

In global society, for which the intercontinental airliner is perhaps a better symbol than the express train, the desire for demarcation may grow, but the opportunities for drawing boundaries diminish. This perhaps makes the late-originating 'territorial instinct' (Enzensberger) both more vigorous and more difficult to satisfy.

National and global modernity: problematizing strangers

National or nation-state democracy is not based on a harmonization, but rather on politically sensitive compromise solutions of the contradictions between '*ethos* and *demos*' (Francis 1965; also Bauböck 1991 and Bielefeld 1991). Internally, the differences and conflicts between ethnic groups are standardized and harmonized out of existence. The road to the nation state is paved with oppression. Its law reads: Either–or. Externally, this implies exclusion, construction of alterity and enemy stereotypes as well as corroborating (operating) them in (threatening) wars; internally it means forced assimilation, expulsion and destroying the culture and life of 'deviant' groups that refuse to give in to the official monotony of the 'mother tongue'. Accordingly, the construction of natives and the transformation of 'strangers' into 'our own kind' was always handled restrictively.

> The success of the integration of immigrants depends on several factors that can be specified, such as relative number, class position, distance from the country of origin and opportunities for communication, as well as, among others, ideological 'factors'. The lack of a focused immigration policy has consequences equally as disastrous as a treatment of foreigners based on false (utopian) ideologies. . . . Neither regionalism nor federalism in themselves help to eliminate the problems of ethnic heterogeneity in the democratic state, as the by now failed 'melting pot' example in the USA teaches us. This applies to all immigration countries, which, moreover, often tend to dictatorship (Latin America) for this among other reasons, as well as to nation states that were set up on the territory of multiethnic communities that were created under quite different preconditions (Yugoslavia). (Francis 1992: 2)

If the nation is essentially a nation of people influenced by the same newspapers, it also becomes problematic in the age of globe-spanning television and telecommunication. This opens up the space of an unlimited public sphere, surmounting and undermining the national construction of 'foreign' and 'indigenous'. It is probably not coincidental that two events coincided in Europe: the abolition of borders and militant eruptions of xenophobia that attempt to re-establish the lost borders in an incendiary way (both materially and rhetorically).

Owing to global mobility, trade relationships, tourism, but also hybrids among 'our own kind' (from migratory movements of foreign workers to the international or national restaurant cultures), as well as the uniformity and standardization of world cultures, the possibilities of a national Either–or are disappearing and the indistinctness of the And are growing and dominating. *Individualization processes, considered globally, abolish prerequisites for constructing and renewing national oppositions of own-group and strangers*. Alterity, and consequently the familiarity of the indigenous, become blurred and deprived of tradition. Which does not imply that they disappear in the And, but quite to the contrary, they turn constructivistic and atavistic. The national becomes a question of power that creates and legitimates itself by forcible means. In this view, the eruptions of xenophobia and ethnically motivated wars in Europe indicate the tendency of borders to become unreal in global risk society. They are not evidence of the revivification of old, still effective popular cultures and ethnic identities suppressed in Marxism-Leninism; instead they are militant reactions to the disappearing possibilities of maintaining and renewing alterity and difference in the modernity of the And.

As Sighard Neckel surmises, this has perhaps even changed the type of the stranger and alterity which Georg Simmel used as the basis for his analyses at the turn of the century.

Does this type of 'alterity' still exist in our encounters with strangers, since the stranger attains significance for us only insofar as we encounter it? The unknown is not strange; it is quite simply unknown, non-existent for us. The stranger is the other which we know about or with which we become acquainted. We encounter the stranger more frequently today than previously and perhaps in a transformed manner. Two prerequisites in the relationship of the indigenous and the strange, a relationship characterized anthropologically by insecurity, appear to me to have become uncertain.

First of all, in the constructed global society we cannot unquestioningly assume that the characteristic uncertainty of mutual expectation is still connected in the same way to the experience of alterity. If global society is characterized by economic interdependence, media cross-linking, spatial mobility and cultural standardization, then this does not leave unchanged our knowledge and expectations in relation to that which is alien to us. As we encounter strangers and strangers encounter us, we belong today to the same communicative context. Mutual knowledge and expectations are already embedded in it by way of the mode of relation to alterity itself, among other things. To illustrate it with the most extreme example, the desire to destroy the stranger, the Holocaust, that is to say, is no longer a latent tendency today, one that can become manifest in a relationship to alterity. It has become manifest and thus it unmistakably enters into our knowledge of and our communication with the strange itself, for instance with respect to the possible consequences of relations to alterity.

A second prerequisite in the classical definition of the relationship to alterity also seems to have become uncertain. The stranger presupposes the indigenous as a distinction; in social terms, this corresponds to the existence of 'we'-groups, by contrast to which the stranger can be distinguished as exception, minority and difference. The indigenous is no less constructed than the alien, and my contention is that the construct of groups and collective identities of one's own has itself become fragile, and therefore the distinction from the stranger as well. The collectively shared forms of 'our own', from which 'alterity' is set off as a difference, are less and less able today to rely on those basal processes by which they are constructed. These are, on the one hand, a stable identification with one's own social group and, on the other, the internalization of collectively shared values. . . . To put it pointedly, that which Simmel takes to be the characteristic of the stranger – 'the migrant who comes today and stays tomorrow' – is about to become the generalized way of life in the age of individualization.

Now this does not mean that the relationship to the stranger has become less problematic, quite to the contrary. If drawing the boundary with respect to strangers can no longer rely on unambiguous and self-evident cultural distinctions, then two things happen. First, the constructed character of the stranger (and also of the indigenous) is laid bare to be visible. This of course has always been attached to these things, but now – laid bare by self-evident cultural evidence – it stands out more clearly as a social construct.

Second, the occasions for laying down boundaries change. They open up in the social respect all the way to pure decision, the foundation of which is no longer the culturally unknown and uncertain aspects which premodern societies still associate with strangers. Cultural relationships to alterity are increasingly being replaced by social competition and political strategy. If one takes into account, for instance, the scepticism of modern European ethnology with regard to the thesis of the seemingly ancient and ethnically based tensions now breaking out in Europe, then the current European civil and gang wars are presented as power conflicts, not cultural ones. Released from rigid cultural ties, the individuals construct notions of own-group and stranger in this view rather arbitrarily, fluidly, temporarily and changeably, more according to the dictates of competition for advantages (rights), resources and the exercise of power than according to the amount of irritation at cultural alterity. Cultural differences here become a particularly easy-to-handle legitimation of power strategies (the politicization of ascribed features, for instance), just as they are suited to be external reference points (by way of that which is allegedly alien) for constructing one's own 'situation groups', whose inner coherence and membership varies with the enemy that has just been constituted. (Neckel 1993: 5ff)

This must now be investigated in greater detail.

Militarily restricted democracy

Nation states have revolutionized war just as much as the constitutions on which they are based. Along with popular rule, democracy created the popular army, along with universal suffrage it also created universal conscription, and along with the national it created and incited the nationalist enthusiasm for fighting and killing in war. Since an arch-enemy is both an honour and a burden, one that is not only granted to others but also adorns existence in the eyes of those others, it conceals the dubious pleasure that one's own enthusiasm for the other side's downfall may stimulate the opposing rage in the other side. One can say that the military was democratized only in the sense that it was *generalized*. The democratically legitimated state arrogated to itself the right to call *all* citizens to arms – by force, if necessary (Mann

1984; Shaw 1988). The 'democratization' of war also applies in a second sense: all civilians, not just the combatants, have their lives, property and possessions threatened. This expansion of war, which ultimately – in nuclear war – makes victors and vanquished equal, is, of course, an 'achievement' of modernity. If democracy implies this type of total equality, then equality, that is, the *égalité* of war, was victorious in tandem with democracy.

A strong military arm of the state, a democratic one in particular, is, as one hears everywhere, the prerequisite for a flourishing economy and a guarantor of its internal order and its sovereignty towards the outside. Even if this is true, it is very easy to deceive oneself: military is to democracy as fire is to water. One need only pick out the values of civil society: the basic rights that set every person equal to every other and declare his dignity inviolable, subjecting those who threaten or infringe these rights to criminal penalties. Anyone who reads these and other fairy-tale theses and has maintained a sense of the poetry of politics feels tears of joy welling up. If he then takes note of the reports and images that tell of wars and preparations for war, these tears of joy become intermingled with tears of horror and anger. The life of a person here is worth less than the lump of flesh in which he dwells. If democracy demands the individual's will, the military demands his subordination. If, in the former case, all power originates from the people, then, in the latter, all orders come from above. While in the former case even the intention to kill is considered a severe crime, in the latter, entire staffs are kept in service and receive honours for being able to bring peace, or, at least, heavenly peace, to as many people (now known as enemies) as possible. Should there be resistance to this, it can easily be broken by state force, the same state force, the same state authority that threatens prison for wrongfully harming a single citizen's hair. Wherever one looks, it is the same: democracy means openness, questioning, power-sharing, transparent decisions. Military is a synonym for secret, command, killing, strictly prohibited. There is no need to recite the rest.

At the same time, it is true that these contradictions are absent, nullified or harmonized in the social consciousness and theory of the modern state. How is that possible?

1 All democracies, including the traditional model democracies in Great Britain, France and the United States, were and are *armed* democracies in the sense that the military and democracy have entered into a mutually excluding and limiting symbiosis in them.

2 There may have been many shortages in previous history, but not of enemies. Enemies and enmities are one of the few 'natural resources' that are not consumed but produced in modernity.

3 The military concept of the state represents a left–right consensus. Military force is one of those social facts of life that are always and only controversial in the hand of the opponent, never in the service of one's own cause. Socialists, communists, social democrats, capitalists and liberals of all types and others have all chimed in, if not to sing the praises of state force, then to proclaim its necessity, and have supported a corresponding militancy of society.

4 Nuclear deterrence, or the residue of reason that still echoes in it, has so far avoided the worst and had a taming effect.

5 The monopoly on military force gives the state authority and sovereignty, to which the parliament and the law add legitimacy. Without force, the state would be a eunuch in the guise of a suitor.

6 Where empirical facts fail, anthropology steps in. Sovereign states are constructs of power that neither know nor respect any binding higher authority. This results, quite independently of any history, in a mutual uncertainty of expectations, an at least latent threat, which makes the military and militarization of society appear indispensable and ineradicable.

7 The necessities of a military organization of force must be balanced against contrary necessities of democracy; this may be successful (under certain conditions), but can also be unsuccessful (under other conditions).

Anyone, therefore, who does not close his eyes to the simultaneous contradictions will face two competing questions.

First, what is able to force, metaphorically, fire and water together? How are military and democracy or military and business bound together in the advanced states and societies of the West, highly developed in both military and democratic senses? To anticipate my answer in a few keywords: nothing unifies as well as the threat from an enemy. The enemy, or, in more precise sociological terms, the successful 'social construction of an enemy stereotype', believed and equipped with all the attributes of reality, empowers the state to restrict democracy. The consensus on democracy competes with the consensus on defence; the former makes it possible to restrict the latter, to play the latter off against the former.

With that, the second question has already almost been asked and answered. The contradictions between military and democracy erupt to the extent that enemy stereotypes pale and lose cultural credibility in the 'state without enemies' (Beck 1993). This may come about because the enemies turn into friends who want to join NATO, or because the cultural prerequisites of the defence consensus lose credibility and wither away in the wake of social modernization and individualization processes.

Thus there is not just the (often emphasized) relationship of mutual justification between the military and democracy. The military empowers democracy and democracy legitimizes the military. These two spheres and logics of action in modern society are also in a state of siege of one another. The military threatens democracy and democracy threatens to restrict and hollow out the military. This is not just a matter of declared goals and intentions, that is to say, putsch or pacifism, cutting the military budget, pruning military privileges and the like. This competition for supremacy can also be conducted, voluntarily or involuntarily, indirectly by means of (latent) side-effects. The power of defence and the preparations for it restrict the opportunities for citizens to move; this becomes physical reality on manoeuvres or in a military emergency. But even the threat of a defence emergency makes itself felt in the legal system, for instance in laws on demonstrations or in domestic policy. If one can succeed in defining the opposition's demands into the vicinity of the enemy's demands, then criticism falls under the jurisdiction of the counter-espionage or espionage authorities. Conversely, the welfare state may break up social ties until ultimately society based on an enemy stereotype, the last bastion of large-group society, decays and a possibly highly armed democracy can no longer be held together and motivated for the defence emergency by the belief in a shared enemy.

In other words, all democracies are *militarily restricted* democracies. Fully established democracy nullifies the ability and readiness for defence just as much as, on the other hand, the militarization of society (business, law, the private ways of life and lifestyles) hollows out and breaks up democracy.

The nation state and industrial society are a restricted version of modernity by design, so that the military restriction of modernity is only one case among many. This can be shown particularly clearly with the contrasts between men and women. These, so one hears, are primeval (like the inevitability of war), based on nature or anthropology and therefore not accessible to change. Actually, however, just as the militarization of society – universal military service – was implemented in tandem with the democratization of society – universal suffrage – work at home and work for pay were separated in the nineteenth century and exclusively assigned to women and men respectively.

The unravelling of this interweaving runs analogously to the inter-weaving itself. With the feminization of education in the second half of the twentieth century, with increasing employment outside the home for women including mothers, with rising divorce figures and the resulting pressures on women to build up a professional existence of their own, that is, to remain mobile and maintain a 'life of their own' even during motherhood, the constructions of modernity become fragile along the male–female axis. Similarly, with the increasingly civilian nature of military organization ('civilian control', expansion of civilian employment), the implementation and claiming of democratic rights and the automation of military technology (which allows a demilitarization of everyday life and customs in modern society), the constructions of restricted modernity become questionable in military democracy. This evolution remained latent during the Cold War, but is now appearing with the collapse of the militarily stabilized East–West world order.[5]

Just like the antagonism between men and women, therefore, the antagonism between citizen and soldier was created in tandem with industrialization. It is also true, however, that the social antagonisms between slaves and freemen or between men and women, just like those between citizens and soldiers, were stable and (largely) accepted over the millennia. There was one not inconsiderable difference, name-ly that the antagonisms between *citoyen* and soldier were in *one* person, separated in one biography between various life phases (edu-cation, civilian career and military service, wartime), and had to be fought out there. Particularly if one considers the dramatic contradic-tions between citizen and soldier, one has to wonder with a certain astonishment how these antagonisms could have been accepted almost unnoticed for so long.

The contradictions between military and democracy point to a cen-tral power base in society, the state's monopoly on the legitimate use of force. In contrast to the antagonisms between capital and labour or between men and women, which also have their basis in the architec-ture of industrial society, the crucial key, the central lever for the balance of power between military and democracy lies in the external threat from enemies.

Enemy stereotypes empower

In all previously existing democracies there have been two types of authority, one coming from the people and one from the enemy. The contradictions between military and democracy, military and business do not exist so long as the prevalent perception is that enemies are threatening the life and order of the citizens with their hostile intentions and means.

The concept of 'enemy' is the strongest possible antithesis to the concept of 'security'. All the dimensions (order, values, life) of security, and more precisely *collective* security, are *collectively* threatened, not latently or inadvertently, but deliberately and intentionally by all the means and capabilities of the opposing military power.

Antagonisms and contradictions melt away in the face of this threat. The enemy compels a defence and the defence consensus by virtue of his existential threat. He creates community, not only by values but also by forcing a counterreaction. The special aspect of posing, or, better, opposing enemies – to bar the door to ontology from the start – certainly lies in the intensification of the decision between life and death (cf. Schmitt 1976), not in the private/individual sphere or the intermediate zone of crime, but in the open opposition of state organizations. Enemies are equipped with the all the trappings of state legitimacy on *both* sides. Enemies are not criminals. They do wantto do each other in, but all persons are known and generally occupy well-paid positions with eligibility for pensions. Everyone has his own law on his side and can boast of all the trappings of legitimacy: laws, parliamentary resolutions and social approval. The special aspect of enemies (compared to criminals) is that they are at least ex-criminals who have risen to be the supreme servant of their state and are now able to pursue their own interests in the guise of 'the people's interest'. In their career, they have crossed the boundary that puts even criminals in a position not only to become government ministers, but to dismiss ministers and perhaps even prosecute rivals as criminals.

Enemy stereotypes empower. Enemy stereotypes have the highest priority in the conflict; they outdo class conflicts. They stage and give institutional form with existential force to the great certitude of counter-modernity, the Either–or, that mutes all questions.

The 'justification' for this chosen, producible certitude lies in the tacit compulsion of force itself, and that is of course a 'justification' of a special type. It *creates* the relationships and the behavioural logic of attack and defence, pro and contra, which first kill the questions and then the people. Not only because the best 'argument' still comes from the mouth of a gun, but because the threat abolishes all individuality. The very ordinary chaos of modernity regresses and is simplified down to the forced alternative of he or I, they or we. The threat produces constructed ascription, in which the 'fate' of force and counterforce rules.

Since consensus has become a chronically scarce commodity in all democracies, one can say that democratic states are particularly dependent on a second, para-democratic source, the enemy stereotype, from which consent bubbles up. Enemy stereotypes, turned domestic, open up sources of extra-democratic and anti-democratic consent. Cultivating these makes it possible to become independent of consensus by consensus. Enemy stereotypes are, one could say, alternative energy sources for the raw material of consensus that is consumed in the development of democracy. The internal democratization of a society can be held in check by enemy stereotypes without having to forgo consensus. Enemy stereotypes, seen from the inside, from the point of view of their major domestic side effects, make it possible to dismiss democracy with the blessing of democracy.

The consensus on defence is thus an 'antidote' to the democratic consensus, which is often much more difficult to achieve. Enemy stereotypes, moreover, are subject within limits to the principles of their own construction (mass media, the incitement of competition, the dramaturgy of the foreign). Enemy stereotypes legitimize state force as opposing force. 'Top secret!' is the seal that cuts off all questions, slams the door shut on democracy and then bolts it.

Enemy stereotypes therefore limit democracy in the double sense that they make it possible to put up fences that must call a halt to all self-evident democratic truths and they legitimate the furnishing and delimitation of 'democracy-free or low-democracy zones'. Here, according to established rules, everything can be tried out, planned and implemented which would otherwise be subject to the strictest prohibitions. Examples include: planning and perfecting murder; spending money on horrific weapons systems, the productivity of which 'culminates' in their never being used; and many other things. The consensus on defence is therefore a consensus of empowerment. How far the empowerment reaches depends no longer on the democratic sovereign, the people, but rather on the extent of the threat and the 'necessities' of defending against it, deemed 'necessary', that is, by those who are 'responsible'. Enemy stereotypes are the Golden Goose of necessities. They empower the powerful and siphon off the consent to do it from the powerless.

What is of interest is the interchange and interweaving of outside and inside, of activity and passivity, of force, power and consensus in the construction of the enemy. It operates according to the old 'tell-tale principle': it's his fault, not mine! All the initiative comes from the enemy. He threatens me and not vice versa, a perception, of course, that prevails on both sides. The enemy stereotype is not the enemy itself, but a constructed image of an enemy. Following this 'tattle-tale logic' of the enemy stereotype I can simultaneously wash my hands in innocence. The enemy stereotype makes the foreigner an enemy, but at the same time cancels out the activity of its creator and says: 'He is the enemy who threatens me; my enemy stereotype is no threat to him.'

To simplify considerably, the argument above was that, first, nations are national communities of people influenced by the same newspapers, in which anonymity, individualization, and the opposition between sameness and alterity can develop and flourish according to the national pattern. Second, enemy stereotypes empower. If both of these are true, then that implies, third, that this type of power formation and legitimation is, or at least could be, undercut in the age of global telecommunication. This, in any case, would be a starting point for a peace initiative of the United Nations by global information networks that would work against the national mechanisms of enemy stereotype formation, propaganda in plain language. It would also be conceivable to concede neutral UN journalists information rights (broadcasts and news) on both sides. The drama in the decaying Yugoslavia shows that national sovereignty over broadcasters and broadcast areas is used for merciless agitation, while the means and capabilities for a global tele-public to oppose this classical mechanism of war-mongering go unused. Thus initiatives such as the mothers who rescue their sons from barracks are swept aside by frequently falsified broadcasts of rumbling tanks that whip up fear, aggressiveness and anger and attune people to subsequently exploding horrors (Pešić et al. 1993: 13–20). The targeted abolition of national sovereignty areas for information, from multinational to global broadcasts, would in any case be an important prerequisite for making international conflicts more civil.

Must the loss of the stranger's traditional significance, Sighard Neckel inquires, not lead to a reversal of the classical question?

> [Is] the stranger in individualized risk society now really becoming a problem as a stranger, or, conversely, is it not precisely the successive dissolution of alterity which represents the problem that is used to justify violent exclusions? This could also be an explanation for why we have such difficulty today developing functional equivalents to the ancient institution of hospitality. (One point: the functionality of hospitality relied on inequality, while the situation today is characterized by generalized claims to equality.) Then not just one particular stranger but

potentially all strangers today would be an object of violent aggressions, not by being a stranger or being perceived as an enemy, but by being in a weaker situation than an aggressor and perceived as inferior or defence-less. In that sense, alterity would be a subordinate case, a variant of that general tendency in modern society that was understood by Jean-Paul Sartre as an objectivization of the other. In that sense, freedom is proven by the degree of control I have over others by depriving him [*sic*] of his subjectivity, objectivizing him and making him an object of my own freedom. Precisely this seems to me to be the situation of the stranger, not with respect to his difference, but with respect to his powerlessness. (Neckel 1993: 8)

Alongside violence, there is another star witness of counter-modernity: the *staging of nature*. This can be studied in a number of quite different themes, but probably most impressively in the 'naturalization of femininity', as pointed out and taught by women's studies.

The naturalization of femininity

Women have existed as long as men, and women and men certainly are different, as even the saucy phrase 'vive la différence!' indicated. The idea that these *differentia speculativa* explain the position of women in society is a modern legend. More precisely, the 'natural woman' is an invention of the eighteenth and nineteenth centuries. All the 'evidence' of the incipient human sciences was mobilized in this effort. The French philosopher of the Enlightenment, Denis Diderot, writes, for instance:

Women are subject to an epidemic savagery. . . . They are outwardly more civilized than ourselves, but inwardly they have remained true savages. . . . They are less in control of their senses than we are. . . . O women, you are peculiar children! . . . The ideas of justice, virtue, vice, kindness, or malice float on the surface of their souls. On the other hand they have maintained selfishness and egoism in their entire natural force. . . . Women are seldom systematic, always subject to the moment. (Diderot 1981: 171f; quoted in Bublitz 1992: 60).

'In modern society,' Hannelore Bublitz summarizes the results of research in women's studies, 'in which equal rights were formulated for all people, women occupy the place of the alien, the exotic and the childish.' The feminine is stylized into the antithesis of culture.

The – masculine – subject constitutes itself as a sovereign, autonomous individual who, equipped with self-confidence and the defining power of epistemological competence, delineates himself against nature and

sensuality; simultaneously, women are thrown back to nature and, with
the aid of the newly arising human sciences, formulated by men, tied
down to their organic features, without, of course, any empirical evidence; thus they are excluded from social, cultural and scientific progress,
as well as from the right to have any say in history or society. (Bublitz
1992: 60)

Natural categories are an artifice of the construction and perpetua-
tion of certitude. They subdue the questioning dragon of modernity by
hiding him behind a wall of unchangeability. Nothing that is de facto
constructed here is openly admitted to as such. This only makes what
is happening anyway seem reasonable. Here the bed of *faits accomplis*
is made and padded with self-evidence. Not only is no one compelled
to ask questions here; no one feels the need to do so; one can simply float
along on the stream of complacency. There is always the possibility,
when the time is ripe, of pulling the levers concealed behind the
fatalism of nature to get something done in one's own interest. After
all, we decide who or what is nature, by means of science if need be.
Mobility inwardly and rigidity and stoicism outwardly, which can be
constructed and presented as a compulsion; that is a bit of tangible
paradise in a world that has dissolved into questions.

Nature does not 'legitimate' decisions; that is much too activistically
stated! It absorbs and transforms them into non-decisions. It produces self-evident truths and laws in the guise of necessity rather
than as morality and argument. Questions are raised and pushed
back down under the surface of reflection, sealed there with
necessities and silenced. 'Nature' is not good and not bad, it simply is.
One can bathe in existence here and take part in something otherwise
denied us human beings: eternity, but only as a social construct, of
course.

Nature permits and approves the forgetting of society with all its
unfathomable, undecipherable confusion. Here – at long last! – is a
chance to tidy up and clear things out. 'Nature' is the resurrection of
simplicity. It would have to be invented if it did not already exist so
splendidly in such accessible eternity. The most personal and the most
general of things once again come to participate in one another directly. All of this happens, lest anyone be deceived, after the demise of
nature, after its absorption into society. Only something which does
not exist can be adored so fervently.

Nature cuts all the Gordian knots of modernity. It provides the
pleasures of necessity, and does so permanently, not just once or twice,
but as a social construction. This means: it is certitude cast in institutional form.

This stabilizing principle is the naturalization of social classifications. An analogy is needed, with the aid of which the formal structure of an important complex of social relationships in the natural world, in the heavens or elsewhere can be recovered, with all that matters being that this 'elsewhere' is not recognizable as a social construct. If the analogy is transferred from nature to a complex and from there back again to nature, then this repeatedly appearing formal structure will engrave itself into consciousness and the back and forth of these transfers equips them with a truth that speaks for itself. (Douglas 1990: 84f)

It would be completely false to assume that the natural category is becoming obsolete in fully established modernity. The opposite is the case, because constructed, decidable nature as a basis of counter-modernity is gaining in fascination with the acceleration of modernity, becoming almost alarmingly attractive as an antidote to a scientifically fortified and therefore technologically producible certitude. In that sense one should not underestimate the possibility of founding reflexive modernity on scientized natural categories. These include sociobiology, ecology very much in the centre, but also the disciplines of the physical and lifestyle revolutions that are around the corner: human genetics, reproductive medicine, among others, and the possibilities derived from them for designing a gradual, voluntary 'eugenics' prescribed and certified by 'preventive medicine',[6] 'nature in the age of its technological reproducibility' (Böhme 1992).

The difference between the nineteenth and the twenty-first centuries lies precisely in these radical differences between *ideological* and *technical* 'naturalization'. In those days, it was only possible to naturalize images, people and the world. Tomorrow perhaps, probably?, the conditions for the origin of life itself will be converted into a nature which is literally producible (thus really no longer nature at all) and designable and changeable in this more limited sense.

What frightens us in view of such capabilities, beyond any romanticism or love of nature, is the recovered consciousness that we are speaking of ourselves when we say 'nature', the nature which we ourselves are. Technical reproducibility calls our own self-concept into question. (Böhme 1992)

The abolition of nature, its absorption into a technical project, coincides with the opportunities for a reified, one could say a really real, naturalization. Here the term 'construction of nature' has doffed anything metaphorical. This *modernization of nature* produces the situation of being able to create 'nature' which is no longer that, and not just the image of nature. This places almost unthinkable possibilities in the hands of a future counter-modernity: forms of a reified naturalization of social circumstances, the metamorphosis of these into living physical creatures we cannot yet even imagine.

Dilemmas

The concept of counter-modernity is pure horror for any upstanding defender of modernity. 'Counter-modernity' provokes a reflex: look the other way, deny, suppress, take flight, spit on, lock up, shackle, condemn, smash. In that sense, formulating a value-free concept of counter-modernity is like the attempt to jump out of the window and fly upwards. But if the dialectic of modernity and counter-modernity sketched out here should prove to be true, then that changes the black–white view. The question is no longer: does counter-modernity exist? The question then is: which counter-modernity and how can counter-modernity be substantiated and achieved? Is this to be done by drawing on pre-modernity or by anticipating the as yet unfinished modernity, by negation or by radicalization of modernity against industrial entropy?

The dilemmas of all attempts to escape in one direction or the other can be clearly laid out on the table, contrary to any pedantic interference (particularly if presented with the air of Enlightenment, which has in any case degenerated to little more than a wagging finger of warning).

One dilemma lies in the fact that the universalism of modernity can no more be sacrificed than it can be redeemed. The latter implies abandoning modernity and the former is meaningless, because the institutional vacuum starts outside the national democracies. Enduring both and keeping them open, however, is almost beyond human capabilities.

There are two simple and wrong answers to this problem of the cages of freedom, the prisons of prosperity, the historical unity of the contradictions between modernity and counter-modernity, with which we are involved everywhere in global risk society. One of these answers relies on the correct insight that only separation, that is, boundaries, makes freedom possible. To put it conversely: the destruction of separation is tantamount to the abolition of freedom.

This first answer can be illustrated in the functional differentiation of modern society. Freedom in the private sphere, freedom of research, freedom in law and so on are all based, in Michael Walzer's phrase, on the 'art of separation' which distinguishes liberal society and politics (Walzer 1993: 45).

Walzer justly polemicizes against holistic left-wing hopes of overcoming boundaries, because they open the gate wide to tyranny:

> Marx's vision of individual and collective self-determination requires the existence of a *protected space* inside of which significant decisions can be made (although Marx himself never understood this requirement). But such a space can exist only if wealth and power are surrounded and bounded by walls. . . . Thus the bishops of the Church criticize national defence policy, the universities shelter radical dissidents. . . . In each case, the institutions follow their own inner logic, although they are reacting to the influence exerted upon them by the system as a whole. This play of inner logic can be suppressed only by dictatorial power, border violations and the tearing down of walls. . . . (Walzer 1993: 45)

Yet the argument that 'liberalism is a world of walls and each produces a new freedom' (Walzer 1993: 38) does not break up the universalism of liberalism, which seems to be equally concrete. His argument only looks the other way or disregards it.

On the contrary, it remains quite unclear in this sense how boundaries, whether between subsystems or between countries, cultures and continents, can or should be drawn. That not only implies permeability as to how 'indigenous' is defined and the exogenous can and should be made indigenous or 'naturalized' and similar questions. Put more sharply, it is or is becoming unclear whether in this globalized modernity the mode of the boundary is available to us at all, whether or how much concretely existing boundaries still bound or delimit anything. How suitable are boundaries – no matter how 'unassailable' they may be – in view of the concretely existing universalism of modernity? Of course the affluence is still nationally organized. The dangers, however, already fail to recognize boundaries. The market, money and science are also beginning to perforate the incontrovertibility of borders and the national and are causing modernity to hover transnationally. In other words, the age of And causes even borders that have been drawn and armed to become unreal.

Of course this problem is also nothing new. A long time ago boundaries hardly existed, even on paper. Not until the nation state was the systematic organization and fortification of boundaries advanced. One can say of the Eastern Bloc that not the least important reason for its collapse was the illusion of an 'Iron Curtain', which, after all, was completely non-existent for the Western broadcasters and Eastern television viewers. The issue of the ability of borders to be barriers may be an old one, but it is becoming more and more acute with the emergence and development of a global market and risk society.

The false simplicity of living up to the professed universalism by abolishing borders corresponds on the other hand to the false simplicity of glorifying existing borders as guarantors of freedom. That, after all, is a misapprehension of the creeping unreality of seemingly concrete borders in a globalizing modernity.[7]

A second dilemma can be reduced to a simple question: how much breakdown can a person survive? If it is true that reflexive modernity sweeps away even the bases and instruments for restraining uncertainty, then no one should be surprised if counter-modernity is desired and grasped for like a swig of water in the desert. Reflexive modernization thus provokes counter-modernization, in all forms: religious movements, esotericism, violence, neo-nationalism, neo-racism but also the renaturalization of social relationships by genetic and human genetic trends.[8] All of these live from the same promise to create new certitudes, or, better, rigidities, in one way or another, in order to put an end to permanent doubt and self-doubt.

This yields the same question: not no borders, but what kind of borders; how can there be borders at all? To ask it another way, what kind of counter-modernity? This will be pursued a little using the example of the environmental movement.

Ecological ligatures: on the road to eco-democracy or eco-dictatorship?

'I have come to believe that we must take a bold and unequivocal action: we must make the rescue of the environment the central organizational principle for civilization.' The person who wrote this was Al Gore (1992: 270), the American Vice President. First demonized, then ridiculed, later preached and finally in the government programme – the Horatio Alger story of the environmental issue seemed to reach its culmination.

As we now know, books are not policy, and intentions can be renounced or turn out to be the opposite of what they seemed to be. Still the questions remain: how long can the industrialized world afford to run backwards in this race for the future? What makes the environmental issue so explosive? When does it provoke lethargy and fatalism, aggression and calls for a strong hand? When and how does it motivate a rebellion, perhaps even a reform of industrial society? Is it possible to forge models of order from the environmental issue that counter the dissolution tendencies of reflexive modernization? How can the counter-modernity of environmentalism be restrained, that is, how can its ascetic and dictatorial tendencies be connected to the extravagant tendencies and the freedom of modernity?

Al Gore certainly did not discover the environmental issue. What he did discover and began to exploit was its power to create meaning, politics and structure. The post-traditional world only seems to be disintegrating into apathetic individualization; paradoxically enough, it also possesses a fountain of youth for re-moralization, motivation – and neuroses – in the challenges of self-inflicted imperilment. To put it pointedly, someone like Al Gore replaces status and class consciousness, faith in progress or doom, and the bogeyman of communism with the 'humanistic project of saving the environment'. Socially conservative, religious and emancipatory ideas unite in him and ally in a 'new deal' that would have seemed pure dreaming only a short while ago – and they stimulate the economy. Industry in the United States obviously switched to the Democratic side because of the politics of environmental conviction and its economic promise. Rather than colliding with a business sector trying to make up for opportunities for sales and employment, the utopia of an ecological democracy seeks to form a coalition with it. But this is only one variant, and not necessarily the one that will succeed.

The as yet undiscovered specifics of ecological ligatures can at least be hinted at, laid out dimensionally and outlined, not coincidentally, in the comparison with the national consensus on defence issues. In spatial terms, the national security consensus is both national and anti-national; it ties together the antagonisms internally by mobilization against external outsiders and enemies. By contrast, the environmental consensus (if there ever were or could be such a thing) would be global, that is, supranational, by design. It goes without saying that national or nationalistic colorations are possible or even probable. Perhaps there will even be such a thing as an 'environmental security consensus'; people might mobilize against 'dangerous nuclear power plants' abroad. There is already consideration of supranational rights of intervention and corresponding authorities that are intended to bring environmental violator states to their senses. At the same time the environmental issue, once accepted and internalized, abolishes boundaries of privacy internally. In sorting through the trash for recycling, everyone is compelled to cooperate as a minor activist in the overall rescue mission for the earth and humankind. This produces a total responsibility that no longer leaves any corners to escape to.

Ecological morality and the consensus on defence approach the salvation from the now anonymous, universalized and objectified 'enemies', 'enemy substances' that is, with equal fervour. Even though the consensus on defence has something like conscientious objection, an objection to environmental service seems to be out of the question. Young and old, handicapped and government officials, but above all women are compelled to 'lend a hand' here in the daily battle of defence.

The national security consensus still has peacetime. Ordinarily, it only threatens the 'defence emergency', war, and that already accomplishes a great deal. Its executive powers are limited in social and temporal terms, however. The environmental issue, if it ever came to power, would be a kind of permanent wartime, if one will permit the analogy. Action has to be taken, immediately, everywhere, by everyone and under all circumstances.

Environmental morality could accomplish something that Christianity has always tried and always failed at: swallowing up, devouring and converting all enemies and competing religions, including even the as yet unborn, future generations. Only the dead, of course, would be left out. Otherwise, if one thinks the moral possibilities of the environmental issue through to their logical end, there is really no escape.

Anyone who thinks being an animal is a relief, that being an animal would be wonderful because it makes everything possible which is denied to people – attacking, devouring and other delightful things – is deceiving himself. That is just it, animals and even plants are all embraced as fellow creatures in the grand gestures of ecological morality. Even thoughts will be hard pressed to maintain their original freedom over the long run under the heavy pressure of this new environmental universal. Only think ecologically from now on! Recycling begins in the mind! If this level of morality does not arouse political minds and instincts, then there really is no hope for the world.

One need only recall the humble patience with which the democratization of recycling is endured and carried out today in order to recognize what a structuring power lies in the environmental issue. Not consciously or directly but because of its accepted dominance, reckless industry has turned all of us into its unpaid recyclers working in the field. They follow the motto: if production is not to be democratized, then at least its waste products can be. We do not reject this with screams of outrage (and appeals to the polluter-pays principle), but comply around the clock with masochistic industriousness. No one has a rubbish-free day anywhere, and, even more peculiarly, no one is calling for one. That, among other things, shows the ligatory power of the environmental issue already. Anyone who thinks that this will be satisfied over the mid- to long term by a cosmetic and symbolic policy is misunderstanding the total And that is a threatening prospect here as well.

Quite antithetical realities and social structures – democratic and dictatorial, to cite only the extremes – can be forged out of this moral material. That is precisely why the call for ecological democracy, which will tame the counter-modern dictatorial potential, reconciling and tying it to the freedom and doubt of modernity, is so elementally important and urgent.

3

Subpolitics – The Individual Returns to Society

Modernity and counter-modernity, simple and reflexive modernization, interpenetrate one another. But this interaction – in old-fashioned terms, this dialectic – is directed, not arbitrary. The societalization forms of simple industrial modernity are disembedded at the core, sometimes accompanied by petrifaction and sanctification of their shells, and we call this process individualization.[1] At the end of the twentieth century, people are being cut loose from the ways of life of industrial society, just as at the entry to the industrial epoch they were (and still are being) cut loose from the self-evident feudal and status-based understandings, ways of life and societal forms. The fact that the two processes – the transition to industrial and the transition to reflexive modernity – overlap at the threshold of the twenty-first century in Europe, and in various other countries as well, makes the shocks that have shaken the world since the collapse of the Cold War order comprehensible. This is meant when we speak here of the *conflict of two modernities*.

Individualization – on the unliveability of modernity

'Individualization' does not mean a lot of the things that many people think it means in order to be able to think it means nothing at all. It does not mean atomization, isolation, loneliness, the end of any type of society, or disconnectedness. One also often hears the refutable claim that it means emancipation or the revival of the bourgeois individual after his demise. But if all these are expedient misunderstandings, then what might be a consensus on the meaning of the term?

'Individualization' means, *first*, the disembedding of industrial-society ways of life and, *second*, the re-embedding of new ones, in which the individuals must produce, stage and cobble together their biographies themselves. Thus the name 'individualization'. Both – disembedding and re-embedding (in Giddens' words) – do not occur by chance, nor individually, nor voluntarily, nor through diverse types of historical conditions, but rather all at once and under the general conditions of the *welfare state* in advanced industrial labour society, as they have developed since the 1960s in many Western industrial countries.

In the image of classical industrial society, collective ways of living are understood to resemble Russian dolls nested inside one another. Class presumes the nuclear family, which presumes sex roles, which presume the division of labour between men and women, which presumes marriage. Classes are also conceived of as the sum of nuclear familial situations, which resemble one another and are differentiated from other class-typical 'familial situations' (those of the upper class, for instance).

Even the empirical–operational definition of the class concept makes use of the family income, that is, the income of the 'head of household', an inclusive word, but one that clearly bears masculine features in practice. Which means that women's labour participation either does not 'register' at all in class analysis or is 'averaged away' (Heath and Britten 1984). Turned the other way around: anyone who takes male income and female income separately as the basis must draw the image of a *split* social structure, which can never be recombined into a single image. These are only examples of how the categories of life situations and life conduct in industrial society presume one another in a certain way. Just as certainly, they are being systematically *dis*embedded and *re*-embedded – that is the import of individualization theory.

They are being replaced not by a void (that is precisely the point of most refutations of individualization theory) but rather by a new mode of conducting and arranging life – no longer obligatory and 'embedded' (Giddens) in traditional models, but based on welfare state regulations. The latter, however, presume the individual as *actor*, *designer*, *juggler* and *stage director* of his own biography, identity, social networks, commitments and convictions. Put in plain terms, 'individualization' means the disintegration of the certainties of industrial society as well as the compulsion to find and invent new certainties for oneself and others without them. That this causes some turbulence is something known to anyone familiar with Charlie Chaplin and Woody Allen movies.

To put it yet another way, the currently fashionable complaining about individualization – the invocation of 'we-feelings', the disassociation from foreigners, the tendency to pamper family and feelings of solidarity, turned into a modern theory: communitarianism – all this is propagated against a background of established individualization. These are mostly *reactions to experienced intolerable aspects* of individualization, which is taking on anomalous traits.

Once again, individualization is not based on the free decision of individuals. To use Sartre's term, people are *condemned* to individualization. Individualization is a paradoxical compulsion for the construction, self-design and self-staging of not just one's own biography, but also its commitments and networks as preferences and life phases change; all this, of course, occurs under the overall conditions and models of the welfare state, such as the educational system (acquiring credentials), the labour market, labour and welfare law, the housing market and so on. Even the traditions of marriage and the family are becoming dependent on decision-making, and with all their contradictions must be experienced as personal risks.

'Individualization' therefore means that the *standard* biography becomes a *chosen* biography, a 'do-it-yourself biography' (Hitzler 1988). Whatever a man or woman was and is, whatever he or she thinks or does, constitutes the *individuality* of that particular person. That does not necessarily have anything to do with civil courage or personality, but rather with diverging options and the compulsion to construct and present these 'bastard children' of one's own and others' decisions as a 'unity'.

Now how should one conceive of the connection between individualization and the welfare state, between individualization and the legally protected labour market more precisely? An example might clarify this, the *work biography*; for men it is taken for granted, but for women it is controversial. None the less, half the women (at least!) work outside the home in all industrial countries, increasingly even while raising children. Surveys document that for the coming generation of women a career *and* motherhood are taken for granted as part of their life plans. If the movement towards two-career families continues, then today and in the future two individual biographies – education, job, career – will have to be pursued together and held together in the form of the nuclear family.

Previously, status-based marriage rules dominated, as imperatives (the indissolubility of marriage, the duties of motherhood, and the like). These constricted the scope of action, to be sure, but they also obligated and forced the individuals into togetherness. By contrast, it is not true that there are no models today; instead there are a number of models, specifically those that are negative: to build up and maintain an educational and professional career of their *own* as women, because otherwise women face ruin in case of divorce and remain dependent upon their husbands' money in marriage – with all the other symbolic and real dependencies this brings for them. These models do not weld people together but break apart the togetherness and multiply the questions. Thus they force every man and woman, both inside and outside marriage, to operate and persist as individual agent and designer of his or her own biography.

Most social welfare rights are *individual* rights. Families cannot lay claim to them, only individuals, more exactly, working individuals (or those who are unemployed but willing to work). Participation in the material protections and benefits of the welfare state presupposes labour participation in the greatest majority of cases. This is confirmed by the debate over the exceptions, among other things: wages for housework or a pension for housewives. Participation in work in turn presupposes participation in education and both presuppose mobility and the readiness to be mobile. All these are requirements which do not command anything, but call upon the individual kindly to constitute himself or herself *as an individual*, to plan, understand, design and act – or to suffer the consequences which will be considered self-inflicted in case of failure.

Here too, the same picture: decisions, possibly undecidable decisions, certainly not free, but forced by others and wrested out of oneself, under conditions that lead into dilemmas. These are also decisions which put the individual as an individual into the centre of things and disincentivize traditional ways of life and interaction.[2] Perhaps against its will, the welfare state is an *experimental arrangement for conditioning ego-centred ways of life*. One can inject the common good into the hearts of people as a compulsory vaccination, yet this litany of lost community remains two-faced and morally ambivalent as long as the mechanics of individualization remain intact, and no one really calls them seriously into question, neither wants to nor is able to.

Politics and subpolitics

This type of individualization does not remain private; it becomes political in a definite, new sense: the individualized individuals, the tinkerers with themselves and their world, are no longer the 'role players' of simple, classical industrial society, as assumed by functionalism. On the contrary, the institutions are becoming unreal in their programmes and foundations, and therefore dependent on individuals. Nuclear power plants that can destroy or contaminate an entire millennium are assessed as *risks* and 'legitimated' by comparison with cigarette smoking, which is statistically riskier. There is beginning to be a search in the institutions for the lost class consciousness of 'up there' and 'down here', because trade unions, political parties and others have built up their programmes, their membership and their power upon that. The dissolving post-familial pluralism of families is being trimmed to fit the still prevailing ideal of 'nuclear family', to cite one example.

In short, a double world is coming into existence, one part of which cannot be depicted in the other: a world of symbolically rich political institutions and a world of often concealed everyday political practice (conflicts, power games, instruments and arenas). These two worlds belong to two different epochs, industrial and reflexive modernity, respectively. On the one hand, a political vacuity of the institutions is evolving and, on the other hand, a non-institutional renaissance of politics. The individual is returning to society.

More or less everything, it would seem, argues against this. The issues that are disputed in the political arenas, or, one would be tempted to say, for which antagonisms are simulated there, scarcely have any explosive power left that could yield sparks of politics. Accordingly, it is becoming less and less possible all the time to derive decisions from the partisan political superstructure. Conversely, the organizations of the parties, the trade unions and so forth make use of the freely available masses of issues to hammer together the programmatic prerequisites for their continued existence. Internally and externally, so it seems, politics is losing both its polarizing and its creative, utopian quality.

That diagnosis rests, in my view, upon a category error, *the equation of politics and state*, politics and the political system; the correction of that error does not completely deprive the diagnosis of its elements of truth, but it does invalidate it as a diagnosis. People expect to find politics in the arenas prescribed for it, and they expect it to be performed by the duly authorized agents: parliament, political parties, trade unions, and so on. If the clocks of politics stop there, then it seems that politics as a whole has stopped ticking. That overlooks two things. First, the immobility of the governmental apparatus and its subsidiary agencies is perfectly capable of accompanying mobility of the agents on all possible levels of society, that is to say, the petering out of politics with the activation of subpolitics. Anyone who stares at politics from above and waits for results is overlooking the self-organization of politics, which – potentially at least – can set many or even all fields of society into motion 'subpolitically'.

Second, the political monopoly of the political institutions and agents, which the latter demand from the political constellation of classical industrial society, is incorporated into views and judgements. This continues to ignore the fact that the political system and the historical and political constellation can have the same relation to one another as the realities of two different epochs. For instance, the increase of welfare and the increase of hazards mutually condition one another. To the extent that this becomes (publicly) conscious, the defenders of safety are no longer sitting in the same boat with the planners and producers of economic wealth. The coalition of technology and business becomes shaky, because technology can increase productivity, but at the same time puts legitimacy at risk. The judicial order no longer fosters social peace, because it sanctions and legitimates disadvantages along with the threats, and so on.

In other words, politics breaks open and erupts *beyond* the formal responsibilities and hierarchies, and this is misunderstood particularly by those who unambiguously equate politics with the state, the political system, formal responsibilities and full-time political careers. An ambivalent, multi-level, 'expressionistic concept of politics' (Jürgen Habermas), which permits us to posit the social form and politics as mutually variable, is being introduced here for a very simple reason. It opens a possibility in thought which we increasingly confront today: the political constellation of industrial society is becoming *un*political, while what was unpolitical in industrialism is becoming *political*. This is a category transformation of politics with *unchanged* institutions, and with intact power elites that have not been replaced by new ones.

We look for politics in the wrong place, with the wrong terms, on the wrong floors of offices and on the wrong pages of the newspapers. Those decision-making areas which had been protected by politics in industrial capitalism – the private sector, business, science, towns, everyday life and so on – are caught in the storms of political conflicts in reflexive modernity. An important point here is that how far this process goes, what it means and where it leads is in turn dependent upon political decisions, which cannot simply be taken, but must be formed, programmatically filled out and transformed into possibilities for action. Politics determines politics, opening it up and empowering it. These possibilities of a *politics of politics*, a *reinvention* of politics

after its 'demonstrated' demise, are what we must open up and illuminate.

The socially most astonishing and surprising, yet perhaps the least
understood phenomenon of the eighties is the unexpected renaissance
of a *political subjectivity*, outside and inside the institutions. In this
sense, it is no exaggeration to say that citizen initiative groups have
taken power politically. They were the ones who put the issue of an
endangered world on the agenda, against the resistance of the established parties. Nowhere is this so clear as in the spectre of the new 'lip-
service morality' that is haunting Europe. The compulsion to engage in
the ecological salvation and renewal of the world has by now become
universal. It unites conservatives with socialists and the chemical industry with its Green arch-critics. One almost fears that the chemical
concerns will follow up on their full-page ads and re-establish themselves as conservation associations.

Admittedly this is all just packaging, programmatic opportunism,
and now and then perhaps really intentional rethinking. The actions
and the points of origin of the facts are largely untouched by it. Yet it
remains true: the themes of the future, which are now on everyone's
lips, did not originate from the far-sightedness of the rulers or from
parliamentary struggle – and certainly not from the cathedrals of
power in business, science and the state. They were put on the social
agenda against the concentrated resistance of this institutionalized
ignorance by entangled, moralizing groups and splinter groups fighting
each other over the proper path, split and plagued by doubts.

Subpolitics has won a quite improbable thematic victory. This
applies not only to the West, but also to the Eastern part of Europe.
There, the citizens' groups – contrary to all the evidence of social
science – started from zero with no organization, in a system of
surveilled conformity, and yet, lacking even photocopiers or tele-
phones, were able to force the ruling group to retreat and collapse just
by assembling on the streets. This rebellion of real existing individuals
against a 'system' that allegedly dominated them all the way into the
capillaries of day-to-day existence is inexplicable and inconceivable
according to the prevailing categories and theories. But it is not only
the planned economy which is bankrupt. Systems theory, which conceives of society as independent of the subject, has also been thoroughly refuted (even if *its* dogmaticians and apparatchiks have not yet been
put out to pasture). In a society without consensus, devoid of a
legitimating core, it is evident that even a single gust of wind, caused
by the cry for freedom, can bring down the whole house of cards of
power.

The differences between exuberant citizens in East and West are obvious and have often been mentioned, but that is much less the case for their quite considerable common ground: both are grass-roots-oriented, extra-parliamentary, not tied to classes or parties, organizationally and programmatically diffuse and feuding.

Of course one could say 'tempi passati'. The insight might be difficult for many people, but even the extreme right-wing headhunters who have been mobilizing in the streets of Germany since the summer of 1992 against 'foreigners' (and whomever they consider to be such), as well as the covert and unnerving support they find all the way to the top of politics (now that everyone is finally willing to modify the fundamental constitutional right to asylum), yes, even this mob is using and acting out the opportunities of subpolitics. This contains a bitter lesson. *Subpolitics is not open to only one side*. This opportunity to fill a vacuum can always be seized and used by the opposite side or party for the opposite goals.

What appeared to be a 'loss of consensus', an 'unpolitical retreat to private life', 'new inwardness' or 'caring for emotional wounds' in the old understanding of politics can, when seen from the other side, represent the struggle for a new dimension of politics.

The still prevailing impression that social awareness and consensus 'evaporates' in the 'heat' of individualization processes is not false, certainly, but also not correct. It ignores the compulsions and possibilities of *constructing* social commitments and obligations, no matter how tentative (the staging of a new general consensus on the environmental issue, for instance). These can take the place of the old categories, but cannot be expressed and comprehended in them.

It makes sense to distinguish between different contexts and forms of individualization. In some states, particularly in Sweden, Switzerland and western Germany, we are dealing with a '*comprehensively insured individualization*'. That is to say, individualization processes arise here from and in a milieu of prosperity and social security (not for everyone, but for most people). On the other hand, conditions in the eastern part of Germany, and especially in the formerly communist countries and the third world, lead to unrest of a quite different dimension.

The individualized everyday culture of the West simply is a culture of built-up knowledge and self-confidence: more and higher education, as well as better jobs and opportunities to earn money, which at least do not rule out in advance the claim to more development and having a say. Individuals still communicate in and play along with the old forms and institutions, but they also withdraw from them in at least part of their existence, their identity, their commitment and their courage. Their withdrawal, however, is not just a withdrawal, but at the same time an emigration to new niches of activity and identity. The latter seem so unclear and inconsistent not least because this inner immigration often takes place half-heartedly, with one foot, so to speak, while the other foot is still firmly planted in the old order.

People leave the 'nest' of their 'political home' step by step and issue by issue. But that means that in one place people are on the side of the revolution, while in another they are supporting reaction, in one place they are dropping out, while in another they are getting involved. All of that no longer fits into *one* design of an order upon which the surveying specialists of the political map can base their analyses.

The individualization of political conflicts and interests thus does not mean disengagement, not the 'democracy of mood' and not weariness of politics. Instead, a contradictory multiple engagement is emerging, which mixes and combines the classical poles of the political spectrum so that, if we think things through to their logical conclusion, everyone thinks *and* acts as a right-winger *and* left-winger, radically *and* conservatively, democratically *and* undemocratically, ecologically *and* antiecologically, politically *and* unpolitically, all at the same time. Everyone is a pessimist, a passivist, an idealist and an activist in partial aspects of his/her self. That only means, however, that the current coordinates of politics – right and left, conservative and socialistic, retreat and participation – are no longer correct or effective.

For this type of practice, which can be more easily comprehended negatively than positively – not instrumental, not dominating, not executing, not role-determined, not instrumentally rational – there are only faded and blurred direct concepts, which boast and mock almost slanderously with words like 'communal' and 'holistic'. All the non-labels can only succeed in denying and missing the state of affairs, but not in getting rid of it. Beneath and behind the façades of the old industrial order, which are sometimes still brilliantly polished, radical changes and new departures are taking place, not completely unconsciously, but not fully consciously and focused either. They rather resemble a collective blind man without a cane or a dog, but with a nose for what is personally right and important and, if scaled up to the level of generality, cannot therefore be totally false. This centipedal non-revolution is under way. It is expressed in the background noise of the quarrelling on every level and in all issues and discussion groups, in the fact, for instance, that nothing 'goes without saying' any longer; everything must be inspected, chopped to bits, discussed and debated to death until finally, with the blessing of general dissatisfaction, it takes this or that particular 'turn' no one wants, perhaps only because otherwise there is the risk of a general paralysis. Such are the birth pangs of a new action society, a self-creation society, which must 'reinvent' everything, except that it does not know how, why and with whom; more likely, how not, why not and with whom absolutely not.

Political science has opened up and elaborated its concept of politics into three aspects. First, it inquires into the institutional constitution of the political community with which society organizes itself (the *polity*), second, into the substance of political programmes for shaping social circumstances (*policy*), and third into the process of political conflict over power-sharing and power positions (*politics*). Here it is not the individual who is considered fit for politics; rather the questions are directed at corporatist, that is, *collective* agents.

Subpolitics is distinguished from politics in that (a) agents *outside* the political or corporatist system are also allowed to appear on the stage of social design (this group includes professional and occupational groups, the technical intelligentsia in companies, research institutions and management, skilled workers, citizens' initiatives, the public sphere, and so on), and (b) not only social and collective agents, but *individuals* as well compete with the latter and each other for the emerging power to shape politics.

If one transfers the distinction between polity, policy and politics to subpolitics (= the inquiry into the structure-changing practice of modernity), then the following questions come up:

1 How is '*subpolity*' constituted and organized institutionally? What are the sources of its power, its resistance possibilities and its potential for strategic action? Where are its switch-points and what are the limits of its influence? How does the scope and power to shape things emerge in the wake of reflexive modernization?

2 With what goals, content and programmes is '*subpolicy*' conducted, and in what areas of action (occupations, professions, companies, trade unions, parties, and so on)? How is subpolicy objectified, restricted, conducted and implemented into non-policy? Which strategies – for example, 'health precautions', 'social security' or 'technical necessities' – are applied for this purpose, how and by whom?

3 What organizational forms and forums of '*subpolitics*' are emerging and can be observed? What power positions are opened up, solidified and shifted here, and how? Are there internal conflicts over the policy of an enterprise or a group (labour, technology or product policy)? Are there informal or formalizing coalitions for or against

certain strategic options? Are specialist, environmentalist and feminist circles or working groups separating out inside occupational groups or plant labour circles? What degree and quality of organization do the latter exhibit (informal contacts, discussion meetings, bylaws, special journals, focused publicity work, congresses, code of ethics or a flag with a special emblem)?

Congestion – the meditative form of the strike in reflexive modernity

Many people are hoping for rescue from the dilemmas of late modernity and the incrustations of the party oligarchy in Western democracies by a subpoliticization of society. The *common good* is the magic word that is to call society to repent. This public-spirited movement is gathered in the United States under the name of *communitarianism*.[3] At the top of its wish list is a society integrated by a shared notion of the ethically good. This idea, writes *Der Spiegel*, 'is fascinating and dangerous in equal measure. It is uncertain, first, who decides what is ethically good and, second, what is to happen to the proponents of evil' (Darnstädt and Spörl 1993: 154).

'Subpolitics' means social arrangement from below. 'The only protection from self-righteous elites,' writes Claus Leggewie in the same article,

> from the failure of the interventions of an overburdened state, from the illusion of the invisible hand of the market, as well as from a regression to authoritarian or worthless populist social patterns is the civil society that we ourselves constitute – without a stable centre, without exact distributions of jurisdiction, without homogeneous convictions, without a presumed consensus and without a finished master plan. (p. 154)

Subpoliticized society is, or, more cautiously, could become (among several other possibilities), the civil society that takes its concerns into its own hands in all areas and fields of action of society. Actually, history, at least the political history of ideas over the last two decades, cannot do without the historiography of subpolitics. Domestic and foreign policy, environmental and technology policy have received substantive grass-roots stimuli from the peace, women's and environmental movements and at least their objectives have been (partially) designed from the bottom up. Even the general disgust with politics and the contempt for parties that are now so popular are, among other things, an expression of civil self-deception. They brush over the fact that society can be and is being shaped subpolitically – including the mobilization of the radical right-wing.

Some exemplary cases of subpolitics can be cited from the history of Germany in the past few years. As an example, consider Wackersdorf [the site of a proposed nuclear reprocessing plant in Bavaria – translator]. The conflicts over this plant intensified. There was an escalation of militancy, on the side of the police as well as among the demonstrators. The political move that defused the situation (although it did not solve it) did not come from the top of the political system. That had long since trapped itself in asserting and reasserting the rightness of its cause. It came from the ranks of subpolitics, in this case the nuclear business itself: the project was stopped and exported to France 'for reasons of cost'. As I said, not a solution but definitely a case of subpolitics.

The second example: speed limits. In the struggle over the transportation system of the future two themes are interwoven: environmental destruction and accident victims. The United States and most of Western Europe have long since implemented one element of a solution, namely a self-limitation of speed. Not so in Germany, which continues to complain about the destruction of forests. In this situation the judges of the Federal Constitutional Court took the – subpolitical – initiative. Something banal and unspectacular became the lever that introduced far-reaching changes. Up to that point a high-speed accident was considered an 'unavoidable event', as if there were a natural law built into a 200 hp engine that unleashes its energy on German autobahns without any human intervention. Now the 'risk liability' of the car owner for the consequences of his action is reinterpreted to coincide with that which is self-evident: anyone who drives a car must be liable for the dangers of operating it. He is responsible for the danger that emanates from his vehicle, his four-wheeled weapon.

This is again an instance of the insurance criterion of risk society. If one can make the allegedly natural fate of a threat – in this case the mad rushing in car traffic and its lethal consequences – calculable, accountable, insurable and therefore expensive for whoever causes it, the transportation system may not be remodelled down to its very foundations, but this action throws a switch-point which, together with other measures, can certainly help bring about a policy of self-limitation, self-control and responsibility. Anyone who cares to can continue to speed in order to get to the site of his accident as quickly as possible. Above 80 mph, however, he does so at his own risk, or, better, that of his comprehensive liability insurance.[4]

Certainly, if one examines this judicial traffic subpolicy in the harsh light of day, it amounts, first, to an appeal with a certain public effect and, second, to an advertisement for comprehensive liability insurance policies. And yet this example illuminates in exemplary fashion the possibilities for a rule-changing subpolicy, here that of the judges. They are, of course, in a better position to do this than others, as their involvement in the highly political decision on missions of the Bundeswehr in ex-Yugoslavia shows. It is usually from unspectacular, seemingly self-evident things that new guidelines can be forged.

Precisely this explosiveness of the small and banal things contains a great part of the effect and secret of subpolitics. It is often necessary to transform empty phrases into instructive precepts and things taken for granted into levers in order to be able to intervene in the opposition of the mutually obstructing forces.

Then there is the example of Italy. Conflicts of interest between the state, business interests and parties had been considered 'government Italian style' for decades, but a judge in Milan interpreted such practices legalistically, investigated, charged, summoned and convicted people, with the result that the republic was shaken. Umberto Eco exulted that Italy was finally experiencing its 14 July 1789. He claimed that the hard-bitten oligarchs from Giulio Andreotti to Bettino Craxi were deserving victims of this storming of the Roman Bastille (Darnstädt and Spörl 1993: 154).

Another example might be the rubbish-disposal plans in Bavaria. In 1991, the threat that a referendum, permitted by the laws of that province, would succeed in establishing a recycling system provoked a curious competition between the [ruling conservative] CSU [Christian Social Union] and the SPD [Social Democratic Party of Germany]. These two major parties, previously relatively uninterested in the problem, each attempted to get ahead of the citizens' initiative with more and more far-reaching programmatic promises. The referendum failed, but the rubbish-disposal plan was pushed forward by the CSU. 'Those are methods of a tenacious "siege" against the state and the parties', writes *Der Spiegel*, 'which even Jürgen Habermas praises as a promising procedure for rebellious citizens' (Darnstädt and Spörl 1993: 158; Habermas 1996).

Even when administrations or local politicians situate hostels for asylum seekers in towns or neighbourhoods where the residents can be protected from violence only with difficulty, if at all, or when they move these residences to residential neighbourhoods where the unemployment rates are high and the activities of right-wing radicals are notorious, this is also subpolitics in a certain sense. The fire-bombings and the attacks on people make it possible to shift the political coordinates and priorities of the republic to the right. It is equally true, conversely, that the candle-light marches against racism and persecution of foreigners owe their success in no small measure to their exclusive grass-roots origin – against parties and their limitations.

Yet it is also necessary to warn against false optimism. What appears from below to be the sphere of influence of subpolitics results, seen from above, in the loss of enforcement power, the shrinkage and minimization of politics. In the wake of subpoliticization, opportunities to consult and participate are growing for groups which have so far not participated in the substantive process of technification and industrialization: citizens, the public sphere, social movements, expert groups, employees on the scene, even the opportunities for individuals with civil courage to 'move mountains' in the nerve centres of change.

Subpoliticization therefore implies the decrease of centralist control-lever policies, the fizzling out of previously trouble-free processes against the obstinacy of controversial plans; situations in which the various groups and levels of decision-making and participation in it mobilize the legal means of the state against one another. This does not occur only in the confrontations of individuals and citizens' groups, but also in the conflicts between national and local politics, between a Green-spirited administration and an old-fashioned industrial management, and so on. In the end, no one prevails, neither the opposing power nor the established power, so that these terms actually become as relative as they should be conceptualized to be. A general 'relative powerlessness' arises (a powerlessness of citizens' groups as well, naturally) which is the other side of subpolitical activism. But this very petering out of the implementation process formerly so well oiled by consensus, which produces losers on all levels, *decelerates* the process, and is thus the precursor of an unregulated, anarchic self-restriction and self-control.

There are two paradigms of involuntary deceleration: *risk* and *congestion*. Congestion refers not simply to traffic congestion, but rather to the quite general modernization infarct in all sorts of phenomena and areas of society. A general congestion and overflow is threatening everywhere, in the mass media for instance, where the prospect of a thousand channels is bringing an end to the [traditional German] system of publicly operated media and opening wide the door to randomness.

One of the instruments of power in subpolitics is 'congestion' (in the direct and the figurative sense) *as the modernized form of the involuntary strike*. Here it can be seen how congestion and politicization – and their ambiguities! – cooperate and blend into one another. It is being recognized that things cannot go on this way, that they are not moving – congestion. This 'dammed up' citizen protest is a bit of 'life politics' (Giddens 1991; cf. pp. 152ff as well) and can explode in any direction. In any case, traffic policy has an everyday depth dimension that takes effect in a political way that can be experienced by everyone.

Congestion thus always means the *experience of congestion*, so that it is a category of cultural experience, in contrast to *class experience*, which, as we know, must be split into an 'in itself' and a 'for itself' to guarantee its objectivity. Congestion also has an egalitarian effect. All classes of cars are equal in its eyes. The phrase that Munich motorists, or, better, parkers, can read at a typically congested location, 'You're not in the bottleneck, you are the bottleneck', illustrates this direct and involuntary 'socialism experience' in automobile class society, as well as the parallel between strike and congestion. Congestion, unlike the strike, is not dangerous. Nothing is happening, after all. It is a kind of involuntary passive resistance to the modernization attack that is threatening everywhere.

The forced meditation on congestion in all topics and levels of the overdeveloped society could, paradoxically enough, start the rethinking and re-acting that prevents things from flowing smoothly. Politics can and must develop its shaping and creative radicalism from this, justify it and create new forms of consensus-building.

Put less positively and more sceptically or realistically, the subpoliticization of society initially comes down to preventing any kind of politics, or at least making it more difficult.[5] In the legitimation vacuum of a technological and industrial evolution that is playing with doom on the instalment plan, claims, contradictions, fissures and coalitions are pressing forward. They have only one certain effect: seeing to it that technological developments with predictably unpredictable side-effects that are dubious in a deeper sense eventually come under fire. This applies, for instance, to the plans from the bag of tricks of the sorcerer's apprentices in genetic engineering and human genetics, but also to highways, rubbish incinerators, dangerous new industrial sites or nuclear power plants (not to mention their waste-disposal programme). All these become entangled in a thicket of contradictions and resistance that ultimately demands either an authoritarian police response or an alternative modernity that would tie technological and industrial development into its new consensus procedures (see below 'On dealing with ambivalence: the "round table" model', chapter 4, p.121).

In order to understand what is happening in Europe today, it is also necessary to look at what is not happening, but could happen if the necessary political institutions, which we must invent, already existed. Everywhere only those political forces and institutions that already exist are acting and not those that must be invented and established. But that means that the lack of a 'sense of possibility' (Musil) and creativity has become the source of the prevailing misery.

> If one wants to pass through open doors easily, one must bear in mind that they have a solid frame; this principle . . . is simply a requirement of the sense of reality. But if there is a sense of reality . . . then there must also be something that one can call a sense of possibility. . . . This might be defined outright as the capacity to think how everything could 'just as easily' be, and to attach no more importance to what is than to what is not. . . . Such possibilitarians live, it is said, within a finer web, a web of haze, imaginings, fantasy and the subjunctive mood. . . . The possible, however, covers not only the dreams of nervously sensitive persons, but also the not yet manifested intentions of God.

In the eyes of others, a person who can see 'possible truth', Musil continues, often has

> a fiery, soaring quality, a constructive will . . . that does not shrink from reality, but treats it, on the contrary, as a mission and an invention. . . . Since his ideas . . . are nothing else than as yet unborn reality, he too of course has a sense of reality; but it is a sense of possible reality . . . (Musil 1953: 12, 13)

4

Ways to Alternative Modernities

There is only one word for the viewpoint with which the previous chapter closed: naive. This is a point of agreement for those who otherwise paint the changing realities of late modernity in exactly the opposite colours and emphases, the believers in progress and the sceptics of progress. If there is any certainty in the eye of the hurricane, the centre of disenchantment, then it would be that the law of techno-economic innovation is inviolate and implacable.

The modernization machinery that sets social circumstances in motion is a bit of transcendence in this world. One can love the technological god – or devil! – of modernity, or one can rage and curse against him, but there is only one thing one cannot do: shut down or reprogramme this out-of-control human machinery. In the social dynamics of modernity, a transition like that from the railway train to the aeroplane is just as much out of the question as the attempt to replace cars with bicycles.

What is possible, and is indeed happening, is to evaluate the modern fate antithetically. Some emphasize and welcome the increase in options that this allows. They are proven correct by the fact that states where options are 'flourishing' have now begun to put up protective walls against their attractiveness. Other people, by contrast, either see the entire gigantic undertaking heading straight for the abyss or sliding over into a new type of barbarism. There is one point on which these clashing perspectives are united: nothing can really be changed. Despite all the secularization, this faith has not been shaken.

A paradoxical situation has arisen with the end of the Cold War. Something that had been completely unexpected, in fact, proven to be out of the question – the political renaissance of Europe – has led not to a revival of Europe's ideas, to a purgatory and paradise of questioning, but rather to a general paralysis. Sometimes positively, sometimes negatively, one type of fatalism contradicts and corroborates another. Thus, despite Europe's inclination to realism, scepticism and nihilism, people misunderstand and cast aside the very thing that constitutes Europe's vitality: the ability to renew itself through radical self-criticism and self-destruction. Enlightenment is the exception where the vanquished gains from defeat. Optimistic and pessimistic fatalism agree in one respect: that there is only *one* shape of modernity, that of industrial society, whose compulsion produces that beneficent mixture of the consumer society and democracy at one time, and the next accelerates the general decline. *Tertium non datur. Tertium datur!* Many modernities are possible; that is the reply of reflexive modernization.

'But just as, at that time, those with acute hearing were able to perceive the rumblings within the ordered calm, the sharp-eyed can see within the present chaos a new order,' writes Kandinsky, as quoted in the introduction to this book. 'This order departs from the basis of "either–or" and gradually attains a new one – "*and*". The twentieth century stands in the shadow of the device "and".' This 'and' experiments with the excluded middle.

> The differences, laid down almost by Providence, between art and science (especially 'positivistic' science) are being consistently examined and it is not particularly difficult to see that the methods, the materials, and their treatment in each case are not essentially different in the two areas. The possibility arises for the artist and the scientist to work together on one and the same task. . . . A further impetus and the researches leading from it, which were likewise the product of painting, has the same value in principle – the collapse of the wall dividing art from technology, and the consequent reconciliation of these two sharply divided and, as people in general thought, hostile realms. (Kandinsky 1982: 711, 714)

Sociology, or, let us say more precisely, the (ironically) ageing sociology of modernization, must become a bit of an art, that is, a bit playful, in order to liberate itself from its own intellectual barriers. One could call this the *chemistry of premises*; oppose pseudo-eternal verities, rub them together, agitate them against one another and fuse them together until the intellectual test tube starts giving off sparks and smoking, smelling and sputtering.

How does the image of 'functionally differentiated' industrial society change when one applies the premises of 'functional differentiation' to it? Why do the varieties of sociological functionalism always paint an image of the differentiated society in the sense of a final differentiation, while further differentiations of industrial society operating right now are possibly opening up paths to new types of modernity?

Why should modernity be exhausted in autonomization and culminate, of all things, in 'self-referentiality' (Luhmann)? And why not in the opposite, specialization in the context? Perhaps the autonomy premise of modern systems theory, raised to the level of virtual autism, is only the basic multiplication table, while decimal arithmetic starts only where one autonomy is cross-linked with another, where negotiating institutions come into being, and so forth? Does reflexive modernization perhaps begin where the logic of differentiation and dissection ends and is combined and opposed to a logic of mediation and self-limitation?

Is the continual tracing of the disintegration of the old world in 'binary codes' not somewhat boring (all right, that is not a scientific category, so let us say: somewhat insufficiently complex)? Is it not time to break this great sociological taboo against simplification and, for instance, inquire into *code syntheses*, to search for *where* and *how* these are already being produced today? Is the combination of art and science, technology and ecology, economics and politics resulting in something Neither–nor, some third entity, as yet unknown and yet to be discovered, really out of the question simply because the basic multiplication table of functionalism considers it out of the question? Why must science itself, which changes everything, be conceived of and conducted as unchangeable? Or is it perhaps possible that the way a change in the framework of science is considered and rejected pushes out of sight the very possibility of self-limitation and change which is available to and incumbent upon the sciences? This would be the *self-opening of the monopoly on truth* that is becoming possible and necessary in and along with the methodological doubts to which science itself pays homage.

No doubt, fatalism has its good sides. It prevents, for instance, the activism of a modernization of modernity which would open Pandora's box. But it also acts as a lobotomy for sociologists, who, in their awareness of the autonomy of modernity, forbid themselves even to raise and discuss the issue of alternative modernities in any systematic way. 'Self-application' is the magic word which is supposed to loosen and overcome these old cognitive barriers. In spelling out this thinking we intend to proceed methodically and name the respective principle of industrial modernity which is to be applied to industrial society itself (in the thought experiment). Then we shall inquire what *face of modernity* results if what is unavoidable becomes true, that is, what might happen if modernization overruns even industrial society?[1]

Self-application is made concrete, first, in the key concept of 'functional differentiation' and, second, in the parallel concept of 'functional autonomy'. It is distinguished in the former case along the dimensions of future and past, and in the latter case along the dimensions of inside and outside, leading to four test categories. Anyone who inquiries into the 'functional differentiation' of 'functionally differentiated' society is raising (1) the issue of the (revolutionary) *further* differentiation of industrial society in the dimension of the future, and (2), in the dimension of the past, the issue of the *ageing* of 'modern' society and its systemic logic and institutions.

If one uses the key concept of 'functional autonomy' as a basis, then two questions of reflexive modernity can be obtained: externally, (3) the issue of the *intersystemic mediation and negotiation institutions* and, internally, (4) the inquiry into the conditions that enable '*code syntheses*'. These very different signposts to alternative modernities will only be cognitively approached, illustrated with examples, and pursued for a few steps.

Further differentiation of industrial society: feminization and naturalization of society

The way *into* industrial modernity was blown open, one has to say, by the French Revolution. It disembedded the *question of power* from its feudal–religious ascriptions and proscriptions. Contrary to all the professions of impossibility and against conservative rhetoric, the *plebs* became sovereign – at least in aspiration and procedure. This set the standards for the political grounding of power, to which even dictators still have to subject themselves, at least verbally.

The Industrial Revolution also led *into* industrial modernity. It permanently gave the owners of capital, the business middle class, the right to permanent innovation. One change after the other, followed by more change, unstoppable and uncontrollable, something that appeared completely inconceivable, even blasphemous, to earlier periods, came to be taken for granted, a certainty that is now becoming more and more dubious; it is the law of modernity to which everyone must submit at the risk of political demise.

This reminder that 'functional systemic differentiation' is another word for revolution is sorely needed. Only then can it be understood what is meant when people ask which functional systemic differentiations might lead *out* of industrial society. Two such are becoming clear today: the earthquake of the *feminist* revolution, on the one hand, and the systemic differentiation of *nature* 'in the age of its technical reproducibility' (Böhme 1992), on the other. Another one can at least be thrown into the arena of possibilities as a hypothesis that makes the unthinkable thinkable: *technology* that escapes the constraints of the economy, throws off its yoke of economic and military utility and becomes modern, nothing but technology, technology for technology's sake.

The revolt of *women*, unlike the explosion of the French Revolution, is a *creeping* revolution, a subrevolution moving not on cat's paws but on claws. Wherever it touches it changes industrial society's soft underbelly, the private sphere, and reaches from there into the peaks of male domination and certainty. The subrevolution of women which directly cuts up the nervous system of the everyday order of society, despite setbacks, can certainly give society a different face. One need only venture this thought experiment: a society in which men and women were really equal (whatever that might imply in detail) would without a doubt be a new modernity. The fact that walls to prevent this are built from nature, anthropology and ideas of family and maternal happiness with the deliberate cooperation of women is another matter. It is not least of all the shocks precipitated by the failure, in the view of many women, of the permanent feminist revolution which serve as a measure of the changes that will face us from its success. As social science studies show, the broad variety of fundamentalisms are patriarchal reactions, attempts to re-ordain the 'laws of masculine gravity' (cf. Riesebrodt 1993).

It is already becoming recognizable that *nature*, the great constant of the industrial epoch, is losing its pre-ordained character, turning into a product, the integral, shapeable 'inner nature' of (in this sense) post-industrial society. The abstraction of nature leads *into* industrial society. The integration of nature into society leads *beyond* industrial society. 'Nature' becomes a social project, a utopia that is to be reconstructed, shaped and transformed. *Re*naturalization means *de*-naturalization. Here modernity's claim to arrange things has been perfected under the banner of nature. Nature becomes politics. In the extreme case which can already be observed today, it becomes the field for genetic engineering solutions to social problems (environment, social and technical security, and so on). That means that society and nature fuse into a 'natural society', either by nature becoming socie-talized or by society becoming naturalized. That only means, however, that both concepts – nature and society – lose *and change* their meaning.

What directions will be taken here can be determined in advance only by prophecy – and by a little application of the principles of industrial production; industrial systems that are converted to natural production are transformed into natural systems which make social changes permanent. Constructed 'nature' (in the non-symbolic, materi-alized meaning of this word), 'decided nature', makes the production of matters and bodies of fact possible. Here a *policy of creation* produces a world of living creatures which can conceal its constructed character in the physical compulsion it creates and represents (see 'Counter-modernity means constructed certitude', p. 62 above).

The environmental issue and movement, which appear to be calling for the salvation of nature, accelerate and perfect this consumption process. There is a penalty in the fact that the word 'environmental' is so ambivalent that everything from prophecies of doom to hypertech-nologism can find a place and a rank in it.

Freedom for technology!

There is always an attempt to protect the hair-thin coating of legitim-ation for mega-technological systems, which can crack and chip away in the next major accident, by calls for retreat, stopping and more monitoring. Why not simply, as a thought experiment at least, venture more modernity: freedom for technology!

That implies releasing technology from the shackles (including the internalized self-restrictions) of business and the state and exposing it to the cold wind of doubt. Technology and its practitioners must ask themselves: is technology possible? How is technology possible? Is, or, more radically, how is, a non-utilitarian technology not concerned with effectiveness possible? How are fundamental alternatives possible, aesthetic, political, ecological, non-instrumental designs and images of technicity that perceive and take seriously the materiality of the world? What would a technology look like that accepted doubt rather than denying it? When in doubt, opt for doubt!

One can explain this utopia of a technology that is both radically modern and liberated with a parallel to art, specifically painting. Arnold Gehlen quotes Rimbaud, who anticipated the leap into abstract painting in 1871:

We must disabuse painting of its old habit of copying in order to make it autonomous. Instead of reproducing objects, it must force agitation by means of the lines, the colours and the outlines drawn from the outside world, but simplified and tamed.

In the same passage Gehlen quotes Herbert Read:

The forms that an artist realized and perfected step by step have a life of their own and follow a logical development which the artist could not change if he wished to. There are actually two sources of inspiration. One is found in that which is called nature and the other lies in the work of art itself. One could say, there is not just a form of life, there is also a life of form. (quoted in Gehlen 1965: 66)

We must disabuse technology of its old habit of copying economic necessities and military purposes in order to make it autonomous.

There are two sources of inspiration in the field of technology. Economic utility, effectiveness, enhanced speed or functionality are the first source; the second source of inspiration is the *technical work itself*. This must be developed. Technology could, like painting, become pure and abstract, discovering and trying out its 'agitations of the lines', its laws of point, surface, colours, and so forth.

This of course presupposes that technology and engineering science divest themselves internally and externally of the dogmatism of *extrinsic instrumental rationality* and *controllability* and open themselves to the constructed uncertainty, ambivalence, contextuality and fundamental dubiousness of their designs. With its elaborated scientific spirit and professional ethics, this 'technology of doubt' would make itself the advocate of the insecurities it creates. Precisely that would constitute its pride, its dignity, its independence and its autonomy. What would it mean if, instead of economy and effectiveness, technicity itself becomes the source of inspiration?

First, the discovery and support of technology for its own sake. Under these criteria of a 'value-free' or 'pluralistic-valued' technology, industrial research, for instance, would be refused; it would be considered the epitome of extrinsic control. Only in that way can scientists and the creators of technology stumble across and expose conceptually and creatively that which Kandinsky calls 'inner necessity' – the inherent value and inherent logic of materials, the specifics of designing, of the mechanical and of constructivity.[2] In the same breath, these creators of an 'abstract technology' (conceived in analogy to abstract painting) criticize the economic serfdom of technological tradition, its subservience to the 'mediocrity' of extrinsic instrumental rational technology, which has glorified itself as an anthropological absolute.

Second, such a technology could free itself from one-dimensionality and linearity and open itself to the And, developing, elaborating and internalizing other guiding principles besides economy and effectiveness. Perhaps it would be possible thereby to overcome its fate of blindness to consequences. That is, it could establish a type of technology that would replace secondary study and technology of side-effects with technologies and technological developments that would *minimize* them.

An 'ecologically sensitive' technology in this sense would need to be invented just as much as a technology that makes alternative thinking and doubt the fundamental principles of its development and methodology.[3] This implies that, third, this type of technology would abolish the *objective constraint* by its internal logic and replace it with the ethics and practice of the *objective alternative*.[4] That alone would liberate society from the dominance of technology by enabling and requiring political, ethical and public decisions. By methodically cultivating doubt, constructive fantasy and technical pluralism, a bundle of possibilities would be worked out and presented here, contradicting one another, forcing a non-technical decision, which makes talk of an 'objective constraint of technology' seem antiquated.

Only this 'abstract' and, in the artistic sense, 'non-objective', pluralistic technology, which has advanced further along the path of modernity and climbed to the level of self-doubt, opens up the possibility of classifying and autonomously organizing the issues of technology marketing and technology utilization. It is possible and necessary here that institutions for public consultation, ethical controversies, shared decision-making and voting be invented and put into place. This is of course the opposite of what is currently going on and serving as the guideline for technology policy, namely the emphasis on the optimal intermeshing of technological development and economic utilization to accelerate the spiral of innovation.

Technology development in simple industrial modernity is subject, as we know, to the dictate of profitability. Enterprises invest not in order to benefit humanity or to protect it from problematic side-effects, but rather to open up markets and areas of expansion with promise for the future. They evaluate what the competition is doing and, on the basis of market prognoses, make decisions they consider binding regarding their future focuses of research and production. 'The central problem is that this type of entrepreneurial development of consumption and planned innovation does not normally happen as a response to social sensitivities and articulations of interest but in advance of them, thus largely uninfluenced by democratic debates on the future outlines of technological development and oriented only to the standard of business efficiency and profitability criteria' (Dolata 1992: 352). The first great project of this supply-side technological development and implementation was and is nuclear power and the related industry, which requires a corresponding amount of state financing and public legitimation. From the moment of its origin, the new problem child for the apologists of technology, genetic engineering, is likewise subject to this pressure to assert itself on the market. How can one do research, particularly on side-effects and risks, under the guillotine of investments in the billions that have already been made?

Governmental policy, which ought to assert the common good against the hustle and bustle of an industry that produces prosperity and dangers in equal measure, remains

> largely obligated to the high-speed system of modernization oriented to the global marketplace. Instead of attempting to apply the brakes to the dangerous speed of development of new hazardous technologies, instead of sharpening perception of their threats and problematic effects, instead of generously supporting the search for technological alternatives and conceding more participation to society in the decision-making processes of technology policy, the handling of the dangers and risks of new technologies has remained an afterthought in the effort to protect international competitiveness and the national business climate. Governmental policy of this type is more likely to contribute to the acceleration, autonomization and entrenchment of problematic technology lines than to a cautious and responsible development of them. (Dolata 1992: 359)

The model of a liberated abstract technology for technology's sake would put an end to this cartel of interests, this political and economic serfdom of technology and engineers. The implication is, among other things, that there would be a slowing of technology development and thus an ability to revise it. Only in that way would a 'fault-tolerant technology' (Christina and Ernst Ulrich von Weizsäcker; see Weizsäcker 1991) become possible. Only that would make it possible to admit error without this admission leading to an economic and social catastrophe. And only then could something become possible that has so far been ruled out by its very structure: saying yes to technology and no to its use.

This model of a radicalized modernity rests on two cognitive pillars. Technology currently rules everywhere with no self-awareness, systemically diffused, and thus is nowhere really in control. The first of these pillars is therefore to extricate technology from the dictates of economics and the militarily committed state, very much in the sense of Walzer's 'art of separation', and thus to liberate it. This is comparable to the task of publicly organizing and financing education and training. If the general demand is: 'Get technology and engineers out of the ivory tower and into industrial practice and commercial fields!', then this model amounts to precisely the opposite, a 'contemplative model' of technology: 'Put technology into the ivory tower (of universities)!' Support for a basic, doubt-oriented science of technology alien to utilitarian purposes would be the motto of a high-tech society that reserves for itself the right to make its own decisions on its technological future.

In the terms of Kandinsky (1982: 712), this implies 'divorce . . . from "life" [i.e. of the economy – U.B.], consistent self-absorption in its own aims, resources, and means of expression and . . . at the same time, a natural and lively interest in the aims, resources, and means of expression of other arts' and fields of intellectual life. Only with this 'ivory tower technology' could it be possible to dream and try out the dream of a really 'modern', autonomous technology discovering its own possibilities. Only this could break up and destroy the *de-anthropologization* of technology – the dogma that technology can only be a *means* to interchangeable extrinsic ends (the counter-modern dungeon of a type of technology that is condemned to subordination by its very self-concept).

To continue the comparison with art, technology is still in the stage prior to the self-discovery and revolutionizing of painting in the twentieth century. It is trapped in a naive realism of utility and profitability. Just as artists in previous centuries painted representatively, portraying saints, rulers or nature, technology now serves governmental and economic 'necessities'. Breaking up this 'naive technology realism' would require a 'cubism of the engineers', a Blaue Reiter school of technicians, a Klee or Kandinsky who would be capable of creating the 'purity of technology' in full view of everyone with a creative revolution.

Only that would make it possible to think out and implement the second cognitive pillar of this intellectual model of a liberated and radicalized modern technology: the *division of powers and shared decision-making in the application and commercial use of technology*, in the technification of society.

An alternative type of regulation for the technoscientific revolution, conceived as an alternative design to the high-speed system of global market-oriented modernization, would in my view have to rest on four cornerstones: (1) on the general recognition and implementation of a socially responsible slowness and caution in dealing with new risk-fraught technologies; (2) on a research and technology policy that takes up social problems, corrects technological misdevelopments and actively encourages alternative paths of technological development; (3) on taking on a deep-seated ecologically sensitive restructuring of those industrial sectors with production or products that are laden with unacceptable risks; and (4) on a thoroughgoing democratization and decentralization of patterns of economic and political decision-making. (Dolata 1992: 362)

This implies, among other things, that the liberation of technology and its practitioners from the yoke of economics would have to go hand in hand with their *disempowerment* in the grey area of technology utilization. Their monopoly in questions of safety and in the allocation of side-effects would have to be broken.[5] This amounts to a second historical step in the *division of powers*, this time between the *development* of technology (which could then invent and elaborate much different principles and views for itself) and the *application* of technology. With democratic and moral legitimacy, the latter could then be independently organized largely detached from the milieu of primary industrial modernity.

The dilemmas of uncontrolled technology are not being replaced, as many believe, by autonomy for technology, but rather the lack of it, by subordinating technology to and intermeshing it with business, that is, by preprogrammed immaturity. In a technology without self-awareness, inventive zeal and discoveries are automatically transformed into uncontrollable upheavals and dangers. Genetic engineering and human genetics remodel the laws of human life. Precisely who is doing this? Technical people, politicians, industry or the public? Ask any of them and the answer will be the same as for Odysseus: no one. In developed modernity, so proud of the triumph of decision-making and control, technology policy is tantamount to 'no one's rule' (Hannah Arendt). Arendt (1976) says that this is the most tyrannical form of government because no one can be called to account in it.

The subordination of technology also causes its semi-professionalism (see, for instance, Hortleder 1970; Kogon 1976; Larson 1977). Technology is considered either the deductive branch office of experimentally tested theory or a mere source for useful things and problem solutions of all sorts. In both cases the design logic and autonomy of technology is denied, although all sciences have long since slipped into the technical sphere and the criteria for usefulness have become pluralized and questionable in substance.

Engineers must free themselves from domination by science, not only in their relative external positions, but also in their own images and concepts of technology, in order to free society from the dominance of extrinsically controlled technology. It may sound paradoxical, but freedom of technology and social liberation from technology could coincide. To put it another way, the radicalization of modernity – technology as 'l'art pour l'art' – could simultaneously create the preconditions for solving the problem of controlling, monitoring and democratizing technology systemically, by separating subsystems and making them autonomous yet coordinated. Liberated technology, having cast aside the yoke of utility, will also smash the automatism of implementation and thus make possible new intersystemic agreements and the establishment of 'filter institutions', institutions of negotiation that consult and decide on approval, refusal, as well as the conditions and the mixtures of the two.[6]

If all this should seem and remain contrary to fact, then we are involved here with a 'realistic utopia' (Giddens) of a radicalized modernity. And even the thought experiment makes us aware that technology, the quintessence of modernity, is organized in counter-modern fashion in the design of industrial society.

On dealing with ambivalence: the 'round table' model

Anyone who no longer wishes to accept the loss of legitimation for techno-industrial development must consider how the 'new ambivalence' can be made acceptable and capable of forming a consensus. The And being tested here takes the form of intersystemic mediating institutions. These exist in rudimentary form in the various 'round table' models or in investigative, ethical and risk commissions. The theories of simple modernization conceive of modernization *autistically*, while the theories of reflexive modernization conceive of it as *cross-linked*, specifically, according to the model of *specialization in the context*. While simple modernization conceives of functional differentiation *post hoc* and 'of natural origin', reflexive modernization conceives of functional differentiation in the sense of a substantive 'dividing process', in which the boundaries between subsystems may be planned differently or collaboratively, that is to say, cooperatively. In other words, the question of system formations that are multivalent, permit ambivalences, transcend borders and intermesh systems is now becoming central (Münch 1991; Willke 1992; on the subsequent text cf. Hoffmann-Riem and Schmidt-Assmann 1990).

In risk society, new expressways, rubbish incinerator plants, chemical, nuclear or biotechnical factories and research institutes encounter the resistance of the immediately affected population groups. That, and not (as in early industrialization) rejoicing at such progress, has come to be predictable. Administrations find themselves confronted with the fact that what they plan to be a benefit is felt to be and opposed as a curse. Accordingly, they and the experts in industrial firms and research institutes have lost their orientation, because they are convinced that they have worked out these plans 'rationally', to the best of their knowledge and abilities, in accordance with 'the public good'. In this, however, they miss the onset of ambivalence. They struggle against ambivalence with the old means of non-ambiguity, but here they overlook at least two things.

First, the benefits and burdens of more or less dangerous and burdensome production or infrastructure plans can never be 'justly' distributed. Second, the conventional instrument of political consultation, expert opinion, fails accordingly. Even the interplay between opinion and counter-opinion does not resolve the conflicts, but only hardens the fronts. There are beginning to be cries for an 'ecological trade union' in many plants that deal with hazardous materials or products. It is the same everywhere: the demand is for forms and forums of consensus-building cooperation among industry, politics, science and the populace. For that to happen, however, the model of unambiguous instrumental rationality must be abolished.

1 People must say farewell to the notion that administrations and experts always know exactly, or at least better, what is right and good for everyone: de-monopolization of expertise.
2 The circle of groups allowed to participate can no longer be closed according to considerations internal to specialists, but must instead be opened up according to *social* standards of relevance: informalization of jurisdiction.
3 All participants must be aware that the decisions have not already been made and cannot now simply be 'sold' or implemented externally: opening the structure of decision-making.
4 Negotiating between experts and decision-makers behind closed doors must be transferred to and transformed into a *public dialogue* between the broadest variety of agents, with the result of additional uncontrollability: creation of at least partial disclosure.
5 Norms for this process – modes of discussion, protocols, debates, evaluations of interviews, forms of voting and approving – must be agreed on and sanctioned: self-legislation and self-obligation.[7]

Negotiation and mediation institutions of this type must experiment with novel procedures, decision-making structures, overlaps of competence and incompetence and multiple jurisdictions. They can no more be had without breaking up monopolies and delegating power than with the old demands and models of efficient non-ambiguity. Everyone, the involved authorities and companies, as well as the trade unions and the political representatives, must be prepared to jump over their own shadows, just as, conversely, radical opponents must be willing and able to make compromises. This is more likely to be attained and amplified the more the old, instrumentally rational order, according to which the task is for specialists to 'enlighten' laypeople, is not even brought up.

Negotiation forums are certainly not consensus production machines with guaranteed success. They can abolish neither conflicts nor the uncontrolled dangers of industrial production. They can, however, urge prevention and work towards a symmetry of unavoidable sacrifices. And they can practise and integrate ambivalences, as well as revealing winners and losers, making them public and thereby improving the preconditions for political action.

In risk-society civilization, everyday life is culturally blinded; the senses announce normalcy where – possibly – dangers lurk. To put it another way, risks deepen the dependency on experts. A different way of handling ambivalence thus presumes that *experience* is once again made possible and justified in society – even against science. Science has long ceased to be based on experience; it is much rather a science of data, procedures and manufacturing.

There are actually two types of science which are beginning to diverge in the civilization of danger: the old, flourishing laboratory science, which penetrates and opens up the world mathematically and technically but is devoid of experience, and a *public discursivity of experience* which brings objectives and means, constraints and methods controversially into view.

Both types have their particular perspectives, shortcomings, constraints and methods. Laboratory science is systemically more or less blind to the consequences which accompany and threaten its successes. The public discussion – and illustration! – of dangers, on the other hand, is related to everyday life, drenched with experience and plays with cultural symbols. It is also media-dependent, manipulable, sometimes hysterical and in any case devoid of a laboratory, dependent in that sense upon research and argumentation, so that it needs science as an accompanist (classical task of the universities!). It is thus based more on a kind of science of *questions* than on one of answers. It can also subject objectives and norms to a public test in the purgatory of oppositional opinion, and in just this way it can stir up repressed doubts, which are chronically excluded by the blindness to threats and consequences of standard science.

In both cases we are concerned with a completely different type of knowledge. On the one hand, specialized, complex, dependent on methodology, and, on the other, oriented towards fundamentals and fundamental errors (for instance, in the setting of maximal acceptable levels, or in the practical and ethical way of dealing with probability calculations).[8] The goal ought to be to play the narrow-mindedness of laboratory science off against the narrow-mindedness of everyday consciousness and the mass media and vice versa (in Popper's sense). That requires stages or forums, perhaps a kind of 'Upper House' or 'Technology Court' that would guarantee the division of powers between technology development and technology implementation (cf. Adam 1990).

Rationality reform: code syntheses

The 'acrobatic gospel of art as the last European metaphysics' (Benn) or Nietzsche's dictum that 'nihilism is a feeling of happiness' has by now reached and penetrated advertising, business, politics and everyday life, that is to say, it has arrived and is becoming a cliché. After nihilism we do not end up with emptiness, but with aestheticism. In post-traditional society, people walk a tightrope between art and artificiality. That was how boundaries, assignments, and commitments formed and determined themselves in tightly woven networks; these make choice, accountability and commitments possible, on the one hand, as well as mass production, design, sales and fashions, on the other.

Gerhard Schulze (1992) forged the concept of 'society of experience' from and for this (and here he has probably, dare one say?, artfully and artificially overstylized an important and accurate partial aspect). Scott Lash (1993) built up this thought into a theory of aesthetic reflexivity. He connects the inquiry into the limits of reflexivity with it, because he assigns aesthetic reflexivity to practical, 'emotional reason' (if such a combination of words is permitted). Here he confuses reflection (knowledge) with reflexivity (self-application) (Lash 1993). I would like to take an essential further step, however. The aesthetic dimension of reflexive modernization, of which Scott Lash speaks, covers only one special case from the large box of, in old-fashioned terms, realistic utopias (critics would say horror visions) at the turn of the twenty-first century. The rigid theory of simple modernity, which conceives of system codes as *exclusive* and assigns them to one and only one subsystem, blocks out the horizon of the future and of possibility, the ability to shape and delimit oneself, in short the 'art of modernity'.

This reservoir is discovered and developed only when code combinations, code alloys and code syntheses are imagined, understood, invented and tried out. The 'aesthetics laboratory' which society has long since become is only one example of this. The question runs (in classic terms): how can truth be combined with beauty, technology with art, business with politics and so on? What realities and rationalities become possible and actually come into being when the communicative codes are applied to one another and fused together and a Neither–nor results, some new third entity, which makes new things possible and permanent?

The problem can be explained with a parallel between the genetic and the communicative codes. The genetic code opens up the generative centre of nature (human nature as well), while the communicative code opens up the centre from which originate the designs of reality for the subsystems and their opportunities to become reality. We are concerned here with the autonomized subrationalities which delimit and exclude the systemically frozen opportunities for action in modernity. This is where the analogy ends. There is no communicative code engineering (in the sense of genetic engineering), no way of opening and manipulating the codes of the subrationalities technically (like genetic codes). What is possible, and has to some extent already been done, is to bring the only apparently 'self-referential' subrationalities into relation to one another and to apply one to another in a meta-rational thought experiment. In the sense not of 'anything goes', but of a focused regrounding, a creation, or more cautiously, a correction of system rationalities that have become obsolete and historically irrational. For instance, does the recognition of the ambivalence forced upon us by the civilization of threat not require a different 'type', that is, a different rationality of science (logic of research, rules of procedure, methodology of experiment and theory) (approaches in Bonss and Hartmann 1985; Bonss, Hohlfeld and Kolleg 1989)?

Doubt, for instance, which not only serves science, but now, applied reflexively, disrupts and destroys its false and fragile clarities and pseudo-certainties, could become the standard for a new modernity which recognizes the 'basic right to err' (Guggenberger 1988). Contrary to a widespread prejudice, doubt is once again making everything possible – science, knowledge, criticism or morality – only different, a couple of sizes smaller, more tentative, personal, colourful and capable of learning. Hence it is also more curious, more open to things that are contrary, unsuspected and incompatible, and all this with the tolerance that is based in the ultimate final certainty of error (cf. the final chapter of this book).

In other words, reflexive modernization also and essentially means a 'rationality reform'. Only this could do justice to the historical a priori of ambivalence in reflexive modernity. This is certainly one of the issues of the century. As it takes its first few steps, this immodest inquiry into a new modesty can certainly move within the horizons of the subrationalities which simple modernity developed and mutually insulated. It can experiment with them, in the sense not of a 'chemistry of rationality' or a 'test tube rationality', but of a creative hermeneutics which turns constructivism positive and dethrones it through itself.

It is not an excess of rationality, but a shocking lack of rationality, the prevailing irrationality, that explains the ailment of industrial modernity. It can be cured, if at all, not by a retreat, but only by a radicalization of rationality, which will absorb the repressed uncertainty. Even those who do not like this medicine of civilization, who find its taste unpleasant, simply because they do not like the medicine men of civilization, will perhaps be able to understand that this playful dealing with the earthly sources of certainty, this type of rationality experiment, is only retracing what has long been underway as a concrete experiment of civilization.

The political bourgeois

Modernity transforms everything – truth, nature, God, objectivity – into decisions. But in the same degree to which this occurs, those who make the decisions disseminate self-portraits of processes devoid of decisions, invoking institutions, systems and inherent dynamics which justify what they do by placing a stamp of unrecognizability on it. Reflexive modernity cannot be conceived without crushing this constructed immunity to action. Possibilities of 'subpolitical' action and design arise in all areas and on all levels of society. A modernity which is fatalistic, at least in people's minds, slides over into a *political* modernity, in which constants are shifted, renovated and exchanged. From the rearrangement of the familial and gender order through the ecological renovation of industrial society all the way to the renovation of Europe (wherever its borders might end up some day), more or less everything is in motion, at least for a historical moment. The image of a 'new modernity' may seem overwrought and mysterious to many. It is haunting the management of companies, political parties, labour unions, and so on, as a question, fear, denial, curiosity. One way to it leads through the fusion of those which are separated according to the system: business and politics.

Arguing using the example of the environmental issue, the intrusion of ecological concerns into the economy opens the economy to politics. Industry and business become a political undertaking in the sense that the arranging of the enterprise itself – its organizational and personnel policies, the range of products and the development of production, large-scale technical investments and organizational arrangements – all of these can no longer be executed behind closed doors as objective and systemic constraints (Deutschmann 1989; Pries 1991). Instead, they are surrounded and permeated by alternatives, which means that other expectations, agents and considerations, as well as consumer consultations, act on the management group, which previously ruled alone and therefore 'unpolitically'. The unpolitical bourgeois of late capitalism as regulated by the welfare state becomes the political bourgeois who must rule in his economic sphere according to the standards of a policy requiring legitimation. Economic action, predominantly economic in character in simple modernity, must adopt and integrate principles of politics in reflexive modernity. It therefore becomes required to justify itself and dependent on negotiation, externally and internally, vis-à-vis the public (consumers) and the (current and potential) staff (Steeger 1992).

These constraints on business to open up to politics in its activities certainly also come from the economic sphere. To use an example, the ecological sensitization of business originates in part from the fact that firms in hazardous industries have or fear problems with recruitment of skilled workers and highly qualified professionals. If one digs a layer deeper, the employees in controversial firms, research fields and institutions are subjected to continual questioning and criticism, often by their closest relatives, but always also involving their closest relatives and their everyday surroundings (acquaintances, neighbours, networks, and so on). More pointedly, that not only means that professional participation in (publicly suspected) dangerous business production activities ends up in a private situation of accusation and threat, all the way to psychotherapy sessions for the children, who are unable to endure the conflict of expectations between their peer group and their identification with their father (or parents). It also means (although this cannot be documented by studies) that opportunities on the marriage market are declining for students and professionals in fields and firms that are stigmatized as 'hazard-producing'. If the industrially produced but denied danger becomes a personal one in this way, then one should expect that, in the long run, professions, firms and sectors with a hazardous image will have problems replacing personnel.

The transmission of public discourse and stereotypes into the economic sphere is obvious, since publics can always also be considered paying customers and must always be attracted and bound, that is, convinced. Under the conditions of simple modernization, this minor problem of image maintenance is trivialized. But such a separation of inner and outer is itself dangerous, because all investments of this type go up in smoke at the next accident or suspected accident or with the next 'toxin of the week' (which will come as certainly as 'amen' in church). This implies that economic activity can assure economic success only if it perceives and takes seriously public consequences and influences, anticipating and integrating them into all internal company decisions, that is to say, if it opens itself to political and social concerns, brings them in and assimilates them.

This is all the more applicable the more consumers begin to organize themselves in publicly effective fashion, everywhere in the world (here too the United States appears to be playing a vanguard role), and moralize the act of purchasing, organizing it publicly. Thus the synthesizing of economy and publicity is interlocked in business and society, intensifies and breaks up the monopoly of the economic side and forces new types of connection and combination of politics and economy.

The political bourgeois creating himself in these processes should not be confused with the *citoyen*, not even with a 'business *citoyen*'. This new type of an open, structure-arranging industrial policy remains quite well distinguishable from\the processes and mechanisms of the political system. The 'political entrepreneur' of the future is not an elected representative; the neutral indicators of wage and profit continue to decide on the participation of organizations and the success of products. Yet the substantive 'how' becomes controversial, subject to shared decision-making, capable and in need of being consented to. Trust becomes central, 'trust capital', which is forfeited in re-enacting the old industrial script. That is the source of the 'new piety' of business: ecological morality, ethics and responsibility are proclaimed for public relations effect on entire newspaper pages and the glossy pages of magazines.

In this way, reflexive modernization becomes *discursive* modernization. The 'discourse society' (Jürgen Habermas) changes the ground rules for techno-economic activity, forcing more than just a different 'style of communication', or different forms and forums of self-presentation. It also devalues previous organizational and strategic knowledge and forces new forms of intra-organizational action and legitimation.

The politicization that is brought into industry by environmental and technical threats has two sides. For one thing, industrial and organizational activity is becoming discursive and dependent on publicity. Additionally, the opportunities for external groups to exert influence are growing, but the same goes for the administration and parliamentary and governmental policy. The old, 'unpolitical' grand coalition of administration, state, business, technology and science no longer works. It is falling apart under the public accusations against the 'tolerated' dangers. Increasing prosperity and increasing danger are mutually interrelated. To the extent that the public becomes aware of this, the defenders of safety are no longer sitting in the same boat as the planners and producers of industrial wealth. The coalition of technology and economy is becoming fragile because technology may raise productivity, but it simultaneously puts legitimacy at risk. The legal order no longer fosters social peace, because by tolerating the dangers it sanctions and legitimates a disadvantaging of people in general.

To put it another way, the impotence of official policy against the industrial bloc is impotence against its classical setting. This can be overcome by a *politics of policy* that elaborates and develops its opportunities for influence in forging environmental alliances. In its double role as consumer and conscience, the public becomes a permanent forced father confessor for a sinful business sector. Things such as monitoring, safety, protection of citizens and the environment from the destructive effects of economic growth, which had previously existed only on paper and had not been taken seriously by anyone, are now becoming levers with which the state, the public, citizens' groups and the administration can plan and execute their political interventions in the fortresses of business in the name of a new band of environmental crusaders.

Losers produce winners. As industry publicly loses its environmental innocence, other business branches build up their 'Green' existence. A business sector that is capable of learning ecologically splits off. This split in turn permits the production of learnability by political means. Just as petty princes were played off against one another by popes and emperors (and vice versa), the distribution of winners and losers initiates a political game with business sectors, companies, taxes and controls, seasoned and prepared with 'scientific risk analyses', passing the buck back and forth and occasionally covering it up. This 'game', which comes into being in tandem with politics itself and is yet to be developed, makes it possible to forge coalitions of pro and contra and play them off against one another for the purpose of *repoliticizing policy*. In other words, it is possible to give strategic tutoring to an environmental policy in the form, to put it ironically, of a Pocket Guide to Ecological Machiavellianism. Only this is capable of stripping the phrase 'ecological reform of society' of its air of technological naiveté and equipping it with political meanings and a power to act that are necessary in the transition from an ecological morality to an ecological politics.

The age-of-And experiment of joining business and politics is therefore taking place simultaneously on several levels and is running in different directions. First, management must be conceived of as a kind of electoral district in which consent must continually be obtained over again, even if it is not organized in the form of a mandate (management training and so forth). Second, it is necessary to open management strategies and methods, including personnel, technology, organizational and labour market policies, to this dependence on publicity and consensus and to criticize and reorganize them on the basis of appropriate alternatives. The flood of corresponding self-help literature – *Beyond Hierarchy* and the like – indicates the reality of the issues and conflicts that are erupting here.[9]

Third, as indicated, the dependence of business on politics can be transformed into an *empowerment of politics*. Accidents and the probability of accidents or public news of toxins are a 'political factor' with an almost revolutionary impact in risk society (it is certainly no longer possible here to speak of a 'political subject'). Near-disasters and covered-up disasters, not to mention real ones, open the rigid circumstances of even the most powerful and 'self-referential' of industries to political action and arrangement from the outside (administrations, municipalities, political parties, citizens' groups and so on). The competition and rivalry between departments, individuals, groups and policies of the organization present similar opportunities from inside for trade unions and others.

Fourth and finally, it is conceivable that industrial operations which have hitherto had certain forms of hazard monitoring delegated to them and have pursued these under their own control may now have these functions organized inside their own operation under a mixture of public and private control. This combination of systemic logics would resemble the *Trojan horse model*, in which the potential dangers are observed and assessed on site under a separation of powers.

These are only the beginnings, the already documentable experiments of synthesizing business *and* politics in the economy.

5

The Reinvention of Politics

The points of the preceding chapter must be made more specific and defended against at least three objections. First, anyone who abolishes the boundary between politics and non-politics deprives himself of the basis of his argument! Where everything is somehow political, then somehow nothing is political any more. Isn't the necessity of political paralysis somehow being counterfeited into the virtue of subpolitical mobility and emotionality, following the motto that if nothing works any more, then somehow everything works? Incidentally, 'The knowledge that everything is politics', as Klaus von Beyme writes, 'leads us astray if it is not supplemented with the insight that everything is also economics or culture' (Beyme 1991: 343).

Second, doesn't subpolitics end precisely where politics begins, namely where the 'real thing', the key question of power, is at stake, in such areas as military strength, foreign policy, economic growth and unemployment? Is the emphasis on subpolitics, then, just another kind of automatic obedience?

Third, doesn't subpolitics reach as far and last precisely as long as it can be certain of the support of politics – law and money? Must one not then turn the argument around: doesn't the development of sub-politics presume a *reactivation* of the political centre and system? It is tempting to suspect that the formulation 'reinvention of politics' is pure wishful thinking. Even worse: is this not invoking and working for the resurrection of a 'statist absolutism of reform' (Thomas Schmid)? I should like to take up and refute these objections by means of a conceptual and typological sharpening and differentiation of politics and politicization.

The politics of politics

The East–West antagonism was one gigantic cementing of politics. The roles were fixed and the antagonisms reached into everything. On the small, everyday scale just as much as on the large geopolitical stage, normality and deviation, 'leadership', 'partnership' and neutrality were staked out and established all the way down to the details of industrial production, municipal politics, family policy, technology policy, foreign aid policy, and all the rest. It was the order of the great antagonism and its eternal prolongation which brought about three things: tension, clear possibilities for orienting oneself and a world political order which could give itself the semblance of being non-political.

If it is permitted to compare the unrestrained character of politics to a creature from the animal kingdom, one can say a lion was sitting in the zoo and yawning. His keepers maintained and protected his cage and threw him a few bloody morsels to scare and amuse the zoo visitors looking on from all sides. 'Symbolic politics' was what many clever minds called this telegenic lion feeding, this political circus. The training was general and omnipresent. Politics became trivial. Everything was stage-management. Things that would have happened anyway and the way of presenting them followed the law of inverse proportionality: the smaller the scope of action and the differences between the parties, the more hot air.

With the collapse of the East–West antagonism, a paradoxical situation has arisen. Politics still takes place in the same old cages, but the lion is free. People pretend to be in the zoo – without the lion. They treat lions running at large like zoo lions, and they consider it narcissistic touchiness if the latter do not dutifully look for peaceful cages to lock themselves up in. A bit of political wilderness, devoid of institutions, has arisen in Europe in all spheres of politics, even in those such as technology, industry and business which, not being politics, had hitherto been able to count on generally smooth implementation of their desires.

We distinguished above between official, labelled *politics* (of the political system) and *sub*politics (in the sense of subsystem politics). This return of politics after the East–West conflict and after the old certainties of the industrial epoch compels and justifies a further distinction, which runs transversely to that above, that is, the distinction between rule-*directed* and rule-*altering* politics. The former type can certainly be creative and nonconformist, but it operates *within* the

rule system of industrial and welfare state society in the nation state
(or, in our terms, simple modernity). Rule-altering politics, on
the other hand, aims at a 'politics of politics' in the sense of altering the rules of the game themselves. There are two things connected
to this type of meta- or super-politics: first, the switching of the rule
system and, second, the question of what system of rules one should
switch to. Perhaps one should play gin rummy instead of bridge or vice
versa.

Even inside simple politics, the bridge game, there are a number
of individual variants of a more or less sophisticated type which
one can play with various degrees of skill and mixed success. A
completely different situation arises, however, if the rules of the
game themselves are altered or switched. The height of confusion
is attained when one plays both at once, bridge and the game
of switching its rules. People play with swapped rule systems in
order to change the rule systems themselves. Some continue to play
bridge and are outraged as others attempt to invent and implement
new displaced rules of the game during the bridge game. We face
precisely this kind of hybrid of normality and absurdity everywhere
today.

The game of classical industrial society, the antagonisms of labour
and capital, of left and right, the conflicting interests of the groups and
the political parties, continues. At the same time, many demand and
actually begin to turn the rule system itself inside out, while it remains
quite unclear, to put it figuratively, whether the future game will be
bridge, ludo or football. Rule-directed and rule-altering politics overlap, mingle and interfere with one another. There are periods when one
side dominates and then again periods when the other does so. While
Europe is experiencing a regression back to rigid, bloody variants of
the game as played by nation states in simple modernity, America is
setting off for the new continent of inventing politics, trying out – and
suffering from – the politics of politics.

The distinction between official politics and subpolitics, which is
oriented to the systemic structure of society, must therefore be contrasted with the distinction between *simple* (rule-directed) and *reflexive* (rule-altering) politics. The latter is measured by the *degree* and
quality of politics. The phrase 'politics of politics', or 'reinvention of
politics', which aims at this need not be meant normatively by any
means. It only brings up for discussion what would have to happen if
the subject of discussion everywhere (including in the opposition!)
were to become reality – independent of whether these are dreams,
nightmares or ideas on the way to realization. Thinking minimalist-

ically, we are dealing today with the *concrete-sounding idea* of the reinvention of politics. Conceiving of it maximalistically, 'society' or groups in society are setting off on that mission.

The distinction between simple and reflexive politics can be applied to both politics and subpolitics as well as to the conditions for their politicization (see Table 1).

Table 1 Categories of the political

		QUALITY OR PERIOD OF POLITICS	
		Simple (rule-directed)	Reflexive (rule-altering)
PLACE AND TYPE OF POLITICS	Politics of the political system	Symbolic politics, economic growth, full employment, technical and social progress	Reactivation or metamorphosis of the state, gutting of politics
	Sub(system) politics	Simple expert rationality, dominance of technocratic, bureaucratic action, private sphere	Reform of rationality, political entrepreneur, occupation as political action
	Conditions of politicization	Strike, parliamentary majority, governmental initiative, collective–individualistic solutions (e.g. car, insurance)	Congestion, obstruction, and as *one* variant, the struggle for consensus and reforms of the modernization inside and outside the political system

Politics, to the extent that it behaves peacefully or can be kept peaceful, takes place within the nation state concept of democracy exclusively as a *rule-directed wrestling match of parties over the feed troughs and levers of power* with the goals of economic growth, full employment, social security and changing of governments in the sense of changing personnel or parties. That is democracy and that is how it takes place and manifests itself. Politics, however, in the sense of a reconstruction of the governmental system, a transformation of government, a self-dissolution of government both upward and downward by delegating decision-making authority to groups, on the one hand, and global agencies, on the other – never! To put it a different way, politics in the nation state structure and rule system is no departure into a new land of politics, the geopolitical or the global risk society. People quarrel over obeying and protecting the rules of the democratic and economic game in the nation states. This model of politics is dubious for many reasons, not least because of a *double inflation of demands*. Governmental politics is supposed to be in charge of everything, and everyone is supposed to take part in it and to be willing to do so.

This cannot be managed by the present obsolete institutions under any circumstances. If one no longer wishes to close one's eyes to this, then one must leave the framework of status quo politics in one's objectives – economic growth, full employment and social security – or at least open them up, expand them, rethink them and recompose them. That is precisely what the *reinvention of politics* aims to do. The same applies to Europe, to the world after the end of the Cold War, to the antagonisms between wealthy and starving regions of the earth which are now appearing openly and radically, to the problem of the economic and political refugees storming Fortress Europe and so on.

Reinventing politics means creative and self-creative politics which does not cultivate and renew old hostilities, nor draw and intensify the means of its power from them; instead it designs and forges new content, forms and coalitions. What is meant is a *renaissance of politics* which 'posits itself', to borrow an image from Fichte. That is to say, it develops its activity from activity, pulling itself up by its own bootstraps out of the swamp of routine. This does not mean a 'politics of convictions' (Max Weber) or a politics of lip service. On the contrary, the reinvention of politics requires a Machiavellian realism (see p. 130), but does not exhaust itself therein. Instead, it practises and struggles for spaces, forms and forums of style and structure formation inside and outside the political system (cf. the Introduction above, p. 7ff).

The façadism in politics

The view of a political issue of modernity in the vacuum of Europe as presented here is at war not just with the empirical study and theory of politics, but also with the spreading experience of impotence in the face of excessive challenges. Is it even possible to talk about rule-altering politics in a comprehensible manner? Must one not, on the contrary, issue a death certificate for politics, as done most beautifully and drastically by Hans Magnus Enzensberger (1992)?

The welfare state, according to a widely held opinion, has ossified, if not suffocated, politically as a result of its successes. Its social and political forces were no longer a match for the dynamism of the economic forces. The debates on alternatives in the seventies and eighties made it sufficiently clear just how immobile the state apparatus had become, in view of unemployment, ecological destruction and chronically empty public coffers. Here and there, particularly for the now unaffordable social benefits, cost-saving citizen initiatives were integrated into public hiring plans. Overall, however, this very besieging of the status quo by alternatives can be considered evidence that such self-refreshment of governmental politics, however desirable it might be from some aspect of the general good, is either superfluous or cannot be assimilated, and probably both, from the standpoint of politics. In any case, its few elements will be spat out at the first opportunity in the ongoing recession. Even this little seed of rule-alteration did not come up and the political system contracted down to its real purpose: the exchanging of political personnel.

'The institutional structure of the Federal Republic [of Germany]', writes Claus Koch,

> combines a minimum of political mobility with a maximum of flexible stability. A reform would have to proceed on the ant principle: everyone carries a grain of sand from the old location to the new one according to an instinctive plan. Viewed in this way the adoption of trace elements of alternative culture in the political apparatuses, while simultaneously excluding that culture, was a good practice for the almost politics-free integration of East Germany into the West. The seeming counter-example, the constitutional debate in the new Germany, shows the same well-meaning bustle that leaves everything as it was. (Koch 1991: 35)

Even when one reviews the leading political ideas and theories, the same picture results. The antagonisms of the political world – liberalism, socialism, nationalism, conservatism – that still dominate people's minds, parties, parliaments and institutions of political education descend from the rising industrial age. However, when they speak of global environmental devastation, feminism, the criticism of experts and technology and scientific alternative views, that is to say, the remodernization of modernity, these political theories are like blind people discussing colours.

Differences in the concept of politics cause and substantiate these contrasting fundamental assessments. But there is more to it; ever since the end of the Cold War, we have been speaking in linguistic ruins in which, behind the shiny façades of words, new realities are nesting everywhere, breeding and being set up. One could call this the *reinvention of politics as status quo politics*. The names of key political institutions are kept constant and therefore the political switches can be reset almost without any need for legitimation, bypassing public attention.

Strictly speaking, this is a *façadism in politics* which is made possible by the collapse of the East–West order. Drastic as it may sound at first, the image from architecture is completely apt. The Biedermeier façades of the old western republic are preserved and at the same time, below the threshold of visibility or criticism, the walls and floors behind those façades are being replaced by new ones. One could say that not a single brick or principle remains in its accustomed place.

Take military policy as an example. The Bundeswehr is still the Bundeswehr (NATO is still NATO and so on). At the same time, the old domestic Bundeswehr is being transformed into a new global Bundeswehr. The Bundeswehr is being 'gutted'. Its Biedermeier appearance remains, but otherwise it bears only a distant resemblance to the military organization of the same name.

Foreign policy is another example. In the East–West constellation, the principle of non-intervention in the affairs of other countries was an iron-clad rule. Anyone who demanded military intervention was suspected and accused of war-mongering, on both sides of the Iron Curtain. Now the opposing principle applies or seems to apply: intervention for humanitarian and moral/political reasons under the aegis of the United Nations, a kind of positive Brezhnev doctrine of the former West. The latter denounces itself as weak and cowardly whenever it does *not* defend human rights in other countries, no matter where or when or on the basis of what independent verdict. Such a defence, however, implies the invasion of a foreign country, that is, attacking and war-making. It must therefore be permissible to inquire how this axial shift of politics and the global political constellation became possible, how it is justified and how it should be handled in a violent world.

These are both examples of a politics of politics, a rule-altering politics which professes to be unpolitical, because it is conducted in unchanging institutions with unchanging names. We are therefore involved here with a rule-altering non-politics, even a policy of non-politics, at least when the constancy of the institutions and names serves as a shield and a screen to exchange the contents behind it.

This also applies to other areas of politics and of society: parties, trade unions, administrations, industrial plants, the private sphere, and so on (see 'The political bourgeois', p. 126). The 'reinvention of politics' often takes place informally, along the pattern of the gutted Biedermeier façade. It goes without saying that this requires proof in individual cases and cannot be used as an alibi.

All this documents a basic state of affairs that is difficult to capture in ordinary unambiguous concepts: a change of the quality of politics with unchanged institutions of the political system and power and functionary elites that have not been replaced, that is, an untouched systemic image of functionally differentiated society. At its centre, the theory of reflexive modernization diagnoses and comments on this unbinding and freeing of politics with a constant organizational society. Alongside these concealed and covert forms of the reinvention of politics there are of course open ones as well.

Metamorphosis of the state

One can say contradictory things about the modern state: on the one hand, it is withering away, but, on the other, it must be reinvented, and both for good reason. Perhaps that is not so absurd as it appears at first. To reduce it to a formula: *withering away plus reinventing equals metamorphosis of the state*. That is how one can sketch and fill out the image of a state that, like a snake, is shedding the skin of its classical tasks and developing a new global one.

'The politicians too are offended that people are taking less and less interest in them,' writes Hans Magnus Enzensberger.

> Rather they should ask themselves what the reason is. I suspect that the parties are victims of a self-deception. . . . The core of contemporary politics is the capacity for self-organization. . . . It begins with the most everyday things: school questions, tenants' problems, traffic regulations. . . . Today the state is faced by every possible kind of group, by minorities of every kind . . . not only old organizations like the trade unions, the churches, the media. Sportsmen and women are highly organized, the homosexuals, the arms dealers, the drivers, the handicapped, the parents, the tax dodgers, the divorcees, the nature conservationists, the terrorists, and so on. You can discover ten thousand different instances of power in our society. (Enzensberger 1992: 140f)

> In the old Europe, the community was always described by reference to the model of the human body. The government was on top, the head. This metaphor is finally passé. A centre which foresees everything, steers and makes decisions, no longer exists. Society's brain can no longer be located, least of all in Bonn. Innovations, decisions on the future stopped coming from the political class long ago. On the contrary, it's only when the new idea has become banal that the penny drops with the parties and governments. . . . The Federal Republic is relatively stable and relatively successful, not because of, but despite the fact that it is ruled by the people who grin down from the election posters. Although the minister for the post does everything he can to ruin the postal services, letters still arrive. Although the ruling chancellor behaves like an elephant in a china shop, trade with the East flourishes. And so on. . . . This paradox allows

only one explanation: the Federal Republic can afford an incompetent government, because ultimately it's not the people who bore us in the evening news that matter. (Enzensberger 1992: 139, 138)

The self-organization mentioned above does not, as Hermann Schwengel points out, 'mean the old liberal topos of the free social forces', for they were turned *against* the political claim of the state. 'Self-organization means, more precisely, a reunification of these free forces in the deepest strata of society, in economic, community and political activity.' Self-organization means (reflexive) *subpoliticization of society*. 'The locus and subject of the polity definition, of a specifically political power technique, of the guarantee of public peace and of the provocative assertion of a political history of this and only this society, [have] moved apart. They [are] just as accessible to economic and cultural institutions as to the political ones' (Schwengel 1987: 18).

The authoritarian action state has given way to the negotiation state, which sets up stages and conversations and directs the show.[1] 'The ability of the modern state to negotiate is presumably even more important than its one-sided hierarchical ability to act, which is becoming more and more problematic.' In late modernity at the tail end of the century, 'the (traditional) state is withering away as a "separate creature", as the structure of a sovereignty and as hierarchical coordinator' (Scharpf 1991: 7). Withering away need not be synonymous with failure, the variation we hear from one end of the country to the other in the accusation of a 'disenchantment with parties'. Success can kill too. The withering away of the state is often just the other side of the self-organization, the subpoliticization of society; it is a bit of *redeemed utopia*. Politics condensed down to symbolism characterizes the intermediate stage, in which the classical problems of the state in simple modernity have in part been solved and in part been forgotten in the thicket of active society, but where the governmental challenges of a reflexive modernity are not yet perceived at all.

Social scientists have difficulties with the concept of death. The collapse of the Eastern Bloc, however, has demonstrated that there can be such a thing as a governmental stroke. Anyone who rules out the concept of an 'institutional death' forgets what we are dealing with everywhere in these days of radical social change: *zombie-institutions* which have been dead for a long time but are unable to die. As examples one could take class parties without classes, armies without enemies, or a governmental apparatus which in many cases claims to start and keep things going that are happening anyway.

If it is true that governmental tasks die and new ones must be defined and constituted, then the question arises of which tasks and how they are defined. Carl Böhret suggests an interesting criterion for this, the 'negotiating capability' of social interests. He considers this to be fulfilled where interests become capable of self-organization, where they are given voice and significance by organized agents in the arenas of society and politics. By contrast, the new government tasks that must be explored are characterized in that they are *not capable of negotiation*, but must be extricated from diffuse generality, shaped and made the object of official policy. Examples would be the wounding of the vital and survival interests of the as yet unborn and the natural world around us, or the construction of a supranational and ideally global order. 'All problem fields that are in principle *"negotiable"* between groups of people and organizations can be "societalized". That means here that they can be worked out in the multilateral negotiating system, with the participation of the state. This increasingly also concerns the legal design where the governmental agent is primarily left with the central control of the context.' Put another way: the classical areas of *symbolic politics* can be moved out and delegated back to the organized subpolitics of society.

> All aspects, however, which are *'not negotiable'*, because there is either the lack of a direct partner or because no interest can be represented effectively by such partners in a reasonable time, should in principle be handled as functional tasks of government. That always applies when the 'maxim of survival' is affected and there is a presumption of a 'generational responsibility' or of protecting succeeding generations, but it also applies in the case of 'creeping catastrophes'. For the foreseeable future, deregulation is only imaginable here at the price of disaster. In these areas, therefore, the state devotes itself to those problems which are without social competition for now, in ecology for instance. It is supposed to be allowed to claim a 'process monopoly' for this. The state must permit and even want the tasks assigned to it in each case not to belong permanently to it, but rather to be worked off again and again ('societalized', that is) by the competition that occurs. (Böhret 1991: 9f)

This is more than just a plea for a redefinition of governmental fields of responsibility; it is the radical question of whether certain seemingly 'eternal' tasks and the institutions with jurisdiction over them have outlived their usefulness. Reflexive politics, then, does not just mean the reinvention, but also the *clearing out* of politics: to put it bluntly, murdering institutions. But how can I kill something already dead? Whether, for instance, a military is part of the essence of the state (as almost all theories of the state from Hegel to Max Weber to Carl

Schmitt would have us believe) is definitely dubious and must be made dubious in the age of ambivalence.[2]

So this is not a plea for new governmental tasks within the old forms. Quite to the contrary, the core of the argument is that this new task simultaneously forces the state into a new *form* of task management. The state must practise self-restraint and self-abnegation, give up some monopolies and conquer others *temporarily*, and so forth.

> Neither the 'laissez-faire' of a caretaker state nor the authoritarian overall planning of an interventionist state is appropriate to the operational needs of a highly differentiated modern society. . . . The goal is the construction of realities in which the constructions of realities of other systems have some freedom of action. In the face of externalities that are no longer internally controllable, what is at stake are self-limitations of fully differentiated functional systems by a process of supervision, in which the perspective of mutual intervention – of politics in science perhaps, or of science in politics – is complemented by the perspective of the invention of mutually compatible identities. (Willke 1992: 296, 303)

The third way to the society of citizens: what will become of the parties?

The mass political parties in the Western democracies, for a long time the paragons of a successful combination of citizen interests and opinions, have come into disrepute in recent years. The signs indicate that a storm is coming; in all 'participation democracies', the party of non-voters is the only party that can record robust growth. Following on its heels are right-wing or even radical right-wing parties that hunt votes more or less openly with hatred and persecution of foreigners. The zero-sum game of power among the established competing parties no longer works; setbacks of the governing party are no longer expressed in increased votes for the opposition. In almost all the model democracies, we are involved with double crises. Ailing and crisis-ridden, governing parties and the opposition vying to replace them must both put up with losses.

Strategies based on weakness are beginning to be practised. People no longer pay attention to overcoming their competitor by performance, but only to keeping the extent of their own crises and scandals below the level of failure and loss of confidence that plagues their opponent. Elections are won not by majorities of assent, that is, because the party presents the better candidates and programmes, but because it drives away fewer potential voters through its scandals and failures than does the other party.[3]

A consensus is emerging on the reasons for this development: the stability of the parties relied in part on their associations with relatively clearly delimited social and moral milieus that were predictable for the parties. In Germany this would mean a social-democratic milieu, the classical working class and trade union milieu, on the one hand, and, on the other, a Catholic milieu which the Union parties could count on. Under such conditions, it was possible, as they say, to put a hat on a broomstick and it would still get votes. Put another way, the mass parties did not need to create consensus; they were able to draw on it, at least in the basic questions of small- and large-scale politics.

This did not just ease the way to the party oligarchy that is now so widely deplored. It also permitted the clear contrasting of programmes and candidates on the left–right pattern, in which everyone, almost as if pre-arranged, knew whom to vote for. In other words, it was an order of Either–or, which is now being displaced and replaced by And. Externally, there was the threat from the one overall arch-enemy, who simultaneously stabilized the antagonisms internally. In this sense it was wrong-headed to conceive of the dynamics of the former West Germany as being detached from East Germany, and vice versa. These two divided German states constituted an 'inborn antagonism' from the very beginning, a type of negative unity, a unity, that is, in which the domestic 'right–left' opposition plan could be asserted and organized within the horizon of the military East–West confrontation. Each represented the opposition against the respective state. East Germany was an 'anti-West Germany', not only diplomatically, but also domestically; West Germany was likewise the antithesis of East Germany, a fact which defined and polarized political conflict here and there. In this sense – not just in the shared language, culture and history – the division was always unreal.

Since the East embodied the left-wing experiment, but simultaneously occupied the position of the enemy in the military East–West conflict, it was easy to stigmatize and strangle left-wing politics and criticism in the West with the accusation of, at best, supporting the opposing cause. Criticism of the system was almost considered a matter for counterintelligence, and therefore scarcely needed any serious debate. In the overlapping of East and West with left and right, democratic and military thinking and language play were mixed together and the latter was played off against the former. The pithy sentence with which opposition was dismissed in West Germany – 'Well go over there then!' – indicates this state of affairs exactly.

While divided Germany was caught in the dilemma where the government on the other side of the Iron Curtain embodied the opposition to the respective system, debate was trapped in that same East–West schematism, with the result that GDR socialism was, one could say, the anvil on which left-wing politics in the West could be hammered down. At the same time, the opposition in the West was left-wing and in that sense compelled to distance itself from Stalinist East Germany, but equally to defend the left-wing pretensions of East Germany against the 'imperialistic hostility' of late capitalist 'crisis managers'.[4]

This law condemning opposition to disloyalty showed its traces in the internal opposition policy. Only after its Bad Godesberg Declaration of allegiance to the Western alliance system and its economic rules of the game did the SPD become 'qualified to govern'. The reform policies of the Social Democratic/Liberal coalition [1969–82] constantly had to struggle against the systematically stirred-up suspicion of planning the East-Germanization of West Germany. It was only able to take off with Western wind in its sails (commitment to NATO, the Swedish model, democratic socialism).[5]

No matter how strangely pressed and folded this order and mechanism of Either–or might appear in retrospect, it had one great advantage, almost worthy of glorification today. It offered a forced stabilization of the play of political forces, one that cannot be offered by the complication of the And which now prevails everywhere.

In the age of And, the delineation and profile of the parties with respect to one another is becoming less and less credible and more and more comical. Parallel to that, the individualization processes make assignments to conviction-based affinity groups in society and politics more and more difficult (see chapter 3 above). Who votes in what way for a given issue and candidate no longer follows any predictable and easily consulted pattern. Individualization destabilizes the system of mass parties from the inside, because it deprives party commitments of tradition, making them dependent on decision-making or, seen from the party perspective, dependent upon construction. Considering the fragmentation of interests, opinions and issues, this is like trying to herd a sack of fleas (Wiesendahl 1989; Starzacher et al. 1992; Wehling 1992).

All these radically changed basic conditions – the disintegration of ready-made moulding forms for political consensus with which one can act and negotiate in the political business, the loss of the unifying imagined enemy and the blurring of unambiguous left–right categories

– cause a return of uncertainty here as well. The mass political parties appear to be dinosaurs from a fading industrial age, in which the Either–or of class, nation and progress prevailed. They seem to belong more to a museum than to a government but they are – still – in power. Not the least reason for this is that the political system cannot be voted directly out of office and parties have occupied power and hold on to it everywhere. They have succeeded, after all, in leveraging the governmental separation of powers, getting control of the justice system, parliaments and ministries. 'Parties', criticizes Dieter Grimm, 'cooperate among themselves in various roles' (quoted in Darnstädt and Spörl 1993: 750). And yet they may none the less face the Brechtian fate of having to dissolve society and elect another one. In this sense, the case of Italy pointed the way to the future.

The combination of the abolition and the re-establishment of the state as presented previously would then of course have serious consequences for interest and party organizations in the liberal democracies. The shift of governmental tasks – moving organized interests back into society and elevating unorganized interests, which none the less endanger or protect the public interest, to be central tasks and axes of the political system – could revitalize politics in the political system. This concrete utopia, however, may be failing from the very fact that it is part of the case to which it refers. It arises from a global interest for which implementation power can scarcely be organized in the ruling party oligarchy. Its realization will be possible only to the extent that a variant which does not even appear to be improbable prevails: *the third way to the society of citizens* (Dubiel, Frankenberger and Rödel 1989; Habermas 1996).

The strengthening of plebiscitarian elements need not even take the constitutional royal road so popular in Germany (introduction of referenda, and so on). It may also be taken indirectly by a structural democratization of political parties and other industrial society mass organizations (trade unions, corporate and professional organizations, and so on) and, if thought through to its logical end it, amounts to a *gutting* of them. That is, they are emptied out and rebuilt while the façades are left unchanged and continue to be kept up. In a certain sense, this is the inverse of symbolic politics. If the latter produces smoke to simulate fire, then in this case constancy is demonstrated in order to hollow out the party-political 'state property' in a participatory manner.

The elements for this have already been thrown into the debate by the [former German] president. 'In our country', says Richard von Weizsäcker in his well-known interview, 'a professional politician is generally neither a specialist nor a dilettante, but rather a generalist with specialized knowledge of how to oppose a political adversary' (Weizsäcker 1992: 150ff). His suggestion along this line is greater participation of voters in nominating candidates. Claus Offe goes an essential step further and demands that non-members of parties be placed on the electoral lists and even be helped to power with the aid of quota arrangements (as quoted in Darnstädt and Spörl 1993: 158). These and other apparently small intra-party reform plans and elements (direct election of the chancellor candidate, for instance) are intended to make the party cartel permeable for citizens, expertise and new ideas. Intra-party factionalization along key issues with a future (women, the environment, welfare policy and renationalization) which permit inter-party cooperation lie along the same line.

If one mentally extrapolates this evolution, things that appear identical change. The party names and organizations continue to exist but are filled out with new contents that destroy the parties' previous patterns of partisanship. The transmission belts of political will formation could be opened to the subpolitical society of citizens in this way (if individualized society does not put a quick end to mass parties at the next opportunity).

The gutting of the trade unions, trade organizations and the professional organizations of doctors and engineers and their opening to new issues and contrary interests can be conceived of analogously. The siege of self-referential institutions by alternatives could become successful to the extent that in such manner the permeability from below upward is enhanced and guaranteed.

This is an image of quarrelsome pluralistic affinity-group parties, which lose their profile and open themselves to temporary, issue-specific, person-dependent consensus formation, create subsidiary forums and offer meeting places and participation in decisions to the diversity of citizen interests on all levels of society. It presupposes, however, that in parallel the institutions of major publicity – television, newspapers, the radio – are expanded and made more independent. It is not only necessary to restrict party access to these levers of power for the fourth estate and to strengthen citizen participation. It is also necessary to protect the relative independence of the publicly supported broadcasting system from death by commercialization and fragmentation. Without falsely levelling out the complications, it is fair to say that the interplay of citizens' groups and mass media publicity put the issues of global endangerment on the agenda of politics. Only this interplay can critically accompany and arrange the reconstruction of the party landscape and the state's tasks compatibly with democracy.

In other words, the democratization of criticism that becomes possible in risk society implies that the necessary attentiveness and clarity of criticism in the interplay of government and opposition will falter if at the same time criticism, even radical criticism, does not prove its principles and expand its footing in the public mass media.[6]

Anti-governmental nationalism?

The year of And, 1989, has faded rapidly. The renaissance of politics emerging from the ruins of the Eastern Bloc appears in an odd way to confirm Carl Schmitt. The liberation from communist centralism, its defeat and fragmentation, rests on the revolutionary power of ethnic differentiations and nationalisms once believed dead. We are not dealing with the end of enemy stereotypes, only with an exchange of them. The single grand enemy, communism, is being replaced by a number of nationality conflicts of potentially war-like scope. The Yugoslavian drama must be taken seriously as the thunder and lightning before the actual storm, which is brewing on the territory of the former Soviet Union and threatening Europe and the world.

This very threat, however, shows what the general rigidity of thinking is doing. We are concerned here with wars and outbreaks of unimaginable brutality, but this is still a nationalism whose enemy stereotypes are, first, directed inward and not outward, and one which, second, is based historically on a synthesis of ethnicity and self-determination. Yet the nationalism in Europe now spilling over from the former Eastern Bloc derives its historical force and legitimacy from the overcoming of the communist central power. More pointedly, it was not the West, but suppressed nationalisms that sloughed off communism. This victory is the source and substance of the mystery of nationalistic fascination that now threatens to drench Europe in blood with new cruelty.

'We are *the* people!' 'We are *one* people!' These were the sentences that brought the Berlin Wall down. The intensification expressed in the exchange of the words 'the' and 'one' is uncanny, at least to Western observers. The run-up and the jump, the foundation in democracy and the explosion of nationalism, cannot be put into words any more directly and succinctly. 'The' stood for democracy and the renewal of East Germany. Only the 'one' overthrew both East Germany and the idea of a socialist utopia. The sequence is just as interesting. Not 'one' but 'the' people broke the spell of powerlessness and found the courage to conquer back the streets. Some Western observers shuddered when 'the' was overrun by 'one',[7] but this was drowned out at first in the intoxicating joy of events. It is only gradually dawning on us that 'one' is not so easy to transform back into and cage up in 'the'. The excesses against foreigners in the eastern part of Germany are in part the aftershocks of an 'anti-governmental nationalism' that draws its authority from the sentence 'We are one people'.

In other words, it is the ethnic modification and coloration of the *principle of self-determination* that have made nationalism so devastating for Europe after the Cold War. This principle, defamed by many as a relic of an antiquated bourgeois ethics and society, ridiculed as a mere semblance in the ideological battle of the systems, is now proving to be a sharp and double-edged sword in and among the states of Europe and the world. Something which previously only wars could do – shifting the boundaries between states, nullifying the balance of power in an entire hemisphere – is possible today, peacefully and thoroughly, because groups and parts of states claim the fundamental democratic right to self-determination of ethnic groups and turn it into a fact. The division of Czechoslovakia is the most recent example.

A second aspect is connected to this. At least in the beginning, this was a neo-nationalism with an inner-directed enemy stereotype. This may in turn be overrun by an aggressive, expansionist neo-nationalism. This appears wherever, as in Serbia, a reactionary Stalinistic nationalism desires to conquer back lost territory by military means. A 'neo-Soviet Union' is also looming on the horizon, threatening ethnic pluralism in the East and consequently in the western part of Europe as well. Characteristically, however, this is a *re*action to the successes of a nationalistic and religious separatism that opposed any attempts at assimilation in communist centralism. Of course, this could well prove to be one of the many intermediate forms that are subsequently replaced by a new authoritarian and dictatorial regime. If one looks at how fast the revolution eats its parents (Bauman 1993) there are alarming symptoms arguing for this.

Beyond left and right?

The attempt to apply the categories of 'left and 'right' to this historical mish-mash points out the conceptual jumble that history has perpetrated. Is the conversion of the communist system into a capitalist system a 'leftist' or a 'rightist' undertaking? Is the resistance to that process, that is to say, the protection of the 'achievements' of what remains of socialism, 'conservative' or 'progressive'? Are those who disturb the graveyard peace on the left by mercilessly exhibiting the perversions of socialism in all their concrete forms still promoting the cause of the 'class enemy', or are they already taking the role of a 'post-socialist left' and laying the basis for their claim on the future Europe?[8]

In the old world order, left- and right-wing politics had their conventional clienteles, their own linguistic forms (cartoon captions), hot-button issues, constellations of allies, opponents and intentional or unintentional gaffes, with predictable effects. But as the strings break on this piano, the music loses it musicality, despite unchanged finger dexterity and score. With the loss of the East–West orientation, politics is becoming a silent movie, or, more accurately, a sound movie without the soundtrack. People move their lips and pound the keyboards, but nothing comes out!

Could it be that we still have the old landscape of political parties in Europe, but already signs and symptoms that it will be eroded down to its very deepest layers in the coming years? Is reflexive modernization then equivalent to a long-term earthquake which is turning the 'party geology' upside down? Might all the unease that already takes our breath away today be just the calm before the storm? Or is one thing true and yet the exact opposite happens, that is to say, because people lose the support of the left–right political order, they restore the left–right order?

Perhaps this left–right metaphor actually has irreplaceable advantages. It applies always and everywhere, its transfer to politics is attuned to history and it tailors the (overtaxing) complexity in a bipolar manner which makes it susceptible to action, an asset whose value rises precisely with the disintegration of the world order.

Certainly, empirical political science confirms the relevance and significance of the left–right pattern in the public perception (Gabriel 1992 is representative of many others). Things may be going the same way for those surveyed as for the social scientists doing the survey: they have no alternatives. In their helplessness, however, they help themselves to move on with the conceptual crutches of the past, even though they clearly sense the inadequacy and antiquatedness of those crutches.

The political left–right metaphor, which was born with bourgeois society (Lukes 1992), is probably unconquerable, unless it be 'dethroned' by alternatives. The coordinates of politics and conflict in the future will be located here and approached conceptually in three dichotomies: *safe–unsafe, inside–outside* and *political–unpolitical*. We are concerned here with three key questions: what is your attitude,

first, towards *uncertainty*, second, towards *strangers* and, third, towards the *possibility of shaping society*?

Why these three key questions and oppositions and not others? We
choose these because, in the view of the theory developed here, they
have greater opportunities for implementation or, more clearly, *opportunities for stylization and stage management* than others. That is what
is decisive, after all, and not the inherent validity or the features of the
aforementioned dimensions and categories. On the basis of the theory
of reflexive modernization sketched out previously, it is plausible to
assume, first, that even in the future it will still be possible to conduct
nationalistic counter-modernization, second, that the continuation of
self-destruction will deepen the battle line between safe and unsafe,
and, third, that the 'conflict of the two modernities' has yet to show
and elaborate on its explosiveness politically and subpolitically.

There is little that should be surprising in the significance for the
future of the inside–outside, us–them opposition. Considering nationalistic wars and looming refugee migrations, it hardly requires a theory
of reflexive modernization to venture this prognosis. There might more
likely be a need for that in explaining the How of those phenomena.
Where institutions disintegrate, avalanches of possibilities descend
upon those who must take action. A corresponding unsatisfiable need
for simplicity and new rigidity arises. If alternative institutions that
enable and relieve action are not available, then the flight into the
masquerade of the old certainties begins. These must be resurrected
even while disappearing, as it were. This purpose is served by 'disguises' (in a quite literal sense) which combine two things: *ascription*
(the strongest antidote to disembedding) and – paradoxically enough –
constructibility (see chapter 2). The void cannot be filled in any other
way.

That is to say, we are experiencing not the renaissance of the people,
but the renaissance of the staging of the people (or the staging of the
renaissance of the people). The latter gains the upper hand, in broadcasting stations and on title pages, because other types of change are
blocked off, and nationalism, bitter as this may sound to many,
exudes the enticing aroma of self-determination. Here the different
possibilities of counter-modernization – nationalism, violence, esoteri-
ca, and so forth – can complement, mix, cancel, amplify and compete
with each other.

Of what help is it to point out the staged nature of nationalism? Does
it lose any of its danger thereby? No, but it does become more helpless,
heterogeneous and unstable; it acquires, so to speak, *postmodern traits*
and loses the fatalistic and demonic quality that seduces people into

dynamic nationalism. This neo-nationalism, which can probably be successfully staged in the long run, is a spectre which, like other spectres these days, needs broadcast space on television and the tacit subpolitics of the (still) democratic majority in the West, in order to be able to haunt effectively (Heitmeyer 1991).

Something which is at heart similar can also be said of the other two types of polarization. The growth of controversies over *constructed dangers* causes the antagonisms safe versus unsafe to dig themselves in. Politicization obviously occurs *issue-specifically*. That means, however, that anyone who asserts safety on one side finds himself in the ranks of the endangered on the other. Niklas Luhmann drew the conclusion from this that this opposition can neither be handled institutionally nor does it lead to clear front patterns. The result, he claims, is a fluctuating conflict potential that can no more be limited than it can be sharpened into political disputes. This always understates how the safety and insurance institutions themselves contain and maintain standards according to which they can be convicted of uninsured unsafety.

And that is precisely what clears the way into *subpoliticization* and triggers the opposing impulses towards 'more of the same' and non-politics. The opposition between old and new modernity is a shock that encompasses and electrifies all fields of action in modern society. Uprisings encounter the resistance of the routines and those caught up in them. Reflexive not simple subpolitics must organize itself. Two patterns can be explored for this: *confrontation* and *coalition*.

A general paralysis comes about along with subpoliticization. The modernizers and their critics alike run in place or get caught in the thicket of agitated points of view and interests. This weakening of the implementation process of industrialization, formerly so well oiled by consensus, slows the process and is the precursor of an anarchic self-limitation and self-control of previously unchecked industrialization as usual (see the discussion above on 'congestion', pp. 104 ff).

The general confusion and conflict inside and outside the institutions forces and favours the formation of support networks crossing the boundaries of systems and institutions, which must be personally connected and preserved. In a certain way, then, the disintegration of institutions makes room for a *refeudalization of social relationships*. It is the opening for a neo-Machiavellianism in all areas of social action. Orders must be created, forged and formed. Only networks, which must be connected together and preserved and have their own 'currency', allow the formation of power or opposing power.

Life-and-death politics

The concept of politics in simple modernity is based on a coordinate system, one axis of which runs between the poles of left and right and the other between public and private. Becoming political here means leaving the private sphere for the public sphere, or, conversely, that the demands of parties, party politics or the government proliferate into every niche of private life. If the citizen does not go to politics, then politics comes to the citizen.

Anthony Giddens calls this model 'emancipative politics' and de-limits it against 'life politics'. 'Life politics concern political issues which flow from processes of self-actualisation in post-traditional contexts, where globalising tendencies intrude deeply into the reflexive project of the self, and conversely where processes of self-realisation influence global strategies' (Giddens 1991: 214).

The exciting aspect of this view lies in the fact that here, in contrast to Christopher Lasch and his talk of the 'culture of narcissism', politics is achieved or makes its invasion in the passage through the private sphere, the back way around so to speak. All the things that are considered loss, danger, waste and decay in the left–right framework of industrial society politics, things such as concern with the self, the questions: who am I? what do I want? where am I heading?, in short all the original sins of individualism, lead to a different type of political identity: life-and-death politics (also cf. Beck-Gernsheim 1991; Bauman 1992).

Perhaps this new quality of politics will become comprehensible if one first pays attention to the hysterias that arise here. The pollution of air, water and foodstuffs certainly increases allergies in the medical, but also in the psychological sense of the word. Everyone is caught up in defensive battles of various types, anticipating the surrounding hostile substances with his manner of living and eating. Those substances lie in ambush everywhere, invisibly. In other words, *the most general and the most intimate things are directly and inescapably intercon-nected in the depths of private life* in ecological culture. Private life becomes in essence the plaything of scientific results and theories, or of public controversies and conflicts. The questions of a remote world of chemical formulae intrude with deadly seriousness into the inmost recesses of personal life conduct as questions of self, identity and existence and cannot be ignored. Global society is thus contained in the microcosm of private life, politics nestles down in the middle of private life and breeds there.

What constitutes the political and politicizing aspect of life politics? First, *inescapability*, which, second, stands in *contradiction to the principles of private sovereignty* and, third, can *no longer* claim the character of *natural constraints* (in the original sense of the word) as justification. In contrast to the claims of modernity to order and decision-making, a new experience of compulsion comes into being, which neither coincides with nor should be confused with the dependence on nature in earlier centuries or the class experience of the industrial epoch.

This is the experience of the 'nature fate' produced by civilization, in which the reflexive ego culture experiences and suffers the relentlessness of its technical constructivity and its global society. Now the microcosm of personal life conduct is suddenly interconnected with the macrocosm of terribly insoluble global problems. In order to take a breath without second thoughts, one ultimately has to – or ought to – turn the ordering of the world upside down.

This arouses an existential survival interest in scientific categories, sources of error, and perspectives, of which the earlier humanists could only dream. The philosophical issues of existentialism, for instance, become part of everyday life, almost burning issues. Søren Kierkegaard's concern with anxiety as the other side of freedom, for instance, or the issues of who defines and makes decisions on life and death and in what way, force themselves upon everyone in the distress of having to make a decision and become great issues which electrify everyone (Giddens 1991).

This new symbiosis of philosophy and everyday life shows up strikingly in the issues which people are forced by advanced medicine and genetic research to decide. Those developments are tantamount to a *democratization of God*. They force people into questions that earlier cultures and religions had projected onto God or the gods. The successes of reproductive medicine and genetic research will soon put parents and doctors in a position to select qualities of the coming generation negatively, or, eventually, perhaps positively as well. It is already possible to recognize certain 'congenital diseases', as they are called, at an early stage, and, in combination with abortion, to prevent the birth of a child with these probability characteristics. It is foreseeable that the choice of male or female offspring could also be 'regulated' in this way – unless there are explicit, difficult-to-monitor prohibitions, which also apply mainly to a certain cultural group. And all of this is just the beginning of a long series of scientific revolutions.

Reproductive medicine and genetic research throw open the door to a new quality of politics (Daele 1986; Hohlfeld 1989; Beck-Gernsheim

1991; Beck 1994: 17–35). This quality is distinguished first of all by the absence of any of the provisions of the official political sphere: no executive, no parliament, no implementation barriers, no administration blocking policy. Here, everyone rules himself and his progeny and can directly implement the values that govern him (intolerance, images of others, fears) under his own direction (arm in arm with the 'genetic counsellor' assisting him). Separation of powers between executive, legislative and judiciary is replaced by direct action in one's own interest, preventive health care for oneself and one's loved ones. This private executive branch, lest anyone be deceived, is in sum precisely the gateway through which the (nightmarish) dream of the 'New Man' can be made a fact, flesh and blood. After the demise of socialism and its nightmare of a New Man, a new nightmare of forming reality in our own image is beginning, this time in everyone's private life and on an explicitly voluntary basis.

It is characteristic of the fusion of nature and politics, the biological social engineering, that is becoming possible here that the promises of the old, stagnated politics are again flourishing. Soon the old educational ideal will be 'improved', watered down and undermined by human genetics (Beck-Gernsheim 1991: 56–77). Why bother with the long arduous road of teaching, training and educational research, if, at least in principle, defects such as inadequate ability to learn can be eliminated and perhaps other positive characteristics can be assured by selection and engineering of the genetic prerequisites? Advances in human genetics are competing with educational policy or, more precisely, they are making possible a long-term biopolitical planning policy that has one enormous advantage on its side: it cuts costs and replaces uncertainties of result with 'efficient pre-planning'.

The curve can be extrapolated further. If one once dares to pull back the conceptual bars and anticipate that everything which could happen were allowed to happen, as has indeed been the case so far, then labour policy and measures for the protection of workers could be replaced by genetic hiring tests. These would then lead by voluntary pragmatism to anticipatory measures in the pre-natal stage. That in turn would imply that people (probably) having certain discriminated properties would disappear; even more quietly, they would never be born in the first place.

One can take any field of conventional politics – environmental policy, economic policy, technology policy, prevention of violence, and, it goes without saying, health policy, which indeed supplies the justification for all the initially invisible major side-effects – all these are finding and developing supplements and replacements in opportunities for private action which are offered by the unfolding of genetic knowledge and inventions. Research is already underway looking for genetic features that favour violent behaviour, in covariance with environmental influences, of course. Environmental policy can be 'effectivized', as is also already happening, by the breeding of toxin-consuming bacteria and toxin-resistant plants and animals (even this distinction is becoming old-world).

The linear rationalization of the genetic code is opening a political space. Its particular features are characterized by representing the exact opposite of politics: private sphere versus public sphere, the prenatal obscurity of test-tube eugenics versus the consent of living persons, the trappings of health versus the trappings of law and justice, direct private access versus barriers to implementation. In certain fields, individuals are beginning to acquire capabilities of intervening and arranging things that were denied even to dictators of earlier ages; they can now select qualities of human nature and thus help design as a collective of individuals the face of the evolving society – private eugenics (Weingart, Kroll and Bayertz 1988: 684).

If I may be permitted a prognosis, these design possibilities will be successful precisely because they are emerging in the private sphere, rather than in the political system, and they will be carried through, in all probability, almost without publicity. Expectations and values are changing accordingly. That which today appears to be a ghastly horror story from the laboratory of some mad scientist in the movies will cease to be so spectacular once enjoyed and experienced. Like so many other things, it will go its own way, frightening at first, then beneficial and perhaps again frightening at the thought of losing the benefit.

Of course, these are dreams or nightmares. But, to be honest, what is there to protect us from this brave new world? In realistic terms, not morality, nor laws, nor prohibitions, nor forbearance (although all that should not be underestimated). The most important thing is the insufficiency of research, working and raging, but not getting as far as the 'hopes' that support it. Inadequacy, paired with external and internal criticism and alternative thinking – these represent the final stumbling blocks that will just possibly save us from gliding into the human genetic paradise. It is one of the guiding paradoxes that the scientists who advance this process with their inventiveness must do two things to protect it: tempt with promises of imminent successes and simultaneously palliate or suffocate all the objections that arise from that prospect by pointing to the futility of their efforts.

The 'executive branch' of the genetic cultural and social revolution in the future is the individual decision of the 'private individual'. The patient will become a revolutionary in his own cause. The genetic revolution is extra-parliamentary. The formula 'the personal is the political' thus acquires a secondary genetic meaning, which can quickly become its primary one. As was said, the history of humanity, its peril and its tragedy, is only just beginning, for technology, in its intensified application to the genetic realm, is becoming the birthplace of religious wars which, unlike their forebears in the late Middle Ages, can no longer be neutralized by the state. First intimations of the fundamentalist conflicts that face late biotechnical modernity can already be felt in the disputes over legalized abortion. In 'body politics', so emotionally charged with identity issues, religious wars between groups with conflicting lifestyles are waiting at every fork in the road.

Profession as political action

One of the key questions will be the extent to which these antagonisms impact back on the guardians of rationality, the experts. After all, the question of power is raised in institutions when alternatives are worked out and expert groups rivalling over substantive issues collide.

'It is empirically documentable', writes Elisabeth Beck-Gernsheim,

> that among human geneticists in Germany there is increasing debate on the positioning of the field, on possibilities and opportunities, limits and dangers. Simply consider, to list two current examples, the pro and contra on the abolition of the age indication in prenatal diagnostics or the beginning dialogue between self-help groups and human geneticists, led by prominent representatives of the specialty. These are committed, passionate, sometimes embittered struggles over substantive issues and procedures; unpleasant questions and accusations are also raised. Comparable discussions hardly ever take place in reproductive technology. This may be tied in no small measure to the fact that a much stronger split within the profession has developed in sterility therapy – the technically oriented school on the one hand and the psychosomatic one on the other. (Beck-Gernsheim 1992: 33; cf. the discussion in the journal *Medizinische Genetik*, 1997f)

Vocations and professions – understood as 'brand-name products' on the labour market, as commodity-like, licensed competence – are the guardians of a certain form of normalized subpolitics. Personal–social identity is tied in these 'labour force patterns' to the right and the duty to arrange the *substance* of work. Occupational groups possess the productive intelligence and the power to arrange things in society (Freidson 1975; Beck, Brater and Daheim 1980: chap. XII).

This can have varying meanings. Some contribute to the public welfare in a policy of small steps, others conduct health policy and still others 'improve the world' with genetic engineering. The professional form provides protection against the injustices of the labour market by protecting opportunities for strategic action even with respect to companies, the purchasers of labour power.

There is a second factor connected to this: vocations and professions are (possible) foci of bourgeois anti-politics (Konrád 1984). In addition to the struggles for social and legal security, the franchise and the right of assembly, this is a centre of obstinacy for the self-assured individualist. The heterogeneity of the intelligentsia, the variability of its situations, intentions and views and the constant internal quarrelling, the contempt and lack of consideration its members practise in their dealings with one another – all of these make the intelligentsia anything in the world except a 'class' in any politically practicable sense of that term.

Third, professions are de facto agents in a global society of specialists, and this real existing supranationality predestines them to be agents of global solutions.[9]

Fourth, the subpoliticization of the experts occurs to precisely the extent to which *alternative opportunities for action* are *produced* and set against one another.

Technocracy ends where alternatives open up in the techno-economic process and polarize it. These alternatives become fundamental and detailed, professional and profitable, found careers and open markets, perhaps even global markets. They divide up the power bloc of business in this way and thereby enable and enforce new conflicts and constellations between and inside the institutions, parties, interest groups and public spheres of all types, and to the extent all this occurs, the image of the indifferent self-referentiality of social systems shatters. The systems themselves become subject to design. Like social classes, social systems also fade in the wake of reflexive modernization. Their continued existence becomes dependent upon decisions and legitimation, and therefore changeable. Opportunities for alternative action will therefore be the death of the individual-dependent systems.

An essential role is played here by the *issue of how deeply alternative activity affects and splits even the ranks of expert rationality*. Until now, this was unthinkable, or at least not a concrete threat. Three conditions have changed this: the transition from simple to reflexive scientization, the ecological issue and the penetration of feminist orientations into the various professions and fields of occupational activity.[10]

Where the sciences and expert disciplines adopt and illuminate each other's foundations, consequences and errors, the same thing happens to expert rationality which simple scientization accomplished with lay rationality. Its shortcomings become discernible, questionable, capable of arrangement and rearrangement (for approaches to this cf. Beck 1992: chap. VI). The ecological issue penetrates into all occupational fields and makes itself felt in substantive controversies over methods, calculation procedures, norms, plans and routines. In any case, the existence of ecological splits in the occupational groups is becoming an essential indicator and gauge of the stability of classical industrial society.

The same applies in a different way to feminist critiques of science and the professions, whenever they are not content with merely denouncing the professional exclusion of women, but go on to criticize the professional monopoly on rationality and praxis and to redefine and compose specialist competence with intra-professional acumen and methodology. They do so, furthermore, not individually, but organized and in a group.

This is how an ideal cracks up. Experts can solve differences of opinion, so the presumption goes, by means of their methodology and their scientific and technical norms. If only one conducts research long enough, then the opposing arguments will fall silent and unity and clarity will prevail. The exact opposite could occur. Research that inquires further and into more difficult questions, taking up all the objections and making them its own, this kind of reflexive research breaks up its own claims to clarity and monopoly; it simultaneously increases both the dependence on justification and the uncertainty of all arguments.

An obvious objection is that all of these things are speculations, which are being pushed aside by the hard maxims of free-market success. After all, many will say or hope, these are fleeting opinions, with agreement that can be revoked once and then granted again, so long as their sails are filled by the favourable winds of the economic climate. A juicy depression (no matter how regrettable its details might be), combined with mass unemployment eroding the substance and the self-confidence of the populace, will drive away these spectres and resurrect the old guidelines of classical industrialization like the phoenix from the ashes.

This objection may apply under certain early conditions of environmental criticism, but is less and less valid when business itself profits from the successes and hazards it has created (Jänicke 1979). If sectors come into existence which build up their existence and their markets on the recognition and elimination of hazards, then even the centres of economic power are split into reformists and orthodox believers, environmental Protestants and ecological converts. If it becomes an established view that ecological solutions, as well as ecological competency and intelligence in all fields of society, are in tune not just with values, but also with the market, in the long run perhaps even the world market, then trenches between losers and winners in the ecological competition for (economic) survival open up and become deeper. Ecology becomes a hit, a self-seller – at least as cosmetics or packaging. The resistance of the one half of business and society faces a grand coalition of the alarmed public, eco-profiteers and eco-careerists in industry, the administration, science and politics. That means, however, that alternatives open up, cooperation becomes uncertain and coalitions must be forged, endured and fought out and in turn cause further polarization. This precisely *accelerates* the disintegration of power in the institutions.

Along with the danger and the general perception of it, a highly legitimate interest in preventing and eliminating it arises. The ecological crisis produces and cultivates a *cultural Red Cross consciousness*, which transforms everyday, trivial, unimportant things into tests of courage in which heroism can be exhibited. Far from intensifying and confirming the general pointlessness of modernity, environmental dangers create a *substantive semantic horizon of avoidance, prevention and helping*. This is a moral climate and milieu that intensifies with the size of the threat, in which the dramatic roles of *heroes* and *villains* achieve a new everyday meaning. Sisyphus legends spring up. Even negative fatalism – 'nothing works any more, it's all too late' – is ultimately only a variant of that. This is precisely the background against which the role of Cassandra can become a vocation or a career.

The environmental issue, the perception of the world in the coordinate system of ecological–industrial self-imperilment, turns morality, religion, fundamentalism, hopelessness, tragedy, suicide and death – always intermingled with the opposite, salvation or help – into a universal drama. In this real-life theatre, this continuing drama, this everyday horror comedy, business is free to take on the role of the villain and poisoner, or to slip into the role of the hero and helper and celebrate this publicly. The cultural stages where the ecological issue is played out modernize archaism. There are dragons and dragon-slayers here, odysseys, gods and demons, except that these are now played, assigned and refused with shared roles in all spheres of action – in politics, law, the administration, and not least of all in business. In the environmental issue, a postmodern, jaded, saturated, meaningless and fatalistic *paté de foie gras* culture creates a Herculean task for itself, which acts as a stimulus everywhere and splits business into 'villains' and 'Robin Hoods'.

In systematic terms, one can distinguish two constellations in the ecological conflict, following the schema of Volker von Prittwitz (1990). The first constellation is the *confrontation*, where polluter industries and affected groups face one another exclusively and spectacularly. This constellation begins to move only in a second constellation, in which (a) *helper interests awaken* and (b) the *cover-up coalition between polluters and victims begins to crumble*. This occurs to the extent that parts of business, but also of the professional intelligentsia (engineers, researchers, lawyers and judges) slip into the role of rescuer and helper, that is to say, they discover the environmental issue as a construction and expansion of power and markets. This, in turn, presupposes that industrial society becomes an industrial society with a bad conscience, that it understands and indicts itself as a risk society. Only in that way can helping and coping industries and careers develop themselves and their heroism, which both motivates and skims off profits. This presumes a turning away from mere criticism and a transition to the *siege of the status quo by alternatives*. The environmental issue must be broken down into other questions: technology, development, production arrangements, product policy, type of nutrition, lifestyles, legal norms, organizational and administrative forms, and so on.

Only a society which awakes from the pessimism of the confrontational constellation and conceives of the environmental issue as a *providential gift for the universal self-reformation of a previously fatalistic industrial modernity* can exhaust the potential of the helping and heroic roles and gain impetus from them, not to conduct cosmetic ecology on a grand scale, but to actually assure viability in the future.

Ecology abolishes the neutrality and objective apoliticism of the economic sphere, which splits up in its sinfulness, all the way into its management, into the personality and the identity of the people on all levels of action. This splitting and susceptibility to division into the sinful and the redeemed permits a 'political sale of indulgences' and restores to politics the power instruments of 'papal jurisdiction and misjurisdiction', the public exhibition and self-castigation of the great industrial sinners, even the public torture implements of an 'ecological inquisition'. Most politicians shy away from this in their publicity-conscious kindness. The professional swimmers-upstream in the ecological movement seem to lack the political charisma and realism to pull those instruments out of the political tool chest by themselves.

6

The Art of Doubt

No one can doubt that Enlightenment, the liberation from self-imposed immaturity, in Kant's words, can be perverted. The list of organized, perfected horrors spawned by this century permits no doubt of this: the Holocaust, Stalinism, re-education camps from Siberia to Cambodia, the octopean State Security Service in East Germany. But in these terrible experiences of a 'dialectic of Enlightenment' (Adorno and Horkheimer) is there not also a certain relief alongside the out-rages and sadness? A relief that an unambiguous Enlightenment, com-pulsory and proliferating like an epidemic, is not possible. Does the barbarism that arises or threatens in modernity as its shadow not also demonstrate the old teaching that freedom also makes destruction and devastation possible?

Isn't there an elemental fundamentalism of self-righteousness and indoctrination hidden in all Enlightenment as practised so far, some-thing which always threatens to turn Enlightenment into its very opposite? Perhaps the decline of the lodestars of primary Enlighten-ment, the individual, identity, truth, reality, science, technology, and so on, is the prerequisite for the start of an alternative Enlightenment, one which does not fear doubt, but instead makes it the element of its life and survival.

What is so terrible in Foucault's insight that the institutions of libera-tion are in fact elaborate systems of subordination? Certainly our disappointed ideals rebel. An entire experimental order of Enlighten-ment proves to be the opposite of Enlightenment. But is this not an expression of the desire to unmask, the quintessential pleasure of En-lightenment, which does not even shy away from its own arrogance and its initial hopes, joyously toppling the monuments of its own tyranny?

Perhaps accepted, self-aware scepticism can lead to a way of life on the human scale? Perhaps the error that is gradually being demonstrated is the only way to bring us to reason? Perhaps scepticism, enriched with irony, removed from itself and the confusion of eras and biographies, as experienced and conserved in language, is the existential form in which modernity will cast off the megalomaniacal presumptions of the industrial era? Perhaps self-confident doubt is preparing the way into a new modernity based on smallness and self-disillusionment? Perhaps the reflected scepticism, which lives and argues completely in touch with its times, will overcome industrialism's arrogant faith in technology and will establish tolerance and curiosity with respect to the otherness of others.

Dubito ergo sum: I doubt, therefore I am! I doubt, therefore I shall become! I doubt, therefore I give you space! You doubt, therefore you acquiesce to me! We doubt, therefore we are! We doubt, therefore we become possible! We doubt, therefore there are many modernities and everything is starting from scratch!

Perhaps doubt, mine and yours, that is, will create space for others, and in the development of the others, for me and us? Could this utopia of a questioning and supporting doubt form a basis, a fundamental idea for an ethics of a post-industrial and radically modern identity and social contract?

Perhaps doubt, which no longer only impels science, but also dethrones it, is the layperson's only opportunity to take revenge on the experts who are constantly patronizing him? Perhaps the common sense of reflexive, also ecologically sensitive, modernity will reveal itself to be common scepticism, which has a double-edged effect: waspish and inconsiderate externally, with regard to the old and new varieties of absolutism, but inwardly small-scale and flexible, forming nests of subversive contentment.

No, the destruction of the old grand illusions is not a loss, but rather a necessity in order to discover the breadth of smallness, the joys of relativism, ambiguity, multiple egos, affirmed drives (which had previously bowed down to the rule of a superego). 'My imperfection is . . . not congenital, not earned,' confides Franz Kafka in his diary. 'The reproaches lie around inside me.' 'I myself' as it were, 'am perhaps the best aid of my assailants. For I underestimate myself and that in itself means an overestimation of others' (quoted in Bauman 1991: 86). Perhaps one reason for the fascination exerted by Kafka's 'scribblings' is based on the fact that in the mercilessness with which he leafs through the linguistic photo albums of his own failed existence it is possible to hear and experience an echo of the liberation from the yoke which the maintenance of the grand façade of the self has represented for its exponents to this day.

In the disintegration of identity, self, truth and reality, the handcuffs and leg-irons with which people have imprisoned and mistreated themselves at the behest of outside powers also burst.[1] One can sense something of the advantage that vagabonds or eccentrics, with their effervescent liveliness, have always had over the puffed-up ego-tyrants of the bourgeois world or the heroic self-asserters of the post-bourgeois world – at least in literature. The sceptic, the ironist, the self-concealing chameleon self, the puppet and butterfly existence that slips out and slips around, knowing nothing, but knowing it more thoroughly and substantially than anyone else – the fascination that such characterless characters exert on the theatrical stages (for the real-life modern Hamlets in the audience) reveals a glowing spark inside people's self-images.

Scepticism, contrary to a widespread error, makes everything possible again: questions and dialogue of course, as well as faith, science, knowledge, criticism, morality, society, only differently, a few sizes smaller, more preliminary, revisable, and more able to learn. That also implies, however, being more curious and more open to contrary ideas, things unsuspected and incongruous, with the tolerance based and rooted in the ultimate certainty of error. After Marx, Engels and Lenin, after Horkheimer, Adorno and Habermas, above all Montaigne would have to be rediscovered as the father of a critical social theory of reflexive modernity.

Dare to use your own doubt – Michel de Montaigne

If someone asked me with childish cruelty: 'What society are we living in anyway?', then I would have to wend my way through several negatives – not capitalism or late capitalism, not industrial society, not a service society and not postmodernity either – to this answer: in a modernity which is beginning to doubt itself, which, if things go well, will make doubt the measure and architect of its self-limitation and self-modification. Doubts *liberate*. Even from the rule of experts which they put into power.

Four hundred years ago, precisely here and in this way, there was a fork in the road for two near-contemporaries, each of whom civilized and perfected doubt in his own way: Descartes and Montaigne (Toulmin 1990). The former uses doubt to escape doubt and reach certainty; that is the road to expertocracy. The latter protects and sharpens with doubt his inherent ability to defend himself against the external, to filter it out, separate it and give space and an ear to his own astonishment, his own voice. This very willingness to raise doubt in any authority and remove it by doubt constitutes the modernity and subversiveness of Montaigne. He is the most radical individualist ever to pick up a pen under God's blue sky. His world view, justified only unto himself and within his own horizon, is also radical because it takes away everything tragic and despairing from doubt. Montaigne's scepticism is cheerful and self-ironic, hence completely 'un-Faustian'. Indeed, it refutes Hamlet.

Kant's demand was *sapere aude* – dare to use your own mind, and this motto of the Enlightenment has perhaps never been put into practice more literally and directly, not even by Kant himself, than by Michel de Montaigne, that country squire who had already been in the grave for more than two hundred years in Kant's day. Perhaps one ought to sharpen it in his sense to 'dare to use your own doubt'. The accent here must lie on 'own'. Today, two hundred years after Kant, this particularly includes resistance to the equation of mind and expert knowledge, which Kant took completely for granted.

No less an authority than Max Horkheimer convicted Michel de Montaigne, quite sincerely, of conservatism and bourgeois apologetics. And how. 'In the present civil wars,' quotes Horkheimer deftly from the *Essays*, 'I use the little intelligence I have so that they do not restrict my freedom of movement' (Horkheimer 1971). The Reformation is at stake. Not a spark of partisanship for the Enlightenment. Nothing is sacred to him except his contemplative life in the tower, his 'freedom of movement'. It gets even worse. 'I abhor innovation, whatever face it wears, and I am right, for I have often seen the bad effects of it.' Montaigne cushions his life with doubts, while the world around him falls to rubble. 'I do not see the totality of anything,' he notes with a wink and dismisses all claims transcending it, 'nor do those who promise to show it to us see it.'

But no one should be deceived; Montaigne is just as conservative and apologetic as radishes are red – on the surface. In his eyes, the status quo is neither good nor bad, let alone reasonable; it has no merit other than the fact that it exists. Order and the state, law and justice, are nothing other than established disorder, lawlessness and violence grown respectable from advanced age, often enough ridiculous, inhuman and absurd.

The position that confronts Montaigne is already irritatingly modern. God, nature, morality, law, justice, custom, everything that gives the world order and obligation, lies outside his horizon, inaccessibly far away. The word 'scepticism' does not even fit his view and attitude, since Montaigne does not even search for the possibility of objective knowledge and therefore does not deny it. For the same reason, he is no nihilist either, or, if so, then he is a pragmatic, one could say an optimistic, nihilist. There is no difficulty for him in uniting being a nihilist with being a Christian, even basing the latter on the former. Precisely because he cannot recognize and distinguish what is the truth, he clings to whatever permits him to lead his life. Even this far exceeds his strength. He lives in the rubble of the religious view of society and the world, in ruins of values that have authority for him, if at all, only through himself. *He* enacts *his* laws – even if they are the old and prevailing ones.

The little prince climbs the hill in the morning to order the rising sun to rise. Montaigne does not do or believe that. Continuing the metaphor, there is no sun in itself, only a sun for him. He can move it by looking at it. A simple turn of his head and it disappears. One jump and it hops and someone who turns his head in a circle can see it dancing in the tree branches. Thus he must patch his world together, hold it together, move it as best he can, must choose, 'and because I am not capable of choosing, I follow the choice of others and stay in the track in which God has placed me. Otherwise I would have to roll and roll without end.' The order of things is based on decisions, more precisely, on the decision against the overburdening that calling the order into question would imply. Nothing else.

Doubts also are extremely imperfect, error-prone and ridiculous, in short, thoroughly doubtful. That is the entire secret of how to tame them. Anyone who is attacked by doubts must chase them away with doubts. Doubts can be tamed like circus lions if they are chased by their own kind, doubts. There can be no doubt of this: only doubts puffed up with certainty are frightening. To doubt by half is to despair. To doubt completely, doubting down even the supreme doubt, is to be able to discover that doubts *empower* us. In dealing with oneself, they become manageable, sharp, pointed or round, depending on how they are compared to one another, set upon one another, turned and used, positively or negatively. They force the doubter to decide, and design himself. Anyone who would learn the 'art of living' (Foucault) must practise the *art of doubt*.

Doubt – reflexive modernity will have more names for it than the Eskimos have for snow! One thing is 'certain', however: a distinction between linear and reflexive doubt will become necessary. The simple, linear doubter gets caught in the trap of infinite regression. He must follow every doubt with another doubt, endlessly. Since the way through the infinite is closed to us mortals, however, there is the threat of despair, interruption of the proceedings or dogmatism. Those are the horror visions of scepticism that have been cultivated and circulated for centuries in the culture of certainty to deter anyone from having a fling with doubt. In this sense, Helmut Schelsky (1965) criticized the 'institutionalization of permanent reflection' in sociology. That is one way to misunderstand the art of doubt.

Linear doubt may therefore be impossible, dogmatic and amoral from the perspective of the culture of truth. One must add, though, that this is precisely the opposite of the type of doubt that is advocated by seekers of truth and that arises from the desire for overcoming doubt. Someone who despairs wants not doubt, but, instead, certain, unambiguous knowledge. Anyone who enters into an infinite regression is searching for something he is obviously not permitted to find. Anyone who chases and chases after doubt and then complains of – dogmatically – having to break off the search wants not doubt, but rather non-doubt. This makes it clear that the usual image of scepticism is constructed refutably. One could say it serves for rehearsing the opposite.

Reflexive doubt, by contrast, breaks the energy of truth, which drives doubt to despair because, first, doubt is accepted as an element of life like air and water; ideas of overcoming it are old wives' tales that leave behind a trail of blood in political history. Second, however, people learn, or become able to learn, that doubt does not drive doubt to despair, but instead breaks it. Doubt itself takes away the caustic and destructive sides of doubt. Doubt turned against doubt calls a halt to doubt. It also allows its apparent opposites: faith, trust, morality, knowledge, and so on, but without that strange pretension to obligatoriness that swallows up and condemns any further doubt, subsuming and destroying the personal in the general.

The believer must be responsible with his personality for this kind of faith, now protected by doubt. It is irredeemably *his* faith, his *personal* faith, one he has chosen and must take responsibility for, even if it should be the old general faith.

Objecting to this with the old bugaboo of 'arbitrariness', 'dogmatism' or 'decisionism' betrays the fact that many still approach doubt skittishly in their inherited attachment to 'truth'.

A wealth of realities

Doubt arising not from ignorance but from greater knowledge and further questioning is the most certain victor of modernity. All the ways, including all the modern and industrial ways, to rebel against it and seek refuge in new certainties – whether from the market, from technology or from science – are condemned to failure. Those who bet on doubt win. This is the law of the weak which pulls out the rug from under the feet of the overwhelming powers of autonomized industrial threats. Doubt, aggressive towards the outside and opposed to all hidden or open absolutism in industrial thought and action, does not just destroy; it also enables, encourages and urges on productivity. The art of this century in particular, but of others as well, gives impressive testimony to this. Its images are one great firework display of self-destruction. Paintings, sculptures and novels should be considered and admired as the flames and ashes of that spectacle. Amidst all the lamentation and adulation, it is seldom seen that this 'aesthetic nihilism' (as Gottfried Benn calls it) is the diminutive form from which the self-restriction of modernity, the ironic humanity of self-confident error, arises – or could arise. Perhaps classical modernism in painting has not just changed and expanded perception, but invented creative self-restriction and self-diminution as human form, a way of living, thinking and acting.

Where the dogma of one single objective reality decays, the result is not nothing, and arbitrariness is not the rule either. Those are just intimidations and half-truths, a type of mental prosthesis to rescue faded certainties. The boundary where multiple reality arises is the contrast of the senses. The reality of the ears contradicts the reality of the eyes and the latter contradicts the reality of the hands, and so on. Language does not reflect, it creates. Only that which has been put into words exists. Everything else is humbug and fortune-telling. 'These thinkers with their ground of being that no one can see, completely shapeless, everything just articles and article writers – they turn on the tap and then a little Plato comes out; they wash themselves in it a bit and then the next one enters the tub' (Benn 1986).

The biographical cage of the self is left behind when passing through the gate of books. While reading one can immerse oneself in other eras and exchange one's own for other existences. 'Words, words – nouns! They need only open their wings and millennia slip by in their flight.' The monopoly of the single reality, 'Europe's demonic concept', shatters and only then can one recognize the narrowness and poverty of a managed expert-controlled 'realism', which has dispossessed the senses and their realities.

Perspectivism, the uncertainty of experience, is not the downfall of reality, but rather the beginning of a wealth, even a surplus, of realities. Nothing more than mobility in thinking and looking is required in order to enjoy the treasures offered by the multiplication of reality and its subjectivization and aestheticization. A single view becomes a multiple view. That means, however, that it is again *directly* accessible – through language, desire, looking, criticizing, thinking and questioning, through the head, therefore, and its attitude. Access is not blocked by any priests with methodological altars. The latches to be opened and closed are in plain view and nowhere else. Language, which opens the eyes, and the eyes that fill out language become the mother and father of our realities. What I become conscious of comes into being. Expressing implies producing. Spaces are created and opened which, once present in language, can be lived through, passed through and taken into possession by others.

Scepticism: the political programme of radicalized modernity

However one imagines the new modernity, it will be characterized in all areas by an enhanced quantum, probably even by a new quality of insecurity: as variation, variety, change and ambivalence, but also as threat and as dangers that exceed the customary standards of calculation. In the conventional view this implies *fear*, with all the expected political consequences. Yet this need not necessarily be the case. This all-encompassing and all-permeating insecurity is not just the dark side of freedom. What is important instead is to discover it as the bright side. The introduction of insecurity into our thought and deeds may help to achieve the reduction of objectives, slowness, revisability and ability to learn, the care, consideration, tolerance and irony that are necessary for the change to a new modernity. In other words, the *contradiction* between the system's promises of security (technical, social and political), on which the megalomania of the industrial era and its institutions is based, and the amount of elemental loss of security, produced by reflexive modernization, pushed through against the continually updated defensive armour and now becoming obvious, is what shakes the institutions and people currently and in the future.

The *political* programme of radicalized modernity is scepticism! Doubt and error are the gravediggers of the old and the standards of the new modernity to be achieved. The grand industrial project requires precisely those types of security that are becoming obsolete with the advent of reflexive modernity. Established doubt requires a new distribution of power, new structures of decision-making, a new architecture of institutions, a new type of technology and technology development, a new science, new learning groups and ways to revise decisions – not least of all the anticipation of side-effects. Everything a couple of sizes smaller, slower and more open to the opposite, to antagonism and refutation, as is proper for self-assured doubt.

There is an internal relationship inside classical industrial modernity between its leading ideas and key categories: nation state, classes, scientific truth, faith in technology and the friend/enemy pattern of politics. This very conviction of wanting, having and standing up for the good and the true is the basis of enmities and wars and of that which both protects against them and prepares for them: the military, armament, secret police and espionage, that is to say, the militarization of all of social and political life. The realism of a Machiavelli, of Hobbes' war of all against all, of Carl Schmitt's politics based on the decision on martial law and the opposition of friend and enemy – all of these theories of politics based on the fall from grace of power presuppose the age of morality and truth.

When it is doubtful whether one is right or in possession of the truth, when the questions lie in that area where correctness and falsity overlap, when self-doubts chew up the arrogance, then enemies are no longer enemies, nor are they brothers with whom one dances in festivals of solidarity; instead, they are fellow or opposing doubters. Their interests may be diametrically opposed. They will be seen as such, relativized, negotiated and arranged. The simple reason for this is that, in the age of doubt, contrasts can no longer be dogmatized into enmities that can justify a mutual killing machine or set it in motion. People laugh at one another, first of all even at themselves, or they meet with 'civil indifference' (Goffmann) but do not bash each other's heads in. Since doubting includes the possibility of designing and viewing the world and oneself from the opposite viewpoint, one would ultimately have to bash one's own head in.

Doubt implies multiple voices, opposing voices on all sides and in each of us. This rules out the confrontation of friend and enemy logically (whether it also does so psychologically or socially is another matter). Conversely, thinking in categories of enemies makes sense only in absolutist black–white thinking; it is out of the question in the generally grey or flowing colour spectrum of thinking informed by doubt. More pointedly, a radical inequality of doubt – the exclusion of self-doubt and the concentration of all doubtfulness on the side of the other, the outsider, is the obligatory precondition for the social and state order threatened by war. A thoroughly doubtful society, beset by productive self-doubt, and therefore incapable of truth, strictly speaking, cannot develop or uphold any construction of an enemy.

In other words, pacifism and doubt are elective affinities. Truth and military originate from one and the same conceptual box.

Civilizing conflict?

All great European movements and periods were in search of a medium for neutralizing conflicts and wars. The Enlightenment proclaimed the rule of the mind, that is, of science, law and education, and attempted to establish and design these spheres. This was supposed to make it possible to settle the conflicts between individuals, groups and states reasonably, which meant peacefully, rationally and justly.

Much has been thought out and built up for the purposes of civilizing conflicts. The latest and most intensive attempt would probably be the 'objective law of technology'. This appeared and still appears to many to be the most neutral of all, to be neutrality and objectivity plain and simple. In its mute language of material evidence, of observable use in daily life, of relief, comfort, enhancement of productivity, saving time, maximizing power and, in the sum of all this, the exponential increase of power, technology pushed all the scepticism that had always accompanied its triumph into the idealistic–pessimistic sphere. The pessimism of the rebels against technology did not and still does not find any lasting resonance in view of the general relief brought by technology.

Now technology is just as neutral as a toxic gas that can kill insects, but also people. Technology is an instrument and a weapon, and because it serves *everyone* it is *not* neutral. The opposite is more plausible: technology, particularly nuclear technology and its many analogues in chemical and possibly also genetically engineered weaponry, produces a power whose threatening gestures are ultimately playing with the fulfilment of absolute negativity.

Even against this pessimistic view, however, it can be asserted that technology remains culturally and politically blind. From pure technology, which many glorify as technocracy, stammering about rationality and the downfall of democracy, it is not possible to establish and obtain a binding neutralization of social conflicts.

Perhaps this dream of civilizing the antagonisms finds new nourishment in concepts and ideas in which doubt rules at the centre? Doubt permits conflict and perhaps even forces it, but it removes the dogmatism from the antagonisms and from the means of waging the conflict. It allows a *pacification of the conflict* that reconciles both sides, conflict and peace, so much that the two extremes, paradise and war, are ruled out, or at least become very improbable. Anyone who doubts is also struggling against false certainty, against the dictatorship of non-ambiguity and of the Either–or. He cannot go to the barricades and will not do so either, since doubt produces self-doubt and cares for it like a father for his son. Anyone who would do justice to doubt can only appeal to the civilian resistance of doubt and its virtues, which tend to belong more to the lower classes of cultural properties than to those which favour dictators, whether they reign in taste, in political decisions or in technology 'for the good of all'.

The culture of doubt, cultivating doubt and helping it into forms of public representation and recognition, does not prohibit anything, force anything or proselytize anyone with anything; instead it makes the most varied and conflicting things possible, but in moderated form, subverted and brightened up by doubt. Doubting, something that appeared as weakness and decay to cultures of faith and certainty, now becomes a virtue, the launching point for productivity, for self-limited development, to which everything larger than life and generally accepted is alien, because it negates the ultimate standards of humankind: reservations, uncertainty and 'yes-but'.

Doubt is kind and deeply humane. It reminds us, irrevocably and implacably with pedantic arrogance, of the limits and the error-ridden forlornness and bottomlessness of even the proudest, most certain thought and action, no matter how much machine power it may boast and regardless of the technical perfection with which it advances. Doubt giggles at this, whispers, roars, bickers and dodges: it's all doubtful! You may use a thousand computers and all the worldly and otherworldly wisdom you wish. You are what you are: a miserable rebellion against the fragility of your existence, a forgetting and a dismissal of the doubts that peep out everywhere. All the pomp and certainty have originated from and been fashioned from this and not from themselves.

In the age of reflexive modernity the course of thought – science and technology – is turned back onto its earthly origin, doubt. It rules in all the disguises and devices that deny it, as well as in the language of boastful certainty that its deniers are so fond of using. The god of fully established modernity is doubt. It is the primeval loneliness of the person confronted only with himself and his reflected failure. The final grace that a god has for those who are intended and want to be a likeness to him some day is doubt. It and perhaps only it makes it possible to transfer the dogmatism of the industrial into the reflected self-limitation of post-industrial modes of production and living. And the inherent force of the earthly things forces thought to its knees, contrary to its proud course of certainty, and rubs its nose in the doubt which is the origin of everything: knowledge, the market, the second creation by technology all the way to the revolutions of genetic engineering and (in)human genetics that are imminent today. Doubt is the anti-religious religion of self-limiting modernity.

Doubt is certainly a strict ruler. It irritates, corrodes and conquers certainty, which ignores it. Certainty is the Judas that denies his master, doubt.

Let us be honest, my dear colleagues! Tell me of a theory in our specialist circles which is *not* controversial, which is *only* accepted and would not have to be balanced out, which, alongside affirmation, would not also have to put up with – and hide! – a mountain of doubts and contradictions. I certainly do not see one and would offer to correct the forgetting on which a doubt-free theory (or even just an empirical investigation including all results) would have to be built in our subject area. We all work in sciences which, if one strictly applies the strict standards of the scientific method, would have to build up their arguments and insights on more or less discredited theories. This sounds bitter, and it is certainly not the case only in the social and human sciences. Even in the 'hard' natural sciences, doubts that cannot be scared away are the constant companions of all knowledge. Here too, the only help is to lock up the doubts in the dungeon of irrelevance in order to build up the palace of knowledge on top of it.

It is high time for science to deal with its dark side, the omnipresent and yet oddly repressed and imprisoned doubt, and this is indeed worthy of a science that has become self-confident and need no longer look for approval like a convert. Even though it is correct that doubt is the shadow of all knowledge, no one should be deceived as to the difficulties that confront our project of throwing light onto the shadows.

The darkness in which doubts remain concealed – despite or because of their omnipresence – recalls in many ways the way in which *sexuality* was (and still is being) dealt with in bourgeois circles. All the parallels match: people whisper about doubts and dubious things, they remain concealed, they are more at home above than below, and in circles where the morality of knowledge prevails it is considered obscene and lecherous to talk about doubts. Even the central function of sexuality, the generation of offspring, has an analogy: the knowledge that is accepted tomorrow is usually produced at night in intimate intercourse with doubts. Knowledge arises not from the affirmation of knowledge, which blithely continues to be true, but only from the love of doubt, which does not let anything stand as valid.

Doubt is the motive force of science. In the same way that sexual fantasies have been studied, someone ought to study the doubt fantasies of scientists – what they really think about themselves and other people's science. There are sadistic doubters and masochistic ones, there are some who prefer to be involved with themselves, and so on. All of them behave, however, as the bourgeois morality of the love of truth demands: neatly pressed and wearing ties, they practise one thing and preach another.

To put it another way, the sciences, even the social sciences, are becoming grown up. Looks become cool, hopes dissipate and sobriety is increasing, even with regard to our own drives. That alone dictates the doubt, the self-doubt, which everyone would rather appease than endlessly confront.

Everyone cringes from the dragon of doubt. This is based on the doubt it spews forth. Can an ecological reform of society, for instance, really be impelled and led by doubts? Does doubt not need to clear out and concede everything? Is it not just the helpless doorman of arbitrariness? Does not doubting, if one is to be consistent, imply despairing? What happens to the possibility of somehow finding one's way in this world, out of joint in any case, on a small scale, in everyday life, in private life as well as on a grander scale, if nothing but doubts control our view? Finally, let us assume that doubt is the essence of science, modernity, Enlightenment; would it not then be advisable to do as the Grand Inquisitor did in Dostoevsky's *The Brothers Karamazov* when religious certainty was fading, and to spread and defend the merciful lie of the certainty of knowledge to oppose this intrusion of nothingness into a world built on knowledge?

Once again, doubt prevents nothing, but makes many things possible. Anyone who would like to trace down the mysteries of productivity (not just in the sciences, but also in art, music, politics and ordinary life) must study the nature of doubt. Its source of energy is, one could say, the genetic code of creativity. Nothing is as invigorating as an established doubt. First, it is the champagne of thinking. Second, I know no foundation of such scope and elasticity for a critical theory of society (which would then automatically be a self-critical theory) as doubt. Third, doubt points the way to a new modernity. It is more modern than the old, industrial modernity we know. The latter, after all, is based on certainty, on repelling and suppressing doubt.

Criticism by doubt

There is a source of criticism, including social criticism, which it is imperative to discover: self-confident doubt, arguing completely in step with its times. A major contradiction of industrial modernity is that simultaneously doubt must be fomented and security asserted for the production and reproduction of power, technology and state. Something Max Weber probably suspected, but did not reveal, is the connection between doubt and freedom, doubt and democracy. Truth is a presumption with which people deceive themselves and others as to one's meaning. 'To err and yet have to go on believing in one's inward self, that is mankind, and its glory begins where victory and defeat end' (Benn 1986).

Only after the end of the grand Enlightenment can *criticism by doubt* be discovered in this way. This art is something more Anglo-Saxon or French [than German], because it is closely related to irony, to plays on words and the emphasis on stylistics. The Germans, on the other hand, with their systematic love of theory, tend to doubt with a despairing gesture. That doubt can be the basis and inspiration for commitment can be learnt from Socrates, Montaigne and perhaps Locke, and, among contemporaries, from Hannah Arendt, Albert Hirschmann and Richard Rorty.

There is no lack of ideas for changing society. Today (just as in revolutions of earlier centuries) many contemporaries carry plans for changing the world around with them in their breast pocket or in their heart. That the transport system cannot continue in its present form (other than one's own car, of course) is evident to everyone. As a matter of course, the demand for an 'ecological reform of society' slips from the lips of even representatives of hazardous industries (and they don't turn green). That women want a different kind of science, a different kind of economy and a different kind of society is admitted just as clearly as it is unachievable. Europe is facing a new departure or a collapse; the two are somehow interrelated. The rain forests in South America and elsewhere need our full attention, just as the ozone hole can only be patched up by concerted action on the global scale. Getting out of nuclear energy is our duty. And please do not hold it against me if I conclude by outlining the global problems in only a few words: hunger, malnutrition, population explosion, mobile poverty.

If one takes the deeds that are considered indispensable as the measure, then scepticism grows as the square of the unfulfilled demands. We are living in a self-critical risk society that is continuing, albeit with restrained pangs of consciousness, in the old routines. This coincidence of a verbal revolutionary upheaval of convictions and conservative inaction may arise from a verbal concession to the spirit of the times. It is still and remains a threat *sui generis*.

The empirical orientation of sociology loses credibility if it walls itself off against these social movements and perceptions that urge reform, and therefore criticism, of existing industrial society. Every skilled industrial worker, every high-school graduate, every conservative with what has now become a quite normal ecological awareness has concrete possibilities of social change which a sociologist as analyst of this society is forbidden by the established super-ego of his profession from even registering.

Risk society is certainly also a society of critical lip service. Advertising is one large subject for critical theory. This field is crawling with (usually perfectly disguised and naively falsified) criticism. By now, everything is environmentally sound and so is its opposite. We are incessantly deluged with promises of paradise, against which our reality is easily revealed to be hell, by simply turning around the promises and checking inside the packaging.

Self-criticism does not end with advertising, however. Ecological criticism has established itself everywhere as a kind of auxiliary bad conscience. Even the cathedrals of industrial power have been seized or are under attack by the ecological counter-reformation – at least conceptually and in what people feel they must profess publicly. Industrial criminals of conscience, fighting and dying under the banner of progress, have become rare.

Was the most important contribution brought by East Germans to their western brothers and sisters perhaps the (initial) sparkle in their eyes, with which they took away the most gnawing aspects of self-doubt? Is the gift of the refugees and asylum seekers to a Germany that rejects them perhaps the now almost uncontrollable mass assent to this country, which numbs the self-doubt that has tortured people in this country from the beginning? None of that will work, however; the very recipe for success – safety demands, tight controls, regulatory self-confidence, this walking bureaucracy which is Germany – makes the barb of criticism stick deep inside all the actions and institutions of this super-industrial society.

'Reflexive modernization' also means that society itself produces multiple and concealed forms of self-criticism which cannot even be perceived and decoded by a sociology that abstains from social criticism. The opportunity for social criticism is therefore that it need not be brought into society normatively from the outside, with an air of knowing it all, but bubbles up from sources in the centre of this society. In the phase of reflexive modernization, social criticism is a question not of a normative option, but rather of *empiricism*, and therefore of conceptualism, which of course also requires the proper sensors.

The self-criticism of modernity which may – possibly! – take effect in reflexive modernization must battle against the suspicion of being *purely immanent*. In the view of Marxist social criticism, this was a declaration of excommunication which affected all competing undertakings that did not borrow from Marx. The equation of criticism to Marxist criticism, as if the two were synonymous, captivated the critical intelligentsia for a century, but it is now inapplicable. Thus it is finally possible to discover and elaborate on something sociologists always knew and always stressed: that sociology can redeem its claims to knowledge only in criticism, that is, critical distance, impudence, frankness and freedom of judgement.

In any case, something so enormous, half-baked and seductively naive as an 'ecological reform of industrial society' cannot be fought out or even accompanied by multi-million DM studies proving once again with (functionalist) acumen that everything is going along independent of people's actions and quite well, thank you. This implies, however, that sociology must change itself if it is to recognize society's need for change and comment upon (I deliberately do not say 'satisfy') it. There is at any rate a need for sociological social criticism that is not being perceived at all by 'bureaucracy-digestible sociology' (Claus Offe).

Sociology merits a special significance; it could become an 'eye' for realities that are repressed and denied by old thinking and the old institutions. This is only possible, however, in a double conflict with the sociologists of simple industrial society (whether they deal with the family, industrial labour, the organization, welfare policy or class and stratum analysis) and with the institutions that are the central audience, patrons, financiers and users of social scientific knowledge. 'Administrative' sociology has made the administrative apparatus, the administrative mentality and administrative pigeonholes into the conceptual, specialized and cooperative foundation for its complicated research. Now it is becoming the antiquary's shop of industrial society, the viceroy of obsolescent institutions, the producer of realities existing only in data, confirming with its unchanging institutional categories the self-centred, vapid arrogance of 'self-referential' systems and organizations.

Sociological criticism would be the acid test that presumes an institutional stability of the type offered in particular by tenured university scholars. At the same time it could publicly strike the spark without which sociology easily becomes just a very expensive subsidy of social certitudes that could be sacrificed in the next wave of budget cutting almost without consequences. The element of provocation is certainly fleeting. 'Fire and brimstone' sociology can easily degenerate to an attitude and is unsuited as a focal point of planned research. Without this spur, however, in the full glow of its institutional presence, sociology may easily no longer be contemporary anywhere.

If society is self-critical, an uncritical society will become false and a critical one conformist. A criticism of criticism, however, is yet to be invented.

I sometimes have a dream and part of this dream is the certainty that I am awake, even wide awake. In this dream I keep repeating to myself everything that argues against my impression. I say imploringly: action is a dangerous illusion. It implies a self that demonstrably has not existed for a long time. Systems and circumstances are in power where people who say their names and nothing else of substance raise their voices and their hands, and so on and so forth. That is hard to reproduce because within me all the arguments are alive that prove as strikingly as possible the impossibility of even stringently conceiving of a concept of action, much less filling it out with actual creative deeds. Yet this overwhelming physicality of the arguments, which completely fill me up, has no credit for me for reasons I know directly but have difficulty naming. The arguments seem incredible, something from yesterday, recited by rote, rattled off, theatrical, dusty and ghostly, so that even I have to smile at this apparition. I note how I react more to their strategic substance than their actual contents. 'Aren't those wonderful excuses?', I have to smile. As monstrously as these arguments act and puff themselves up, their power to convince comes from their comfortable sides. Like cushioned furniture they make it possible to sink down and lose onself. Hopes force agitational activities and are even dangerous, as this century teaches us. Blind alleys are modern gifts of God, in which people can make themselves comfortable and cushion their lives without having to do anything. Viewed that way, the theory of a lack of options and hopelessness is liberating. It frees us to a being oneself that no longer need tolerate the curse of 'egoism', because now the stupidity of hoping is protected from any compulsion to accomplish something beyond just being oneself. Of course, the lack of options must be overwhelming and indubitably objective for this old urge to do things and the accompanying reproaches and pangs of conscience finally to collapse. Only a final lack of options frees one to oneself, but you still hope and you're dangerous – this shoots through my head before I wake up and again lose my sense of reality.

Notes

Introduction

1 There are approaches to this in Beck, Giddens and Lash (1994); this debate is the background of the present book as well and it owes much to it.
2 For discussions see Adam and Beck (1997), Bauman (1992), Beck, Giddens and Lash (1993), Bronner (1995), Giddens (1990), Goldblatt (1996), Lash, Szerszynski and Wynne (1996), Rustin (1994). For reformulations, see Beck (1996a, 1996b), Beck, Beck-Gernsheim (1996).
3 'Institutions perish from their victories,' Montesquieu noted. A puzzling and extremely relevant dictum today. That is, there are two ways of disappearing from history: being conquered or conquering. The first happened to the former East and the second to the West. The second is the topic of the present work.

Chapter 1   The Age of Side-effects: On the Politicization of Modernity

1 On this point see Kohler and Meyer (1994), Beck (1995) as well as especially the volume edited by Leggewie (1994). Helmut Dubiel writes there:

> Only starting from the nineties, that is, after the end of the bipolar world order, does the crisis of the Western model seem to have reached its innermost centre, that is, its economic and political foundations. . . . Even the established liberal democracies of Western Europe are paradoxically becoming victims of a peculiar loss of substance at the very moment of their triumph over the authoritarian systems of South America and Central Europe. We are witnesses of a dramatic loss of reputation for the political class, of the erosion of entire party structures . . . of high degrees of voting abstinence and political apathy in general, of the melting away of traditional voting groups and of the explosive growth of extreme right protest voters. (p. 57)

2 For the history of theory, see Bühl (1990) and Wehling (1987) for a summation, as well as Scharping and Görg (1994) prospectively.

3 Talcott Parsons (1974) deals in one of his last great essays with the centrality of an impending or, possibly, current individualization, as well as reaction patterns to be expected. Parsons clears away the common misunderstanding that equates individualism and egocentrism:

> In the pattern of institutionalized individualism, the keynote is not the direct utilitarian conception of the 'rational pursuit of self-interest' but a much broader conception of the self-fulfillment of the individual in a social setting in which the aspect of solidarity . . . figures at least as prominently as does that of self-interest in the utilitarian sense. . . . That is to say, I expect the new religion of Love will manifest a strong individualistic emphasis, that people will love as individuals, and that they will form attachments of Love to other objects also with a very high valence attached to the individuality of the object. (Parsons 1974: 223f)

4 Not everything that sails under the adjective 'postmodern' is postmodern in this sense; see, for instance, the writings of Bauman (1992).

5 Homogeneity is not to be confused with equality; this is the central point of de Tocqueville in his again very timely *Democracy in America* (1945). Equality is conceived of as the antithesis of hierarchy, but homogeneity is the antithesis of difference. Accordingly this 'culture of global homogeneity' does not (necessarily) lead to the overcoming of social inequality between peoples and cultures, but to the overcoming of differences in nature between people and cultures. Homogeneity establishes the end of ontological difference. Homogeneity implies a 'logic of social recognition' (Honneth) and must on no account be confused with uniformity or monotony, since this principle ultimately amounts to multiplicity and variety; for a later, very stimulating view, cf. Gauchet (1990).

6 I am working on this under the title 'The Search for Reality'.

7 Following the collapse of the regime allegedly founded on Marxism, the landscape now emerging from the ruins bears an astonishing resemblance to the conditions denounced so eloquently by Marx! A minority of bureaucrats who converted to the virtues of free trade at the opportune moment are plundering and speculating, and the majority of the population sinks into poverty. Even in England, the cradle of trade unions and the model welfare state, a comparable phenomenon can be seen. While the number of sterling millionaires has doubled in the last decade, mass unemployment has increased and there was a decline of trade unions along with impoverishment and renewed exploitation of child labour, as the *Observer* recounts. We are therefore returning to the world of Dickens' novels, to Engels' description of *The Condition of the Working Class in England*. Those who cling desperately to the last grotesque representatives of a defunct model, in hopes of defying the arrogance of the victors and saving the remaining inventory from ruin, are only extending the intellectual paralysis and delaying the emergence of a new democratic social contract. So long as Fidel Castro and Kim Il Sung are in power they can serve as the bugbear, and the intellectuals who are aware of the fraud – the bottomless chasm between their speeches and reality – are prevented from basing their effort on a new foundation and starting a counteroffensive to the total market economy, so that the peoples of the world might retain at least a modicum of freedom to determine their fates for themselves. (Goytisolo 1994: 7)

8 Ironically, Kuhn (1970) did not consider the social sciences worthy of the state of paradigm.

9 Presented in Zapf (1967) and given a theoretical explication by Münch (1984, 1986); for sceptical and critical views see Lepsius (1977) and Bühl (1970, 1990), respectively.

10 For instance, Brandt (1972), Wallerstein (1986) and recently, with a self-critical accent, Kurz (1991).

11 Cf. Zapf (1992: 20ff), as well as Berger (1988). On the significance of the keyword 'modernity' for social theory, cf. Bauman (1991), Habermas (1987), as well as Wehler (1975) and, especially, Welsch (1991: 45ff).

12 This contrast conceals productive overlaps and points in common. Thus it would certainly be possible to demonstrate points of agreement shared by the theories of postmodernity and reflexive modernity and asserted against the internally contradictory views of simple modernization (in the tension between functionalism and Marxism). For the productivity of the debate on postmodernism in sociology cf. Vester (1984), Lash (1990), Giesen (1991), Bauman (1992), Crook, Pakulski and Waters (1992), among others.

13 This crude characterization covers up the productivity of these theories and the points in common shared by the theories of reflexive modernity and postmodernity that bind them together against the sociology of modernization. On this point, cf. Giesen (1991), Lash (1990) and Crook, Pakulski and Waters (1992).

14 The sociology of class has become more and more diluted here, until it has been transformed constructively into a theory of social classifications; cf. Bourdieu (1984).

15 On the 'myth' of functional differentiation, see, among others, Münch (1991) and Rüschemeyer (1991).

16 In his book on science, Luhmann (1990) once again dismisses all ontological references – reality, truth, objectivity – in the language and theory of autopoietic systems. According to his own self-understanding, he practises a radical constructivism which he not infrequently presents with ironic or even derisive remarks against all borrowings that exude the old-fashioned European scent of searching for truth. But what a surprise! The centre of his systems theory of science is occupied by the dogmatic assumption of a binary functional code of science, which is able to distinguish *either* true *or* false. And to top it all, this contradiction between a radical constructivism and an almost Augustinian fundamentalism of true and false never comes up for discussion. Luhmann thus practises a constructivism of 'as if', but when the substance of his arguments is at stake, this ends up as the opposite of what was intended, that is, a structurally conservative fundamentalism of true and false, for which he can no longer offer any objective substantiation. Everything that contradicts his binary coding of the system of science is mentioned only at the margins; this begins with calculations of probability, passes through the verifiability of theoretical and empirical statements, and reaches all the way to the reversal of experiment and practical application in industrial technology. It is scarcely noted that technology and technification are playing an increasing role in science as well. The characteristics of modern scientific development – the dominance of technology, the priority of production over experimental testing, the construction of models and scenarios, the long list of self-discreditation by implementable distinctions between true and untrue statements – none

of these is allowed to compete with the quaint schematism with which Luhmann views science. In this 'pure' world of pure science, this functionalist idealism of science, with its constructivistic and sceptical veneer, such nasty things as interests, power, compulsions, money, investment decisions made or cultural and political interrelationships have no role in influencing the automatic course of true–false decisions. Science creates knowledge as science for science's sake – the idyll of pure abstraction as both one-way street and destination of scientific evolution. Luhmann's radicalism lies in his having turned the self-nullifying factionalism of science, which becomes political and technical in the pursuit of its research, into a functionalistic Neoplatonism.

17 The classic examples are his studies on suicide and on the division of labour.

18 On this point, cf. Lau (1989) in particular:

> The new conflicts are typically conducted as a dispute over the social construction and definition of risks and dangers. The definition of risks implies in this sense the redistribution of scarce social resources, such as money, property rights, influence and legitimacy. The dimensions of these definition struggles – victimization, power, knowledge and the costs of avoidance – may indeed coincide, but vary independently of one another. It is this peculiar logic of technological and ecological risks which prevents a permanent anchoring of conflicting group interests. Those who benefit from risks in one dimension can be its victims in another. The unstable and contradictory social anchoring of the interests involved has far-reaching consequences. It has been established by now that all conventional institutions for mastering conflicts largely fail in the face of the new risks, since they presume unambiguous, stable interest organizations. (Lau 1989: 374)

19 On this point, see the study of 'Green' industrial workers by Osterland (1994), as well as Heine and Mautz (1993).

20 Here lies a double meaning in the concept of 'reflexive modernization' which can only be separated analytically: expressed and applied, this theory cancels out the central assertion of the unseen system transformation of industrial modernity; see my distinction between 'reflection' (knowledge) and 'reflexivity' (self dissolution) in Beck, Giddens and Lash (1994: 175–83).

21 The concept of 'counter-modernity' is also in an inflationary boom, cf. Zapf (1991: 443–503), Beck (1992: 106ff), Bohrer and Scheel (1992). For further explanation, see chapter 2.

22 First the shift here from 'post' to 're' clarifies how mistaken any periodization of cultural history in the form of pre- and post-, previously and subsequently, is, simply because it leaves the position of Now unquestioned, that is the position of the present from which one is supposed to be able to survey the chronological sequence of the individual epochs of our history correctly. (Lyotard 1988: 5)

A noteworthy revision for a theorist of postmodernism.

23 This ambiguity refers to an elective affinity between late, reflexive modernity and the line of tradition in early Romanticism as expressed, or, better, as erupts, most strikingly in Friedrich Schlegel's *Athenäum* fragments. In that work, the 'fragment', doubt, irony, self-questioning and self-belittling are driven to perfection, to put it paradoxically, and this occurs in the

consistent and complete modernization of modernity. In his essay 'On Incomprehensibility', Schlegel writes:

> Precisely from this . . . I declare that the word means in the dialect of the fragments that everything is just a tendency, the age is in fact the age of tendencies. . . . Here as well, the best might be to do things more and more annoyingly; when the annoyance has reached a maximum it bursts and disappears and understanding can immediately make a start. We have not yet come far enough in giving offence, but there is always hope of improvement.

24 Wolfgang Zapf writes:

> Commenting critically, I would like to say that the position of *Ulrich Beck* is so fascinating because it adheres to the programme of modernization, as well as to a fundamental critique of contemporary society including the bulk of today's sociology. Beck's intent is to design a 'new modernity' and a more insightful, conscientious, reflected, in a word, a reflexive theory. It can gain the loyalty of adherents to the Frankfurt School of the 1930s and 1960s who believe in Adorno's statement that 'The totality is the untrue'. It is able to take in the disappointed Marxists, whose dreams of socialism may be broken, but who are now being shown that free-market democracies also must fail from their own contradictions. It is a modernized variant of the doctrine of late capitalism, with the ecological crisis now playing the part once taken by the legitimation crisis of late capitalism. It is another theory of the 'third way' transcending capitalism and socialism. (Zapf 1992: 295)

25 'In political science, this mode of thought corresponds to the talk of "rules of the game" and to the very "basic consensus" [on the constitution – U.B.] that had to be presumed from the start in order to be able to carry out authentic political will-formation pluralistically on current objective issues' (Greven 1994: 3).

26 See, for instance, statements from Helmut Schmidt (1994: 19–23) (conservative politician) Kurt Biedenkopf (1990) and Al Gore (1992). Reflexive modernization implies coalitions of the (so far) excluded. In the summer of 1994, the Deutsche Bank [the most powerful German bank – translator] financed a series of three-page advertisements in order to make the policies of the trade unions better known to a broader public. Just imagine that fifty years ago, or twenty years ago, or even five years ago for that matter. Ideology or reality? This distinction does not work here. Many will dismiss it as mere indoctrination along the old pattern of ad campaigns, as a public relations offensive of the third type, a come-together offensive from the Deutsche Bank. That may be true. Or maybe not. It depends on who makes what of it, on what the constellations in the trade unions, in the Deutsche Bank and elsewhere are like. It is also advertising, in any case, a kind of provision of legitimation, a hybrid between advertising and publicity, public relations and discourse. These texts design perspectives, questions and possibilities which bring up existing refutations of the old industrial labour policies and the understanding of the labour relationship in industrial society and weave them into new concepts that span the old antagonisms and principles. They remind trade unions as well as companies and management of their duties and offer perspectives for development to everyone (Riester 1994).

Chapter 2   The Construction of the Other Side of Modernity: Counter-modernization

1 I am indebted to Elisabeth Beck-Gernsheim for these relativizing questions.
2 'Clans and tribal groups have existed since the earth was inhabited by human beings; nations have existed for only 200 years or so. It is not difficult to see the difference. Ethnic groups come into existence semi-spontaneously, "of their own accord"; nations are consciously created, and are often artificial entities . . .' (Enzensberger 1994: 107).
3 This principle of ethnic self-determination has now become a governmental 'principle of individualization' in Europe after the demise of the order created by the East–West conflict.
4 The classical formulation of Georg Simmel clarifies this ambivalence. The stranger is not 'the migrant who comes today and stays tomorrow, but . . . has not quite overcome the relaxed mood of coming and going' (Simmel 1908: 764). The stranger is distinguished by being neither inside nor outside; he is neither enemy nor friend, instead 'the relationship to him is non-relation . . . he is simultaneously near and far' (p. 770).
5 Examples of this are the conflicts over military equipment (and re-equipment), the political objectives of Western armies, NATO and the various (counter-)espionage organizations.
6 Eugenic movements existed long before the racial insanity of National Socialism, and in all political groups. These ideas of creating a better human being by biological and technical means are becoming reality with the capabilities of reproductive medicine and human genetics in the form of private eugenics (Weingart, Kroll and Bayertz 1988: 684); cf. below pp. 153f.
7 The so-called 'asylum debate' in Germany during the autumn of 1992 clarifies, among other things, this very permeability of borders. The German 'solution' is to build a wall of neighbouring states. Asylum seekers will be expelled in the overwhelming number of cases back to the [democratic neighbouring] countries from which they entered – except for the luxury class of asylum seekers who are able to afford a direct flight out of a threatening country.
8 The environmental movement appeals to nature in this way as well.

Chapter 3   Subpolitics – The Individual Returns to Society

1 The individualization debate has drawn wide circles; cf. recently, Beck and Beck-Gernsheim (1995) and, with extensive bibliographical information, Beck and Beck-Gernsheim (1994, 1996).
2 Anyone who thinks individualization is just something that has been dreamed up or that it could be restricted by moralization misunderstands this fundamental state of affairs.
3 For a collection of important works on this issue, see Honneth (1993).
4 This shows how *deceleration* in the literal sense can be made possible by the 'brake' of insurance.
5 In reference to the controversial consensus on energy, for instance, that also means that if the negotiations between the players in society end without

agreement, then in all probability there will be no more new nuclear power plants in Germany for the foreseeable future. It is unlikely that the power generation industry will again invest billions in politically insecure projects. In that sense the dissent could offer a way out.

Chapter 4   Ways to Alternative Modernities

1 This thought experiment remains theoretical, and initially it describes only theoretically possible developmental trends, but it can thereby lead to plans for understanding and analysing the current concrete experiments.
2 Traces could be uncovered and collected in historical studies that start from the shared heritage of art and technology – in the Italian Renaissance, for instance.
3 Technology and technological development are oriented towards security; *controllability* is their credo. There has been no inquiry or thought into what a technological development that accepts the return of uncertainty and takes it seriously would look like.
4 The subpolitics of technology would thus be the politics of plural objectivity.
5 This implies, for instance, that the committees and commissions in the grey area between technology and politics would be staffed on an interdisciplinary basis, opened to agents from the affected groups and the lay public, in short, that the monopoly of scientists and engineers and their organizations on court expert witnesses would be broken.
6 These 'intersystemic systems', however, must not be understood on the pattern of fully differentiated cooperation. That way lies impracticality – even in language.
7 Here of course there are levers of exclusion in this self-obligation that can once again condemn the whole affair to failure.
8 These aspects and bases of social (as opposed to the technical) rationality in dealing with threats and side-effects can certainly be sharpened and codified.
9 Representative of many others and with a considerable bibliography, see Toffler (1990: 165–240).

Chapter 5   The Reinvention of Politics

1 For recent literature on the changed tasks of the state, see Willke (1992).
2 On the contradictions between military and democracy after the end of the East–West conflict, see Beck (1993).
3 Raschke (1982), Kaase and Klingemann (1990), Klingemann, Stöss and Wessels (1991), Starzacher et al. (1992).
4 In this German–German dilemma the intellectual opposition of the old Federal Republic tended to oppose the positive. That meant in turn: capital analysis, socialist models that in defiance of being equated to the GDR were always forced to remain general and were never really thought through and

founded in opposition to the concretely existing possibilities of a barbaric socialism. Thus the left-wing intelligentsia of the Federal Republic took the totalitarianism analyses of Hannah Arendt no more seriously than the accusations of Solzhenitsyn, Bulgakov and Mandelstam or the suffering confessions of Arthur Koestler. Meanwhile, every shot at the Berlin Wall hit the heart of Marxist humanism. It is not difficult to predict that these bitter repressions on the part of a theoretically oriented intellectual and protest socialism are not exactly a good starting position to begin and continue the urgently necessary dialogue with the painful experiences of Eastern Europe.

5 Now at the latest, we must say that anyone who wanted to study West Germany would also have had to examine East Germany, and vice versa. The concentration on the respective seemingly independent part (while the other was screened out more or less in conformity with politics) is a textbook example of the entrapment of social science in the apparently self-evident certainties of its 'object'. This applies not just to the Marxist cadre sociology of the East, but in a different, more subtle way, to Western and West German sociology. In any case, I am not aware of any book or analysis of the political scene in West Germany that refers to the anti-government opposition in East Germany and systematically attempts to elucidate the influence of this cross-border opposition on the social and political dynamics of both states.

6 In this sense, protection of the independence of the mass media is of crucial importance.

7 Translator's note: To the German ear, the phrase 'ein Volk' prompts troubling associations with the Nazi slogan 'Ein Volk, ein Führer, ein Reich'.

8 Since 'leftist theory' has been thrown out of the saddle, the question 'What is left?' (Steven Lukes) is beginning to split the remaining groups and splinter groups (cf. on this point the informative series in the *Frankfurter Allgemeine Zeitung* in the second half of 1992). We observe the novel phenomenon of a *restorationist left*. The old right-wing question is haunting many left-wing minds: was everything wrong just because a couple of Stalins and Honeckers made a mess of things? Even the individual in history is being rediscovered, if the point is to play socialism off against its (mis)leaders and thus protect it. Now the left is practising what it always criticized in the right, namely foreshortening history to the history of heroes, by claiming that individuals and not conditions under socialism brought about the collapse of socialism. Against the triumphal shouting of victorious capitalism, so the question and demand goes, is it not incumbent upon people to stand up for the old principles, to distinguish ideal from concrete socialism, and to justify and proclaim the utopias of socialism now more than ever? Is it not particularly 'Western [German] opportunists' who are chasing after the *Zeitgeist* and opportunistically sacrificing the noble insights and outlooks of Western social critique?

9 In that sense the structure of expectations among colleagues also comprises an international and supranational behaviour pattern, one which characteristically mixes and binds together foreignness and familiarity. In other words, professional rationality embodies a bit of And in the Either–or.

10 Berger and Luckmann (1960) also show that alternatives inside and between expert groups break through the social construction of reality.

Chapter 6 The Art of Doubt

1 This rejoicing should of course not conceal the fact that only special circumstances and personality characteristics permit the creative mastery of insecurity: cf. Keupp (1990).

Bibliography

Adam, K. 1990: Der Staat im Zwielicht. In R. Schaeffer (ed.), *Die technisch-wissenschaftliche Zukunft*. Bonn and Frankfurt am Main.

Adam, B. and Beck, U. (eds) 1997: *Positioning Risk*. London.

Adorno, T.W. and Horkheimer, M. 1979: *Dialectic of Enlightenment*. London.

Albrecht, J. and Rückert, S. 1995: Die Gene sind schuld. In T. Sommer and H. Kessler (eds), *Was darf der Mensch? Zeitpunkte 3*. Hamburg.

Altmann, N., Deiss, M., Dohl, V. and Sauer, D. 1986: E in 'Neuer Rationalisierungstyp' – neue Anforderurgen an die Industriesoziologie. *Soziale Welt 2*.

Alfred Herrhausen Gesellschaft für Internationalen Dialog (ed.) 1994: *Arbeit der Zukunft*: *Zukunft der Arbeit*. *18/19 Jun: 1994*. Frankfurt am Main.

Anders, G. 1980: *Die Antiquiertheit des Menschen*. Munich.

Anderson, B. 1983: *Imagined Communities*. London and New York.

Arendt, H. 1976: *Kapitalismus, Sozialismus, Konzentration und Konkurrenz*. Tübingen.

—— 1989: *Zur Zeit – Politische Essays*. Munich.

Bauböck, R. 1991: Immigration and the Boundaries of Citizenship. Vienna (unpublished MS).

Bauman, Z. 1991: *Modernity and Ambivalence*. Cambridge.

—— 1992: The Solution as Problem – Ulrich Beck's Risk Society. *Times Higher Education Supplement* (13 Nov.).

—— 1993: Die Revolution frisst ihre Kinder. *Soziale Welt 3*.

Bechtle, G. and Lutz, B. 1989: Die Unbestimmtheit posttayloristischer Rationalisierungsstrategie und die ungewisse Zukunft industrieller Arbeit. In K. Düll, and B. Lutz (eds), *Technikentwicklung und Arbeitsteilung im internationalen Vergleich*. Frankfurt am Main.

Beck, U. 1992: *Risk Society*. London.

—— 1993: Der feindlose Staat. In S. Unseld (ed.), *Politik ohne Projekt?* Frankfurt am Main.

—— 1994: *Ecological Politics in an Age of Risk*. Cambridge.

—— 1995: *Die feindlose Demokratie – Ausgewählte Aufsätze*. Stuttgart.

—— 1996a: Risk Society and the Provident State. In S. Lash, B. Szerszynski and B. Wynne (eds) 1996, *Risk, Environment and Modernity* : *Towards a New Ecology*. London.

Beck, U. 1996b World Risk Society. In *Theory, Culture & Society*.

Beck, U. and Allmendinger J. 1993: Individualisierung und die Erhebung sozialer Ungleichheit: Methodenentwicklung für den Allbus 1993. (Application to DFG [German Research Society].)

Beck, U. and Beck-Gernsheim, E. 1993a: Nicht Autonomie, sondern Bastelbiographie. *Zeitschrift für Soziologie* 3.

—— (eds) 1994: *Riskante Freiheiten – Zur Individualisierung der Lebensformen in der Moderne*. Frankfurt am Main.

—— 1995: *The Normal Chaos of Love*. Cambridge.

—— 1996: Individualization and 'Precarious Freedoms': Perspectives and Controversies of a Subject-orientated Sociology. In P. Heelas, S. Lash and P. Morris (eds), *Detraditionalization: Critical Reflections on Authority and Identity*. London.

Beck, U., Brater, M. and Daheim, H.J. 1980: *Soziologie der Arbeit und der Berufe*. Reinbek.

Beck, U., Giddens, A. and Lash, S. 1994: *Reflexive Modernization: Politics, Tradition and Aesthetics in the Modern Social Order*. Cambridge.

Beck-Gernsheim, E. 1991: *Technik, Markt und Moral*. Frankfurt am Main.

—— 1992: Wider das Paradigma des Kriegsschauplatzes. *Ethik und Sozialwissenschaften* 3.

—— 1994: Auf dem Weg in die postfamiliale Familie. In U. Beck and E. Beck-Gernsheim (eds), *Riskante Freiheiten – Individualisierung in modernen Gesellschaften*. Frankfurt am Main.

Beckenback, N. and van Treech, W. 1994: *Umbrüche gesellschaftlicher Arbeit* (Special Volume 9 of *Soziale Welt*). Göttingen.

Bell, D. 1973: *The Coming of Postindustrial Society*. New York.

Benn, G. 1986: *Das Gottfried Benn Brevier*. Munich.

Berger, J. 1988: Modernitätsbegriffe und Modernitätskritik. *Soziale Welt* 3.

Berger, P.A. 1993: Staatsunsicherheit und Erfahrungsvielfalt: Sozialstrukturelle Individualisierungsprozesse und Fluktuationsdynamik in der Bundesrepublik Deutschland. Munich (unpublished MS).

Berger, P.A. and Hradil, S. (eds) 1990: *Lebenslagen, Lebensläufe, Lebensstile* (Special Volume 7 of *Soziale Welt*). Göttingen.

Berger, P.L. and Luckmann, T. 1960: *The Social Construction of Reality*. New York.

Beyme, K. von 1991: *Theorie der Politik im 20. Jahrhundert*. Frankfurt am Main.

Biedenkopf, K. 1990: *Zeitsignale – Parteienlandschaft im Umbruch*. Munich.

Bielefeld, U. 1991: *Das Eigene und das Fremde*. Hamburg.

Böhme, G. 1992: *Natürlich Natur – Über Natur im Zeitalter der technischen Reproduzierbarkeit*. Frankfurt am Main.

Bohrer, K.H. and Scheel, K. (eds) 1992: Gegen Moderne? *Merkur* 522/523.

Böhret, G. 1991: Die Handlungsfähigkeit des Staates am Ende des 20. Jahrhunderts. Speyer (unpublished MS)

Bonss, W. 1993: Unsicherheit als soziologisches Problem. *Mittelweg* 36.

—— 1995: *Vom Risiko. Ungewissheiten und Unsicherheit in der Moderne*. Hamburg.

Bonss, W. and Hartmann H. (eds.) 1985: *Entzauberte Wissenschaft* (Special Volume 3 of *Soziale Welt*). Göttingen.

Bonss, W., Hohlfeld, R. and Kolleg, R. 1989: *Risiko und Kontext*. Hamburg (Hamburg Institute of Sociology discussion paper).

Bourdieu, P. 1984: Espace social et genèse de classe. *Actes de la recherche en Sciences Sociales.*

Brandt, G. 1972: Industrialisierung, Modernisierung, gesellschaftliche Entwicklung. *Zeitschrift für Soziologie* 1.

Bravermann, H. 1974: *Labor and Monopoly Capital: The Degradation of Work in the Twentieth Century.* New York and London.

Bronner, S.E. 1995: Ecology, Politics and Risk: The Social Theory of Ulrich Beck. *Capitalism, Nature, Socialism* 6.

Bublitz, H. 1992: Geschlecht. In H. Korte and B. Schäfers (eds), *Einführung in die Hauptbegriffe der Soziologie.* Opladen.

Bühl, W. 1970: *Evolution und Revolution: Kritik der symmetrischen Soziologie.* Munich.

—— 1990: *Sozialer Wandel im Ungleichgewicht: Zyklen, Fluktuationen, Katastrophen.* Stuttgart.

Bürklin, W. P. 1988: *Wohlverhalten und Wertewandel.* Opladen.

Covello, V., Menkes, J. and Mumpower, J. 1986: *Risk Evaluation and Management.* New York and London.

Covello, V. and Mumpower, J. 1980: Risk Evaluation and Management. In R. Schwing and W. Alberts (eds), *Societal Risk Assessment.* New York.

Crook, S., Pakulski, J. and Waters, M. 1992: *Postmodernization.* London.

Daele, W. von der 1986: *Mensch nach Mass?* Munich.

Darnstädt, T. and Spörl, G. 1993: Streunende Hunde im Staat – Die liberale Demokratie am Wendepunkt. *Der Spiegel* 13.

Deutschmann, C. 1989: Reflexive Verwissenschaftlichung und 'ultureller Imperialismus' des Managements. *Soziale Welt* 3.

Diderot, D. 1981: Über die Frauen. In *Erzählungen und Gespräche.* Frankfurt am Main.

Dolata, U. 1992: *Weltmarktorientierte Modernisierung.* Frankfurt am Main.

Douglas, M. 1990: Risk as a Forensic Resource. *Daedalus* 4.

—— 1992: *Risk and Blame: Essays in Cultural Theory.* London and New York.

Douglas, M. and Wildavsky, A. 1982: *Risk and Culture.* New York.

Dubiel, H. 1992: Der Fundamentalismus in der Moderne. *Merkur* 522/523.

—— 1994: Der entfesselte Riese? Die 'zivile Gesellschaft' und die liberale Demokratie nach 1989. In C. Leggewie (ed.), *Wozu Politikwissenschaft? Über das Neue in der Politik.* Darmstadt.

Dubiel, H., Frankenberger, G. and Rödel, U. 1989: *Die demokratische Frage.* Frankfurt am Main.

Enzensberger, H.M. 1992: *Mediocrity and Delusion: Collected Diversions* London.

—— 1994: The Great Migration. In his *Civil War.* London.

Ewald, F. 1993: *Der Vorsorgestaat.* Frankfurt am Main.

Fourastié, J. 1954: *Die grosse Hoffnung des XX. Jahrhunderts.* Cologne.

Francis, E. 1965: *Ethos und Demos.* Berlin.

—— 1992: Der mögliche Beitrag der Soziologie zur Lösung von aktuellen Problemen, die die sogenannten interethnischen Beziehungen betreffen. Munich (unpublished MS).

Freidson, E. 1975: *Kritik des Experten.* Freiburg.

Freyer, H. 1930: *Soziologie als Wirklichkeitswissenschaft. Logische Grundle gung des Systems der Soziologie.* Leipzig.

Gabriel, O. W. 1992: *Erklären von Parteikonflikten.* Bamberg (unpublished MS).

Gauchet, M. 1990: Tocqueville, Amerika und wir – Über die Entstehung der demokratischen Gesellschaft. In U. Rödel (ed.), *Autonome Gesellschaft und libertäre Demokratie*. Frankfurt am Main.

Gehlen, A. 1965: *Theorie der Willensfreiheit und fruehe philosophische Schriften*, Neuwied, Berlin.

Gellner, E. 1964: *Thought and Change*. London.

—— 1983: *Nations and Nationalism*. Oxford.

Gibbons 1991: *Politics in the Postmodern Age*. London.

Giddens, A. 1983: Klassenspaltung, Klassenkonflikt und Bürgerrechte – Gesellschaft und Europa in den achtziger Jahren. In R. Kreckel (ed.), *Soziale Ungleichheiten* (Special Volume 2 of *Soziale Welt*). Göttingen.

—— 1990: *The Consequences of Modernity*. Cambridge.

—— 1991: *Modernity and Self-Identity*. Cambridge.

—— 1994: Living in a Post-Traditional Society. In U. Beck, A. Giddens and S. Lash, *Reflexive Modernization: Politics, Tradition and Aesthetics of the Modern Social Order*. Cambridge.

Giesen, B. 1991: *Die Entdinglichung des Sozialen*. Frankfurt am Main.

Goldblatt, D. 1996: *Social Theory and the Environment*. Cambridge.

Gore, A. 1992: *Earth in the Balance: Ecology and the Human Spirit*. Boston.

Goytisolo, J. 1994: Der Rückzug der Demokraten. *Text und Kritik* 124.

Greven, M.T. 1994: Die Demokraten fallen nicht vom Himmel. *Das Parlament* 50 (16 Dec.).

Guggenberger, B. 1988: *Wenn uns die Arbeit ausgeht*. Munich.

Habermas, J. 1987: *The Philosophical Discourse of Modernity*. Cambridge.

—— 1988: *Legitimation Crisis*. Cambridge.

—— 1996: *Between Facts and Norms: Contributions to a Discourse Theory of Law and Democracy*. Cambridge.

Halfmann, J. 1990: Technik und soziale Organisation in Widerspruch. In J. Halfmann and Japp (eds), *Riskante Entscheidungen und Katastrophenpotential*. Opladen.

Handke, P. 1994: *The Jukebox and Other Essays on Storytelling*. New York.

Haraway, D.J. 1993: Modest Witness, Second Millennium: The Female Man. Santa Cruz. (unpublished paper)

Heath, A. and Britten, N. 1984: Women's Jobs Do Make a Difference. *Sociology* 18/4.

Heine, H. 1992: Das Verhältnis der Naturwissenschaftler und Ingenieure in der Grosschemie zur ökologischen Industriekritik. *Soziale Welt* 2.

Heine, H. and Mautz, R. 1993: Die Herausbildung beruflichen Umweltb wuss seins im Management der Grosschemie angesichts öffentlicher Kritik. *Mitteilungen des Soziologischen Forschungsinstituts Göttingen* 20.

Heitmeyer, W. 1991: *Rechtsextremistische Orientierungen bei Jugendlichen*. Weilheim and Munich.

Hildebrandt, E., Gerhardt, U., Kühlen, C., Schenk, S. and Zimpelmann, B. 1994: Politisierung und Entgrenzung am Beispiel ökologisch erweiterter Arbeitspolitik. In N. Beckenbach and W. van Treeck (eds), *Umbrüche gesel schaftlicher Arbeit* (Special Volume 9 of *Soziale Welt*). Göttingen.

Hitzler, R. 1988: *Sinnwelten*. Opladen.

—— 1996: *Der gemeine Machiavellismus – Beiträge zu einer Soziologie politischen Handelns*. Frankfurt am Main.

Hitzler, R. and Koenen, E. 1994: Kehren die Individuen zurück? Zwei divergente Antworten auf eine institutionentheoretische Frage. In U. Beck and E. Beck-Gernsheim (eds), *Riskante Freiheiten – Individualisierung in modernen Gesellschaften*. Frankfurt am Main.

Hoffmann-Riem, C. and Schmidt-Assmann, H. (eds) 1990: *Konfliktbewältigung durch Verhandlung*. Baden-Baden.

Hohlfeld, R. 1989: Die zweite Schöpfung des Menschen. In K. Schuller and Heim (eds), *Der codierte Leib*. Zurich.

Honneth, A. (ed.) 1993: *Kommunitarismus*. Frankfurt am Main.

Horkheimer, M. 1971: Montaigne und die Funktion der Skepsis. In his *Anfänge der bürgerlichen Geschichtsphilosophie*. Frankfurt am Main.

Hortleder, G. 1970: *Das Gesellschaftsbild des Ingenieurs*. Frankfurt am Main.

Hradil, S. 1987: *Sozialstrukturanalyse in einer fortgeschrittenen Gesellschaft*. Opladen.

Jänicke, M. 1979: *Wie das Industriesystem von seinen Missständen profitiert*. Cologne.

Japp, K.P. 1992: Selbstverstärkungseffekte riskanter Entscheidungen. *Zeitschrift für Soziologie* 1.

Jaspers, K. 1962: *Der philosophische Glaube angesichts der Offenbarung*. Munich.

Kaase, M. and Klingemann, H.D. 1990: *Wahlen und Wähler*. Opladen.

Kandinsky, W. 1982: And, Some Remarks on Synthetic Art. In his *Complete Writings on Art: Volume Two (1922–1943)*, K. Lindsay and P. Vergo (eds). Boston.

Kant, I. 1983: *Perpetual Peace and Other Essays on Politics, History and Morals*. Indianapolis and Cambridge.

Kaufmann, F.X. 1973: *Sicherheit als soziologisches und sozialpolitisches Problem*. Stuttgart.

Kennedy, P. 1993: *Preparing for the Twenty-first Century*. New York.

Kern, H. and Schuhmann, M. 1985: *Das Ende der Arbeitsteilung?* Munich.

Keupp, H. 1990: *Riskante Chancen*. Munich.

Kielmansegg, P. 1977: Demokratieprinzip und Regierbarkeit. In R. Kielmansegg, W. Hennis and U. Matz (eds.), *Regierbarkeit*. Stuttgart.

Klingemann, H.-D., Stöss R. and Wessels K. (eds.) 1991: *Politische Klasse und politische Institutionen*. Opladen.

Koch, K. 1991: Die Sache mit dem Staat. *Die Zeit* 38.

Kogon, E. 1976: *Die Stunde der Ingenieure*. Düsseldorf.

Kohler, G. and Meyer, M. (eds) 1994: *Die Folgen von 1989*. Munich.

Konrád, G. 1984: *Antipolitics: An Essay*. San Diego.

Kreckel, R. 1992 : *Politische Soziologie der sozialen Ungleichheit*. Frankfurt am Main.

Krohn, W. and Weyer, J. 1989: Gesellschaft als Labor. *Soziale Welt* 3.

Kuhn, T. 1970: *The Structure of Scientific Revolutions*. 2nd ed. Chicago.

Kurz, R. 1991: *Der Kollaps der Modernisierung*. Frankfurt am Main.

Lakatos, I. 1970: Falsification and the Methodology of Scientific Research Programmes. In I. Lakatos and P.W. Musgrave (eds), *Criticism and the Growth of Knowledge*. London.

Larson, M.S. 1977: *The Rise of Professionalism*. Berkeley.

Lash, S. 1990: *Sociology of Postmodernism*. London.

—— 1993: Reflexive Modernization – The Aesthetic Dimension. *Theory, Culture & Society* 10/1.

Lash, S., Szerszynski B. and Wynne, B. (eds) 1996: *Risk, Environment and Modernity: Towards a New Ecology*. London.

Lash, S. and Urry, J. 1994: *Economies of Signs and Space*. London.

Lau, C. 1989: Risikodiskurse. *Soziale Welt* 3.

—— 1991: Gesellschafts diagnose ohne Entwicklungstheorie. In W. Glatzer (ed.), *Die Modernisierung moderner Gesellschaften–Ergänzungsband*. Frankfurt am Main.

—— 1996: *Risikokonflikt*. Frankfurt am Main.

Leif, T., Legrand, H.-J. and Klein, A. 1992: *Die politische Klasse in Deutschland*. Bonn.

Leggewie, C. (ed.) 1994: *Wozu Politikwissenschaft? Uber das Neue in der Politik*. Darmstadt.

Lepsius, R.M. 1977: Soziologische Theoreme über Sozialstruktur der 'Moderne' und die 'Modernisierung'. In R. Koselleck (ed.), *Studien zum Beginn der modernen Welt*. Stuttgart.

Luhmann, N. 1986: Kapital und Arbeit – Probleme einer Unterscheidung. In J. Berger (ed.), *Die Moderne – Kontinuitäten und Zäsuren* (Special Volume 4 of *Soziale Welt*). Göttingen.

—— 1990: *Die Wissenschaft der Gesellschaft*. Frankfurt am Main.

—— 1991: Verständigung über Risiken und Gefahren. *Die politische Meinung* 17.

—— 1994: Inklusion und Exklusion. In H. Berding (ed.), *Nationales Bewusstsein und kollektive Identität*. Frankfurt am Main.

Lukes, S. 1992: What is Left? Essential Socialism and the Urge to Rectify. *Times Literary Supplement* (27 March).

Lüscher, K., Schultheis, F. and Weberspann, M. (eds) 1988: *Die 'postmoderne' Familie*. Konstanz.

Lyotard, J.-F. 1988: *Reécrire la modernité*. Lille.

Makropoulos, M. 1989: *Modernität als ontologischer Ausnahmezustand: Walter Benjamins Theorie der Modernisierung*. Munich.

Mann, M. 1984: Capitalism and Militarism. In M. Shaw (ed.), *War, State and Society*. New York.

Menzel, U. 1994: Der Kern des Entwicklungsdilemmas: Zur Revision der internationalen Politik. In C. Leggewie (ed.), *Wozu Politikwissenschaft? Über das Neue in der Politik*. Darmstadt.

Müller, H.-P. 1994: Abschied von der Klassengesellschaft? Über ein 'Menetekel' im Spiegel der soziologischen Diskussion. In C. Görg (ed.), *Gesellschaft im Übergang – Perspektiven kritischer Soziologie*. Darmstadt.

Münch, R. 1984: *Die Struktur der Moderne*. Frankfurt am Main.

—— 1986: *Die Kultur der Moderne*. Frankfurt am Main.

—— 1991: Der Mythos der funktionalen Differenzierung. In W. Glatzer (ed.), *Die Modernisierung moderner Gesellschaften – Ergänzungsband*. Frankfurt am Main.

Musil, R. 1953: *The Man without Qualities*, trans. E. Wilkins and E. Kaiser. New York.

—— 1967: Der deutsche Mensch als Symptom. In his *Gesammelte Werke*, II, A. Frisé (ed.). Hamburg.

Neckel, S. 1993: Kommentar zu Wolfgang Bonss: Das Problem des Anderen in der Risikogesellschaft. Hamburg (unpublished MS).

—— 1994: Gefährliche Fremdheit. *Ästhetik und Kommunikation 69* (May).

Nietzsche, F. 1966: *Basic Writings of Nietzsche*, W. Kaufmann (ed.). New York.

Nisbet, R. 1974: Citizenship: Two Traditions. *Social Research*: 612–637.
Offe, C. 1972: *Strukturprobleme des kapitalistischen Staates*. Frankfurt am Main.
—— 1986: Die Utopie der Null-Option – Modernität und Modernisierung als politische Gütekriterien. In J. Berger (ed.), *Die Moderne – Kontinuitäten und Zäsuren* (Special Volume 4 of *Soziale Welt*). Göttingen.
Ortmann, G. 1994: Dark Stars: Institutionelles Vergessen in der Industriesoziologie. In N. Beckenback and W. van Treech (eds), *Umbrüche gesellschaftlicher Arbeit* (Special Volume 9 of *Soziale Welt*). Göttingen.
Osterland, M. 1994: Der 'grüne' Industriearbeiter: Arbeitsbewusstsein als Risikobewusstsein. In N. Beckenback and W. van Treech (eds), *Umbrüche gesellschaftlicher Arbeit* (Special Volume 9 of *Soziale Welt*). Göttingen.
Parsons, T. 1974: Religion in Postindustrial America: The Problem of Secularization. *Social Research* 41/2.
Pešić, H., Fleinert, M., Müller, K. von, Mugaša, P., and Marsh, L. 1993: Der Medien-Plan. *Süddeutsche Zeitung-Magazin* 11.
Peterson, T. 1991: The Urban Underclass and the Poverty Paradox. In C. Jencks and P. Peterson (eds), *The Urban Underclass*. Washington.
Prantl, H. 1994: *Deutschland – leicht entflammbar*. Munich.
Pries, L. 1991: *Betrieblicher Wandel in der Risikogesellschaft*. Opladen.
Prittwitz, V. von 1990: *Das Katastrophen-Paradox*. Opladen.
Raschke, J. 1982: *Bürger und Parteien*. Bonn.
Riesebrodt, M. 1993: *Pious Passion: The Emergence of Modern Fundamentalism in the United States and Iran*. Berkeley.
Riester W. 1994: Die Zukunft der Arbeit: Die neue Rolle der Gewerkschaften. *Alfred Herrhausen Gesellschaft* 17/18.
Robertson, R. 1992: *Globalization: Social Theory and Global Culture*. London.
Rüschemeyer, D. 1991: Über Entdifferenzierung. In W. Glatzer (ed.), *Die Modernisierung moderner Gesellschaften – Ergänzungsband*. Frankfurt am Main.
Rustin, M. 1994: Incomplete Modernity: Ulrich Beck's 'Risk Society'. *Dissent*.
Scharpf, F. 1991: Die Handlungsfreiheit des Staates am Ende des 20. Jahrhunderts. Frankfurt (unpublished MS).
Scharping, M. and Görg, C. 1994: Natur in der Soziologie: Ökologische Krise und Naturverhältnis. In C. Görg (ed.), *Gesellschaft im Übergang – Perspektiven kritischer Soziologie*. Darmstadt.
Schelsky, H. 1965: *Auf der Sache nach Wirklichheit. Gesammelte Aufsätze*. Düsseldorf and Cologne.
Schmitt, C. 1976: *The Concept of the Political*. New Brunswick.
Schmitt, K. 1967: *Neue Politik in alten Parteien*. Cologne.
Schulze, G. 1992: *Die Erlebnisgesellschaft*. Hamburg.
Schumpeter, J. 1950: *Capitalism, Socialism and Democracy*. New York.
Schwengel, H. 1987: Die Zukunft des Politischen. *Ästhetik und Kommunikation* 65/66.
Senghaas, D. 1994: Frieden und Krieg in dieser Zeit: Sechs Thesen. In C. Leggewie (ed.), *Wozu Politikwissenschaft? Über das Neue in der Politik*. Darmstadt.
Shaw, M. 1988: *The Dialectics of War*. London.
Simmel, G. 1908: Exkurs über den Fremden. In *Soziologie. Untersuchungen über die Formen der Vergesellschaftung*. Berlin.

Starzacher, K. Schacht, U. Friedrich, Leif, S. 1992: *Protestwähler und Wahlver-weigerer*. Cologne.

Steeger, W. 1992: *Future Management*. Frankfurt am Main.

Tocqueville, A. de 1945: *Democracy in America*. New York.

Toffler, A. 1990: *Power-Shift*. New York.

Toulmin, S. 1990: *Cosmopolis: The Hidden Agenda of Modernity*. New York.

Touraine, A. 1974: *The Post-industrial Society*. London.

Vester, H.-G. 1984: *Die Thematisierung des Selbst in der postmodernen Gesell-schaft*. Bonn.

Wallerstein, I. 1986: Typologie von Krisen. In J. Berger, (ed.), *Die Moderne – Kontinuitäten und Zäsuren* (Special Volume 4 of *Soziale Welt*). Göttingen.

Walzer, M. 1992: *Zivile Gesellschaft und amerikanische Demokratie*. Berlin.

Weber, M. 1968: *Gesammelte Aufsätze zur Wissenschaftslehre*. Tübingen.

—— 1978: *Economy and Society*. Berkeley.

—— 1987: *Politik als Beruf*. Hamburg.

Wehler, H.-U. 1975: *Modernisierungstheorie und Geschichte*. Göttingen.

Wehling, P. 1987: Ökologische Orientierung in der Soziologie. *Sozialökologi-sche Arbeitspapiere 26*.

—— 1992: *Die Moderne als Sozialmythos*. Frankfurt am Main.

Weingart, P., Kroll, H. and Bayertz, P. 1988: *Rasse, Blut und Gene*. Frankfurt am Main.

Weizsäcker, R. von 1992: *Im Gespräch mit Gunther Hofmann und Werner A. Perger*. Frankfurt am Main.

Weizsäcker, E. U. von 1991: Geringe Risiken durch fehlerfreundliche Systeme. In Schüz (ed.) *Risiko und Wagnis*, vol. I. Pfullingen.

Welsch, W. 1991: *Unsere postmoderne Moderne*. Weinheim.

Wiesendahl, E. 1989: Etablierte Parteien im Abseits? In P. Wasmuth (ed.), *Alternativen zur alten Politik?* Darmstadt.

Willke, H. 1992: *Die Ironie des Staates*. Frankfurt am Main.

Wilson, W. J. 1991: Studying Inner-city Social Dislocations: The Challenge of Public Agenda Research. *American Sociological Review 56*.

Wolch, J. 1991: Urban Homeless: An Agenda for Research. *Urban Geography 12*.

Zapf, W. 1967: *Theorien des sozialen Wandels*. Cologne.

—— (ed.) 1991: *Die Modernisierung moderner Gesellschaften*. Frankfurt am Main.

—— 1992: Entwicklung und Zukunft moderner Gesellschaften. In H. Korte and B. Schäfers (eds), *Einführung in die Hauptbegriffe der Soziologie*. Opladen.

Zürn, M. 1994: Das Projekt 'Komplexes Weltregieren': Wozu Wissenschaft von den internationalen Beziehungen? In C. Leggewie (ed.), *Wozu Politikwissen-schaft? Über das Neue in der Politik*. Darmstadt.

Index